P9-BYH-876

THE LAST COWBOYS

ALSO BY JOHN BRANCH

Boy on Ice

JOHN BRANCH

THE LAST COWBOYS

A Pioneer Family in
the New West

W. W. NORTON & COMPANY
Independent Publishers Since 1923
New York   London

For information about permission to reproduce selections from this book,
write to Permissions, W. W. Norton & Company, Inc., 500 Fifth Avenue,
New York, NY 10110

For information about special discounts for bulk purchases, please contact
W. W. Norton Special Sales at specialsales@wwnorton.com or 800-233-4830

Manufacturing by Quad Graphics, Fairfield
Book design by Ellen Cipriano
Production manager: Anna Oler

ISBN: 978-0-393-29234-3

W. W. Norton & Company, Inc.
500 Fifth Avenue, New York, N.Y. 10110
www.wwnorton.com

W. W. Norton & Company Ltd.
15 Carlisle Street, London W1D 3BS

1 2 3 4 5 6 7 8 9 0

To Charlie Waters,
a newspaperman of the West,
who always loved a good cowboy story
and encouraged me to tell this one.

Contents

■

PROLOGUE

CODY WAS STILL A BOY then, all of five years old, alone on a horse crossing the rising waters of the Virgin River. The warm, lingering days of late spring melted the deep snowpack in the mountains on the other side of Zion National Park. Miles downstream, there between Hurricane and La Verkin, the ebb and flow came on delay. The water rose in the late afternoon, crested overnight, and fell a bit by dawn.

The boy's father, Bill Wright, knew the rhythm of the river as well as anyone. He was the water boss in Hurricane, which the locals pronounced "her-uh-kin" for reasons no one quite remembered. For nearly ten miles upstream, there was a dirt ditch carved into the side of the canyon wall. It flowed with water siphoned from the river and diverted through a settling pond to feed the farms and ranches in the valley, filled with fields of hay, wheat, and alfalfa.

Part of Bill's job, beyond opening the valves to ration the water, was to ride the canal on horseback every day. Rocks sometimes fell from the canyon cliffs and clogged the flow, or the steep bank of the ditch gave way from erosion and gravity and let the precious water spill out before it could do any good downstream. Bill rode up the canal, looking for problems, then rode back down the river toward town. It could be a dangerous ride. Twice, he had lost horses over the edge to missteps. The second started to tumble as Bill was on it. Bill leapt off, lucky not to get his mud-crusted boots caught in the stirrups, and landed in the dirt just as the horse fell to its death far below.

The runoff made spring the most dangerous season, and this particular one thirty-some years ago was rougher than others. For weeks, the meltwater had rushed fast and risen high with the falling sun. By the time Bill made his way back down the river toward home, right around dark, it teased the banks. There were always places where the contours of the river required that it be crossed, but when the water was especially high it would swim the horses, lifting them off their feet and carrying them downstream until their hooves felt the muddy bottom again and they regained their footing. For a rider accustomed to the cadence of a horse's gait and the comfortable solidity of its support, it was a disconcerting and unwelcome sensation, like when a driver loses control on a sheet of black ice and helplessly hopes for the feeling of the Earth's grip again.

There was an especially tricky crossing point near the Pah Tempe Hot Springs, not far from town, where Bill knew that the spring runoff sometimes got too deep for horses. They had to drift down and across the river for twenty feet or so until they could touch bottom again on the far side.

Cody was not yet in school, so he came with his father. He had been riding horses before he walked—first on Bill's lap, where he fell asleep, nuzzled between his father and the horn of the saddle. By the age of three, he was riding horses alone outside the corral. He mostly rode a gentle little gray mare called Paleface. Its face and legs were white.

"You need to stay with your horse, no matter what happens in the water," Bill told Cody as they approached the crossing. "You cling to your horse."

It was deep into dusk when the horses moved into the river, the water rising higher against their legs with every step. Bill felt his horse drift, its feet paddling invisibly for traction and then binding to the hidden bank. But Cody's horse caught a pocket in the rushing water and was swept into the current. It was quickly turned face-first downstream, water up to its neck, feet adrift invisibly under the surface, the boy clinging to its rein and trying to steer it back to solid ground.

"Cody!" Bill screamed as Cody and Paleface floated past. His heart racing, his mind panicked, Bill spun his horse around and spurred it back into the deep water. He hoped to catch up to Cody and Paleface and snare his son from the horse's back, but Bill's horse was quickly caught in the same current. There was no way to gain ground. The river had them all. Bill could barely see Cody ahead as he slipped downstream in the deepening shadows. The boy disappeared with every dip in the river's urgent tumble, then bobbed back into view where it slowed, rising and falling like a boat on an ocean swell.

"Hang on!" Bill shouted.

Cody fell out of sight again, as if the river poured into a hole, before he and Paleface rose again on the face of a high rapid. But the face was too steep and the churn too heavy. The horse and boy hit the crest of the wave and tumbled backward into the rushing water, then disappeared. A few beats later, Bill and his horse did the same.

Bill was underwater, off his horse, tumbling in the current. When his head popped back into the air, he still had hold of a rein and his horse had found footing. They pulled themselves to the river's edge. Bill, scared and soaked, desperately scanned the banks and the water, now dark as ink, for silhouettes in the flat light of dusk. The rushing river bent out of sight, and Cody and Paleface were nowhere. Bill climbed back atop his dripping horse and raced it down the shallows of one side of the river. The father's eyes searched for breaks in the water's reflection and scanned boulders to make sure they weren't a motionless boy or horse. He looked downstream, and then upstream, and downstream again. For a few moments, he didn't know what to do or where to go. He felt a wave of sickness.

"Dad!"

Bill swore he heard a little voice through the hopelessness of dark.

"Dad!"

Cody stood wet and trembling on the bank nearby. His hat and one boot were missing. Bill's insides collapsed in relief.

"I woulda come and found you sooner," Cody said, "but my horse wouldn't go."

Paleface was on its belly, legs splayed across a sandbar, as if dropped from the sky. The pony had tumbled through the water and made it to the riverbank, a little boy clinging hard to its back, just as the father had told him to do.

"I about lost your boy in the river tonight," Bill told Evelyn as he carried Cody into the house, wrapped in a blanket from the back of the truck. She drew her son a bath, and he fell asleep in the warm water. For a long time, now and again, the boy would be startled awake by the nightmares, he and his horse lost in a rushing river, unable to find his father. Even now, decades later, a grown man with a family of his own, Cody didn't like to talk about it much.

1

Branding Day

MORNING BROKE SLOWLY on Smith Mesa, as if in half time. The sky and land emerged subtly from black to grayish purple before the sun topped the sandstone cliffs and added the full riot of color. Across a brick-dirt prairie of thin grass, dotted by prickly pear in bloom, black cattle stood in small constellations and cast long shadows. A few had already squeezed into the shrinking bits of shade under clusters of piñon pine. More than a hundred three-month-old calves grazed next to their mothers.

Branding day was practically a family holiday for the Wrights. In the shade of the hollow, Bill emerged from a worn metal camper wearing a felt cowboy hat smudged with red dirt, a plaid shirt with snap buttons, a blue denim jacket, and Wrangler jeans cinched with an old silver rodeo buckle he'd won forty years before. As usual, his cowboy hat was pulled low on his forehead and his mouth settled into a slight downward curl. Bill didn't give away his mood easily.

He walked past the tiny log cabin his parents had built decades before. The windows had been broken for years and the only occasional inhabitants were the mice that lived inside the walls. Bill was used to being alone at Smith Mesa, but now there were a dozen other trailers and pickups scattered around. Everyone else was still asleep. Empty chairs surrounded the gray ash of last night's campfire.

He walked uphill to the horses, in a pen next to a shallow metal water tank where the grandchildren sometimes swam on hot days. He put a blanket on his black mule's back and lifted a worn saddle from a horse trailer. The saddle was heavy, but Bill was still strong enough to lift it without much trouble and wiggle it into place. As he had done a million times before, he strapped the front cinch and tied it off, then buckled the back cinch under the mule's belly. He tugged on the saddle to make sure it was snug. His hands were tan, almost the color of the dirt.

Bill sighed and looked around, impatient for his boys. Daylight was not a thing to waste. Neither was a cool morning in late spring, when the high desert's only promise was heat.

Down at camp, the boys stirred, careful not to wake their families, and quietly pulled on their boots. They wiped dryer sheets on their faces, because it was the best thing they'd found for fending off the swarms of gnats that came from nowhere on hot, breezeless days.

Cody was the first to appear through the trees, and he came and stood alongside his father without a word. He was deep into his thirties now, the oldest of the seven brothers, twenty years older than the youngest. The brothers had similar builds—like a litter of puppies, Bill always said—not too tall, lean but strong.

One by one the others appeared, in boots and chaps and cowboy hats, and without much chatter, the boys finished saddling the horses. They climbed aboard with ease, swinging a leg up and over and sitting tall in the saddle like it was something they did every day, which it was. They moved into the pasture and into a loose formation around the small bunches of cattle. They shifted the livestock into bigger groups, a dozen or two at a time, by riding behind and beside them, maneuvering their quick-footed horses with a tug of the rein and a subtle squeeze of their spurs to cut down the escape angles of any cattle that leaned toward breaking away. Whoops and twirling lariats were secondary measures to keep order. Dogs dashed among the hooves, back and forth, marking an invisible boundary. Dust encircled each procession as it moved in slow clumps uphill toward the corral. Guttural dissents carried half a mile.

The corral the family built years ago sat at the corner of the pasture, at the right angle in the rutted dirt road that led to and past the Wright property. The faded sign warning drivers of a ninety-degree turn was riddled with rusted bullet holes. The sides of the corral were lined with concrete pilings, like logs driven vertically into the ground, five feet tall. Real logs of lodgepole pine were lashed horizontally across them, making the fence taller.

Cattle were funneled into a chute on one side. Their moans grew loud and mournful as the cows were separated from their calves. An argument ensued. Cows mooed. Calves bleated. Cowboys barked and whistled.

"Hey hey hey! Woo-woo!" the cowboys shouted. "Git up! Hey hey hey!"

Branding day had workers as well as watchers, and a crowd of watchers gathered. The children sat impatiently on a bulkhead where the road bent. Adults followed and set up lawn chairs behind them. Others sat on horseback, holding babies. A few dozen calves pressed together at the far end of the corral. They called out in high pitches to their mothers, who stood outside the fence, calling back in deeper tones. There was dust and noise and anticipation in the air.

Cody recruited an army of younger boys to gather wood, which he fed into two fires inside the corral. When they were hot enough, he placed a few branding irons into the orange and gray coals. He drove three stakes deep into hard dirt nearby. Each stake held one end of a long, black inner tube. At the other end of each tube was a metal harness that looked like a medieval torture contraption.

Near the fence, Bill kneeled and dug through a plastic bin of supplies—pistol-grip ear punchers, plastic ear tags, syringes, and medicines. He pushed his hat back to his hairline and squinted at the labels. One medicine was for a litany of diseases, from tetanus to black plague. The other was an upper-respiratory vaccine, which helped with breathing disorders worsened by dust. He pulled his phone from its leather holster on his leather belt and called someone. He read the labels into the phone while absent-mindedly unbuckling the spurs from his boots.

"Is that set on two?" he asked one of the boys, holding a syringe and a cell phone.

"That one's on two," his son said, "and that one's on five."

Cody's four school-aged sons—Rusty, Ryder, Stetson, and Statler, all miniature versions of Cody, like unnested cowboy dolls—loitered nearby on horseback, coiled ropes in their hands. Bill gave a nod.

The ropers lassoed calves by their back feet and dragged them on their sides, across the dirt to the other end of the corral, where a team waited at each stake. When a calf arrived, they scrambled in side-by-side fits of action, like pit crews at a racetrack. Everyone had a job. One person wrestled the calf's head into the metal harness as the cowboy on horseback kept its hind legs pulled taut with the rope. The calves, moaning and wild-eyed, were stretched long onto their sides. Once the animal was secured and still, the rest of the team converged. Two with syringes stuck the calves in the hip. One with an ear punch tagged the ear with a colored plastic marker that identified it as belonging to the Wrights.

Someone called out "steer!" when the calf was male. Another

person pulled a white-hot branding iron from the nearest fire. With someone else resting a knee on the calf to hold it still, the brand was pressed hard against its back hip. The hide sizzled, smoked, and sometimes flamed. The air, already swirling with dust and noise, soon filled with the putrid scent of burning hair and flesh.

"It smells like money," someone said.

■ ■ ■

Wrights had run cattle on Smith Mesa for 150 years, long before there were any roads to get there. These days, it meant taking old Highway 9 toward Zion National Park and ditching most of the tourists in Virgin by turning left at the corner where Bill's grandparents once lived. The twisty road followed North Creek for a few miles. At one bend, at the base of a bluff on the left side near a stand of cottonwoods, was a small corral made of gnarled logs. It marked the lower end of the Wrights' range.

But to get on top of Smith Mesa, the narrow road climbed a ridge until it was a squiggly snake of pavement between steep drops. It used to be a series of switchbacks, and Bill's dad once told him that a family lost its brakes on the way down one time and plunged over the edge, killing everyone in the car. Bill wasn't sure about that, but it was a story he passed along. The road entered the national park, with no ranger gate and no fanfare but a small wooden sign. Then it split into a Y.

To the right, still paved, was the way that a small fraction of Zion's millions of annual visitors ever went. It led to a claustrophobic backcountry of soaring sandstone spires with names credited to Mormon pioneers, like North and South Guardian Angel and Tabernacle Dome.

Cut to the left, where pavement turned to dirt, was Smith Mesa

Road. It did not rise and disappear into the towering formations, but hung and teetered on the edge of the sandstone cliffs that formed the western boundary of the park. Most of the road was hardpan, sculpted into a chassis-chattering washboard in some places by summer thunderstorms. On a few steep corners, the wheels of trucks churned the road into loose, squirmy sand. It was a precarious ride, especially in weather and especially when pulling a rickety trailer of a dozen horses or a double-decker cattle pot full of a few tons of livestock. The road left the national park after a mile or so, the exit announced only by a cattle guard. That's about where it disappeared from the glossy Zion map handed out at the visitor center. But the road went for miles more, curling through the wide, big-sky land that the Wrights had worked for generations.

And at one hard turn was the family's larger corral, the center of the Wrights' modest ranching operation at Smith Mesa. The family owned 1,200 acres, which sounded like a lot until you saw it in the context of faraway horizons. Bill leased about twenty thousand more acres of the surrounding landscape from the federal government to graze cattle during the winter months.

Bill's cattle ventured into the park sometimes, through open spots in the barbed-wire fence, startling hikers and campers. Bill routinely got calls from park rangers asking him to come and get his cows. The Wrights and the park were friendly neighbors, even counting the time that Bill's three-legged dog peed on a ranger's leg as the men were talking.

Most of the grazing land at the foot of the thousand-foot cliffs was a shelf of open meadows among clusters of junipers. That was Smith Mesa. As a boy, Bill helped clear some of the trees for farming, a vocation that most folks always found hardly worth the trouble, since there wasn't much water around.

The earth dropped away among the trees to the west, sometimes with little warning, tumbling over a series of crumbling stair-stepped plateaus like giant choir risers. The last step fell away several hundred feet into a red-tinted chasm that the Wrights called, with typical understatement, "the wash." It was a canyon, a deep and jagged gash in the forever landscape of southern Utah, seemingly carved by impatient gods with a dull knife. The slashes in the earth might have been their discarded mold for the towering and rugged formations of Zion.

■ ■ ■

Generations ago, and miles to the north, the vast Great Salt Lake Valley was established as the new center for the Mormons, and in 1849, Bill's great-great-grandparents were part of the Mormon migration. They had come from England, enticed by the ideals of religious freedom and open space, and made their way across the plains and the Continental Divide in wagons and on horseback on the Mormon Trail.

Joseph Wright's young family was among the thousands to settle in the area. Joseph Wright farmed and raised livestock, and was close enough to Brigham Young that Young performed the ceremony when Wright took a second wife in 1857. By then, Young was starting to send families south to lower elevations and warmer climes to grow crops, especially cotton, for the burgeoning empire. In 1862, as the American Civil War was being fought back east, the Wrights were one of 220 families called to be part of the Cotton Mission.

They moved three hundred miles south of Salt Lake City to a creased region of red formations and green valleys. The Mormons called it Dixie. Joseph Wright raised livestock along the Virgin River and helped establish several businesses, including a co-op store in Virgin City. He bought the Kolob Cattle Company from the church.

Now he lay beneath the hardpan dirt of Virgin's Pioneer Memorial Cemetery, under a sandstone slab resting atop sandstone bricks, a few miles from where his family—four, five, six, and seven generations later—had gathered for the spring roundup and for branding day.

"To the memory of Joseph Wright," the headstone read, "who departed this life the 12th of June 1873 in the 56th year of his age." That was a few years younger than Bill was now.

Nearby, amid a smattering of other Wrights, was William Wright, Joseph's son. He shared a grave with his wife, Lovenia. They were Bill's great-grandparents. Her family had come from England in 1856, and her father and a younger brother were among at least 145 members of the 576-person Martin Company who died on the Mormon Trail after being stranded in a blizzard. Lovenia and her mother were rescued and taken in by a family, the Parkers, that was also sent from Salt Lake City to be part of the Cotton Mission. They settled in Virgin in 1863.

Both the Wrights and Parkers farmed and raised cattle and sheep in the area, and William and Lovenia married in 1864. He worked for his father's cattle company. They ran the cattle all the way to Kolob Terrace, and they wintered them on what they later called Smith Flats. After a while, it got to be called Smith Mesa.

"Smith Mesa was named after an old outlaw who used to pilfer and pillage down in the communities, in Virgin and Rockville and La Verkin," Bill told a group one day when the subject came up. "He had a Native American girlfriend and a lookout, and he never really was caught up with. That's the story I got, anyway."

According to records down in Hurricane, the name actually came from Charles Nephi Smith, a Mormon bishop down in Rockville. He ran cattle on the mesa and built a ranch house along a creek, and both the mesa and the creek got named after him. He had two wives, at least, but there was nothing about a Native American girlfriend or a lookout.

People who followed Smith tried to farm the red sand, but no one made much of a living at it. They tried winter wheat, mostly, and beans and squash and corn, but there was never any irrigation on the mesa. So they had to piece together their livings however they could, living hard in the scrub brush and piñons between arroyos, the skyline to the east taller than that of any city anywhere. And among those families who came and never really left were the Wrights.

The West was settled and built by families like the Wrights, in places like Smith Mesa, one parcel, one generation at a time, puzzle pieces that quietly filled in the vast spaces between unmarked boundaries and high skies. Americans weren't always known for their roots, but the Wrights had them planted in the red soil of Smith Mesa before the transcontinental railroad was connected up north, decades before Utah was an official state. They were there before the invention of the light bulb, the telephone, the car, the airplane, radio, and television. It was before Coca-Cola, the player piano, even barbed wire.

"My boys will be the sixth generation to run cattle on this land," Bill said. His mouth never opened far when he spoke. "And Cody's boys will be the seventh."

Smith Mesa was a time capsule of stone and sand, and if Bill had it his way, he would pass it on to another seven generations. His long-range plan was to build the herd big enough to support his children and their children and let them take it over, if they wanted it.

But Smith Mesa was blessed and cursed by rugged beauty and increasing accessibility. Like the Wrights themselves, it squatted at the intersection of the old and new Wests. The time capsule was being unearthed. Developers were coming. Feds were circling. Conservationists were knocking. Land prices were rising.

Bill was boxed in, surrounded by federal land and some private parcels that had gotten too expensive to plant a bunch of cows on. The economics of his ambitions at Smith Mesa had stopped making sense. Bill had already had some offers, some from developers looking to build on Smith Mesa and some from conservationists looking to protect it. He had been out looking at other places, bigger places he could buy with the money from Smith Mesa, places farther away from the encroaching world, places like Smith Mesa used to be. More and more, he took Cody with him.

"I enjoy it, too, the beauty and everything else," Bill said. "But beauty don't pay the bills."

It didn't seem right that a family that had been doing the same thing for seven generations might have to move to do it for the eighth. You didn't just dust off 150 years like a day's worth of dirt.

It weighed on him. For a time, Bill thought that the family, if it ever had enough money, could buy up some scattered parcels of private land near them and scoop up government permits here and there and expand the operation and stay at Smith Mesa. The boys had started winning big rodeos on bucking horses, and the Wrights became the best-known family of bronc riders in the game. Rodeo payouts could go into land, permits, and cows—some of it already had. That's why Cody owned almost half the herd.

The timing wasn't perfectly aligned. It wasn't yet clear that all the boys wanted into Bill's old-fashioned version of the future, and Bill wasn't the type to ever go asking for their money. They'd come around if they wanted to, when the time felt right and they decided what was best for their young families.

There wasn't much to do about it now. The future would get clearer, the way the view does when the dust settles. Bill was no romantic. He wasn't blind to change. He was just the kind of man who figured that hard work was always the best approach to solving the most complicated problems. The way he saw it, until he figured out something different, the best way to keep doing what he and his family had been doing, no matter the forces squeezing in against him, was to do it some more and do it harder. Keep his head down and his mind open.

"I think that this is what it's goin' to take to feed my family, and their families," Bill said, away from the others. He pulled a neckerchief from his pocket, tipped his hat back, and wiped away the sweat on his forehead. "I think agriculture is going to be one of the safest, most stable means of support when things get worse and worse, which we can see they are."

So Bill focused on doing what he was doing, which was really what he wanted to do all along—run his own operation and spend his days in the sun on a trusted horse, knowing that people depended on him. It wasn't often that the entire family got together, because with thirteen children and thirty-some grandchildren—Bill could never keep track of the number—getting everyone together was hard. Besides weddings and funerals, it happened twice a year. One was at Christmas. The other was at branding day.

Bill didn't say it out loud, but he wondered if this might be the last time the Wrights gathered at Smith Mesa.

■ ■ ■

"The irons gotta get hotter!" Jesse shouted. "They're cooler'n hell."

Since roughly half the herd belonged to Cody, the year's steers were marked with Cody's brand, a pair of interlocking 7s. He designed the brand to reflect that he had been born in 1977 and was one of seven boys, but he regretted registering it after someone pointed out that it looked a little like an unfinished swastika once it was seared onto the side of a cow. Heifers got two brands: Bill's CV, a design abandoned by someone else in Utah and inherited by Bill years ago, and a 4 to tell Bill the year of their birth, should they join the herd and grow old as birthing cows. A few were marked for Bill's third son, Alex, who had taken over about ten cows that belonged to his older brother Calvin when Calvin needed the money, with a sideways 3 that looked like a drunken W.

Someone with a knife gashed the tip of each calf's ear, usually causing a spritz of red blood. The cuts were another identifying marker. Bill's heifers were notched straight across, the tips of the ears sliced off. The right ears of Cody's steers were notched with a V.

Castration was quick. Bill or one of the others familiar with the procedure pulled a knife from a holster, tugged on the scrotum, and sliced away the testicles. They dug their fingers inside the steer and pulled out bands of tissue and sliced them away again. Young boys, cousins and grandkids, sprayed the area with an antiseptic. Some years, they collected the testicles to fry and eat. This time, the pen of the corral was littered with dirt-covered testicles. They looked like dusty pearl onions.

Each calf took little more than a minute, never more than two. The men and boys on horseback slacked the ropes as someone pulled the harness off the head. The calf clambered to its feet and rushed away from its torturers, bleating for its mother. They were reunited in the freedom of the pasture.

For most of the day, the temperature spiking in the nineties, the scene repeated—another batch of cattle funneled in, the calves cut temporarily from their mothers, the dust and cacophony rising over the corral—until all the calves in the pasture had been branded, tagged, and inoculated, and the steers castrated.

A few hours later, the corral empty, the crowd gone, and the nearby pasture dotted with cattle grazing on thinning grass, Bill kneeled in the dirt and scribbled numbers on a box with a broken pencil. His hands were brown from the dirt and smeared red with dried blood. He slid one into his shirt pocket, pulled out a roll of Smarties, and popped a few of the tart, chalky candies into his mouth. Alex stood nearby, drinking a cold beer.

"I'm short sixty head," Bill said, looking at tallies of cows, heifers, steers, and bulls that had been rounded up, including 108 calves branded, tagged, and inoculated. "How can I be sixty short?"

He shook his head. His eyes, hidden below the brim of his cowboy hat, gazed hard at the numbers. He added again and finally remembered. He had already moved thirty-six cows north to the summer range in the mountains above Beaver, trying to get a jump start on the heat amid the drought that suffocated Smith Mesa. That meant he was short twenty-four. They were sprinkled somewhere among the twenty thousand acres of canyons and pastures around him.

"A good cowman is always out a couple," Bill said. He laughed, stood, and gazed out at the pasture, where cows and their calves dotted the grass in front of the red cliffs, now glowing in the afternoon sun.

The family would pack up and leave later in the day. The boys would head back onto the rodeo circuit, toward the thick of the summer season. Bill would be left alone, again, as he usually was at Smith Mesa. He sighed.

"Next few days," he said, "I'm going to be back and forth, looking for these cows."

2

Rodeo Cowboy

ODY HAD GROWN into a lean and compact man, about five foot eight, and if he had any body fat it'd take a doctor's exam to find it. He had a gap between his two front teeth and a scar that ran from his temple to his cheek near his right eye. He had sustained too many rodeo injuries to name, but if you could get him to talk about them, the busted eye socket and the knocked-out teeth and the perpetually sore broken wrist usually made the short list. The tibia and fibula bones on both of his lower legs were held together with plates and screws.

Cody knew that every rodeo career could end with the next ride. He'd seen it a hundred times before. And with five children, he needed to figure out how he was going to make a living whenever that happened. Cattle ranching was the obvious answer. Cody had already taken a $100,000 grand prize check from Calgary and invested the money in cows, just about doubling the size of his dad's herd overnight. He let Bill do the accounting.

"One of these days, I'm goin' to nail him down and figure out what I've got," Cody said. Like all the Wrights, he had a hint of a drawl that didn't sound Southern so much as rural. He looked you in the eye when he talked. "I know I have at least seventy-eight cows. If I don't, he's been sellin' 'em off."

He started rodeoing as a teenager, and Bill took him everywhere, hundreds of miles in all directions, because Cody was too young to drive. Then he got a used sedan to drive himself, one with a back seat big enough for sleeping in fairground parking lots. Then he got a minivan he could share with a couple of other cowboys, which helped for splitting expenses and time behind the wheel. Then he bought himself a truck with a cab big enough to seat four and a camper where everyone could sleep. It was the usual progression of a professional rodeo chaser. A truck with a camper meant you were serious, because neither of those things came cheap. Owning one meant you were in it for the long haul.

Now Cody's Dodge had his name on the side, announcing him as a two-time world champion in saddle bronc riding. It wasn't really his personality to drive a truck with his name on it, but the sponsor paid for it, and sponsors were the only things that kept cowboys from going broke when they were too hurt to ride or got themselves tangled in a bad losing streak. The truck sometimes earned him an admiring pull of a trucker's horn on the highway or the handshake of a random fan in a truck-stop parking lot.

Cody was not the oldest child of Bill and Evelyn's thirteen, but he was the oldest boy, the one that his six younger brothers looked to for advice and direction. He was about as close in age to his mother as he was to his youngest brother. That, along with his temperament and age, made him a sort of bridge between two generations.

"He's the kind of guy, when he goes to 31 Flavors," Evelyn said, "he comes out with vanilla."

He had always taken to horses. When he was in grade school back in Hurricane, he rode them around town and through the drive-through window at Frost Pop. He was ten, trying to break a horse in the vacant lot next door, when the horse took off with Cody dangling from its back. It ran and bucked across the property in one direction, reversed and came all the way back, stopped, and dumped the boy to the dirt.

Evelyn caught a glimpse of her son's wild ride through the kitchen window. She ran outside to find Cody slowly standing and dusting himself off.

"You OK?" she asked him.

"Yeah," he said. "That was kinda fun until I fell off."

By twelve, Cody was working as a ranch hand on a cattle operation of a family friend in Nevada, and he spent most of his summers there as a teenager. The other workers, gritty men with leather faces and scarred hands, thought he was a quiet, hardworking kid. Cody never said much. He always thought he could learn a lot more by listening than by talking. Still did.

Cody found his dad's old bronc-riding gear in the rafters one day and tried on the chaps and spurs. Bill had done some rodeoing as a boy. His first was a county fair in Hurricane, when he was twelve. He won the bull-riding event and made forty bucks. He thought it was a pretty good deal, getting paid to ride animals, so he competed in high school and then a bit in college in St. George. But he put it aside as he found jobs and started a family. The gear went into a box that went undiscovered until Cody spotted it and opened it.

Bill was soon putting twenty thousand miles a year on his truck, driving Cody, Calvin, and the younger boys to as many as forty rodeos a year. They were all-around cowboys, good ropers and bull-doggers, but they were even better riders. When Cody was in high school, he qualified for nationals in bull riding, bareback riding, and saddle bronc riding. The next Wright boy, Calvin, looked to be just as good. They went on to college on rodeo scholarships. The rest of the boys followed along, trying their hands at all the different events.

Slowly, surely, they all settled into saddle bronc riding. That was largely Bill's doing. He remembered what his father told him: "Cowboys ride horses—saddle horses. Cowboys don't ride bareback." And a real cowboy would never sit on the back of a bull unless he was drunk or dumb, or quite a bit of both.

Riding a bull was like being in an eight-second car accident, all jerks and spins, horns and hooves, dirt and snot. Bareback bronc riding, saddle bronc's closest cousin, was an inelegant display of neck-snapping, back-bending torture. Instead of holding a rein, bareback riders tied a fist to a handle on the saddle and tried to withstand eight seconds of getting whipped from front to back. Both bull riding and bareback riding were a hell of a way to get old in a hurry, which is why most everyone who did it was so young.

Saddle bronc riding, more poetry than chaos, more grace than mayhem, was the classic, original rodeo event. It was the one depicted in the cowboy silhouette of the Wyoming license plate. Cowboys had always strapped saddles onto the backs of unbroken horses and tried to tame them into something useful. It was a legitimate task, breaking horses, and saddle bronc mirrored real life more than the other rough-stock events. It took balance and rhythm, brains and guts. It was harder to learn, harder on the mind, but easier on the body. Not easy—easier.

"I just think it's a little more fulfilling," Bill said. "It's more of a skill. You have to work harder on it."

Cody was the best. He had fast feet and a fearless mind. He was confident enough to do it and stubborn enough not to quit. Bill gave him a credit card to get his professional career going until he made enough in winnings to pay it back.

Cody already had a family of his own when he turned pro at twenty. He won the Wilderness Circuit title at twenty-three, won some big national rodeos at twenty-four, and made the National Finals Rodeo in Las Vegas at twenty-six, when he won three rounds and finished third in the world standings.

Five times he made the top fifteen in the season standings to qualify for the National Finals, and five times he came up short of winning it all. At age thirty, he had a huge ride in the final round, dismounting to thunderous applause, thinking he had won the world championship. But a flag had been thrown. A judge ruled that Cody had missed his mark out—his spurs hadn't been above the bronc's front shoulders when it landed on its front feet the first jump out of the chute. At least that's what the judge saw. No score. No title.

Bill was livid, certain it was a bad call. Evelyn was distraught. Cody was calm, as usual.

"Son, you were robbed," Evelyn said.

"Mom, we'll get 'em next year," Cody replied. And Evelyn cried all the way home to Utah.

Then, on the sixth try, when he was already thirty-one and had rods and screws holding his legs together, a broken bone in his wrist, and a busted eye socket and teeth that had been knocked back a couple of times, and he and ShaRee had four boys of their own and a little girl on the way, Cody won Round 4 on Sundance and Round 7 on Round Robin and Round 9 on Wild Bill, and that was more than enough to send his idol, Billy Etbauer, into retirement without one last title. Cody won his first world championship.

They had a parade for Cody in Hurricane, where he rode down State Street on a fire truck, and another parade in Milford a few days later, where the town's fire engine carried him up Main Street. He won again two years later, and now he was the one chasing all the rodeo records and building a legacy among the all-time best. He finished in the top four in the world standings every year for a decade and made millions of dollars in earnings and sponsorships. And people noticed that he had some younger brothers who might be pretty good bronc riders, too, now that a few of them were racking up titles in junior high, high school, and college and were turning pro themselves.

They grew up imitating Cody's style on the horse and his manner off of it. They would be lucky to imitate at least part of his career arc. He was the one with the rodeo arena named after him back in Milford, where the Wrights resettled when Cody was in high school. He was the one with the signs on the highways that announced to visitors that Milford was his home. He was famous, in his town and in his world. He was Bill's trusted right hand, his brothers' mentor, his sons' hero. It seemed like everyone wanted to be a little bit more like Cody.

■ ■ ■

As Bill had taught Cody, Cody taught his brothers, and they had the advantage of one another. The other boys learned from the worn notebooks that Cody kept on all the horses he had ridden—each animal's bucking habits and the right length of rein to hold to keep taut—so that he knew for next time. The other boys started adding to the book themselves.

Cody taught them how to work the schedule, to enter rodeos so that they could maximize their time and miles—to get there an hour before and leave before the rodeo ended to beat traffic, to drive at night when the freeways were empty, to avoid the cities at rush hour, to play dot-to-dot with the truck stops for refueling. You could do four rodeos in a weekend, with luck and desire, but it might cost you a hundred hours, three thousand miles, and a blown gasket on

U.S. 50 through Nevada, and it might not win you anything. Then again, it might. It might win you a lot. Which is why they all did it, and why they found it hard to stop.

Most of them had their own trucks now, dividing and conquering the West in a platoon of Dodges. It was usually the identical twins, Jake and Jesse, in one truck and Cody in another, and depending on the season or the weekend or the draw of a particular rodeo, they carried with them some combination of other Wrights—Alex and Spencer and their brother-in-law CoBurn, married to the youngest Wright girl, Becca. Cody kept tabs on everyone and sent news and results to Evelyn in a text message every night.

And now Cody's oldest boy, Rusty, was finishing high school and going pro, and Ryder wasn't far behind, and a new generation of bronc-riding Wrights had mixed in with the old, which happened in families when nephews and nieces were older than some of their uncles and aunts.

The trucks had hundreds of thousands of miles on their chassis, rebuilt engines under their hoods, and new sets of tires a couple of times a year. They had worn leather seats and seatbelts that went unused. They had dust on the dashboards and floors covered in empty bottles that would be tossed out at the next stop, or probably not. Each had a steel grille welded onto the front, like the facemask on a football helmet, to protect the truck from deer and livestock that might be in the middle of a dark road or might spring out on the far end of a blind bend somewhere in Texas or Montana or California.

The tall campers that rode piggyback could sleep four, and several more could fit in a pinch. The saddles and chaps and all the rest of the cowboy gear were stashed inside an oven-sized box strapped to the back bumper. Whatever didn't fit there was usually piled into the shower, because that wasn't used much. There were two big bunks, one above the other. Duffel bags full of clothes fit under the lower bed. Crisp rodeo shirts, long-sleeved with pearl snap buttons, embroidered with logos of sponsors, hung on a closet bar inside their dry-cleaning bags.

The cowboy's most important relationships were with his wife, his horse, and his traveling partners, but not always in that order. The circuit was hard living, a cycle of twelve-hour drives for eight-second rides. A traveling partner, or two or three of them, were the ones you shared most everything with, but mainly time and tight quarters, two things that can be hard to divide to everyone's satisfaction. Traveling partners had to agree on which rodeos to go to. They had to decide who drove, who picked the music, where everyone ate, who paid for gas, who bought the beer, and where everyone slept. They might snore and fart. They might be lovesick for girlfriends back home or go missing for hours at a time after a rodeo as they chased beers and girls. They might talk too much or not enough. You had to look past the cons and find the pros. There were no secrets. There were no bad attitudes. Rodeo didn't have much patience for selfishness. You had to appreciate the other voices and not mind long silences. That was a lot easier to do when the traveling partners were family and some of the most dominant cowboys in the sport.

■ ■ ■

For most cowboys, rodeo was a zero-sum game. It was a hobby on the side, a hope out of reach. No one got rich in rodeo from January to November. The goal for anyone trying to make a living out of the sport was to reach the National Finals Rodeo in Las Vegas each December. That was where lives changed.

To get there, winnings from the rest of the year had to be in the top fifteen in one of seven primary disciplines: bareback bronc riding, steer wrestling, team roping, saddle bronc riding, calf roping, barrel racing (the only women's event), and bull riding. The best might have reached six figures. Those who squeaked into the last slots might have won $60,000 all year. That was as much as more than two hundred professional golfers made each season on their men's tour, where they flew in jets and slept in fancy hotels and had people carry their gear and plied their trade at country clubs without ever getting dirty. For top bronc riders, the winnings might just cover expenses for the chase itself—things like gas, truck repairs, entry fees, and food. The toll on health and family was the unaccounted and unrecoverable cost.

"If you don't make $65,000 or $70,000, I don't think you can break even," Cody said. "Depends on how many guys you travel with."

But if a cowboy or cowgirl could navigate a fraction of the six hundred or so rodeos sanctioned by the Professional Rodeo Cowboys Association each year and earn just enough to finish in the top fifteen in the money standings, he or she might double, triple, or quadruple their winnings in ten nights in Las Vegas. Earnings got pushed over $200,000, even $300,000. Those who finished the year with the most money in their discipline were crowned with the gold buckle, the sport's biggest prize.

It was a sparkly hubcap of gold and sterling. It weighed more than half a pound and was almost five inches across, about the size of a decent cup saucer, but oval. It was made in Montana, and the design hadn't changed much in fifty years. The edges were cut by hand in a braid outline that made it sparkle. The flowers were green gold, the filigree was rose gold, and the center of it had a gold saddle bronc rider in relief—and in perfect form, feet up on the horse's neck, arm to the sky. No one could really put a value on the buckles, because every one was one of a kind, engraved with the name of the winner and the year of the championship. A lot of pro athletes in other sports, far richer sports, said they played for the ring or the trophy. Only in rodeo did they compete for the buckle.

The Wrights were aligned for a buckle dynasty. The year that Cody won his second gold buckle, Jesse, one of the twins and twelve years younger than Cody, finished sixteenth in the standings. He probably would have made the top fifteen had he not crushed vertebrae in his back, between the shoulder blades, when a horse smashed him inside the chute in Omaha at the end of the season. But an injury to another cowboy opened a slot for Jesse in the National Finals, and he figured he was healed enough to go, putting two Wrights in the field.

Jesse had not ridden a bronc for two months, and then he broke his foot in the first round. It swelled so much that he couldn't get his boot on and off, and Cody told him he should slice open the side of the boot with a bunch of vertical slashes to give it room to expand, because he could always buy new boots after the finals. Jesse did as Cody said and rode so well and so consistently that the Wrights had two of the top five saddle bronc riders in the world. Cody got the gold buckle. Jesse's prize was the sliced boot that he kept at home and the bone chip that still floated in his ankle.

A year later, Cody and Jesse were in the finals again, and Jake missed out because he finished $85 out of fifteenth place after a season's worth of rodeos. But Cody and the twins were all there the year after that. Nobody could tell the twins apart, except that they wore different-colored shirts and Jesse held the rein with his right hand. Bill wanted the boys to ride left-handed, because it was more natural for a cowboy on the range to hold the rein with his left hand and swing his rope with his right. But Jesse broke his left arm in junior high. He'd held the bronc rein in his right ever since.

Jesse, twenty-three then, entered the National Finals in first place, but his grip on the top spot loosened like a slipknot when

he was knocked unconscious in the eighth round. It looked like he wouldn't win a gold buckle of his own after all.

"I got me tipped into my right stirrup comin' outta there when he left, and I kept trying to move to my left and I was tipped to my right, so I was trying to get back in my saddle," he told a television interviewer two nights later. "I never could get back in. And all of a sudden, it felt like his butt come around and he clipped my legs or something, and I just hit and it just flipped me, like a quarter. And then I don't remember much after that."

"You could've lost the championship right there," the reporter said.

"To tell you the truth, I thought I did," Jesse said. "But then my dad come over and said, 'Pull it together and you might be able to finish on these two.' So I just tried to ride 'em the best I could and kept my nose clean the next couple days."

Jesse held on to the championship by a mere $797, one of the closest races ever. Cody was third and Jake was sixth. And now the Wrights had two world champions and three of the six best saddle bronc riders in the world. And more Wrights were coming.

Jesse soon used some of his new money to buy permits to run cattle on federal land near Beaver, and that extra summer range helped Bill add some cattle to the herd and gain some flexibility in moving them around. They never really talked about it, because that wasn't the way the Wrights were, but it was becoming clear that one peculiar way for the family to hold on to a dying tradition in the West was by dominating another.

Maybe the best way to build a herd and hang on to Smith Mesa was to win a lot of rodeos.

3

Pioneers

THE DESERT WORE the dark like a heavy blanket. Yellow light glowed from the square windows of a camp trailer parked in the red dirt, near horses that stood in silhouetted silence. Inside the door, Bill sat with his legs spread and his knife open, carving strings of potatoes into a pot at his feet. He opened a can of stew. A small television got decent reception from a couple of stations in Salt Lake City and had a video player, too. There was a stack of old movies, most of them forgotten Westerns, most of those starring John Wayne. Bill had seen them all too many times to count. He'd put one in now and then to keep him company.

The trailer was almost as much home as home was, at least through the winter and spring, when Evelyn was teaching and the boys were home with their families or on the rodeo circuit. Bill liked to work alone, and sometimes he would go days at Smith Mesa without talking to anyone but his dogs, his horses, or his cattle. He might bump into a ranger from Zion or talk to the man hired by the government to trap coyotes and the occasional mountain lion and bear, or to strangers and neighbors who happened down the road past the ranch. Sometimes people camped in the trees because they didn't want to pay the fees in the national park. They got startled when Bill came along on his horse.

It made Evelyn nervous, Bill being by himself, mending fences and checking on cattle from dawn to dusk and sometimes later. She worried that he would get hurt and not be able to get himself help, or wouldn't be found in time to be saved. Even the best horsemen got thrown, she knew, when their horses got spooked by a snake or a nervous cow, backed into a barbed-wire fence, or lost their balance on a loose rock or a steep incline. And she hoped that when it happened to Bill, someone would be there to pick him up if he couldn't do it himself.

A few years before, Bill was bucked off his horse and his hand got caught in the rein. The horse was jumping wildly and Bill was dangled and kicked before he slipped free and was dumped to the dirt, unconscious. Bill broke his scapula and dislocated his shoulder. The fingers of his left hand were cinched so tight in the rope for those few seconds that they almost instantly turned blue. Bill thought he might lose them. He never got the full feeling back.

But Jake had been nearby, by a stroke of luck, and kneeled at his father's side as Bill frothed at the mouth and eventually came to. "Dad, you're OK," Jake said to him. "That's not the lights of heaven you're lookin' at. That's just the sun shining down on you."

Bill wasn't handed much in life but tradition and roots. His parents, Calvin and Zona, didn't have a lot of money. Calvin quit school to care for his father, who was crippled from a fall off a horse that had been spooked by a cow. Zona was born in Hurricane but grew up on the Arizona Strip, the vast and remote expanse between the Grand Canyon and the Utah state line, where her parents raised alfalfa and sorghum and 125 head of cattle. When she was a teen-ager, her parents needed another hand, and they sent for Calvin Wright because they heard he was a hard worker. He was eighteen and fell in love with Zona, a couple of years younger, as she washed the family dishes late at night. They decided they wouldn't marry until she finished high school. They got married the day after she graduated.

They lived in a sheep wagon for years, and Calvin built ponds for a dollar a day. The family always had a few cattle, but that wasn't what paid bills. "My dad was a rancher by trade," Bill said, "but in this country, you had to do a lot of things to make ends meet." He worked for a time at a turkey farm and spent about ten years doing maintenance for Coleman, which built a test track up on Hurricane Mesa during the Cold War and ran rockets off the end to test ejection systems for pilots, back when Bill was a boy.

No, when Bill started out, he was on his own, left to make a living somehow, like his father and just about everyone else he knew. Now he was past sixty and it had come to this: a beautiful piece of land, a tangle of grazing permits, a couple hundred cows, and a bunch of boys off on the rodeo circuit.

Five of the seven boys were professional bronc riders, and getting themselves to all those rodeos and caring for their own families didn't leave them much time to tend the herd. The second-oldest, Calvin, named after Bill's father, had been a promising rider, too, until he broke his wrist in college, crushed in the chute by a fidgety bull. The painkillers he took led him into a drug addiction that he fought for years, between jobs as a ranch hand and a farrier, but Bill hoped he would get his life stable and someday become a trusted partner. Stuart, the youngest of the family, was still in high school, playing baseball, singing in the choir, and just starting to ride broncs. He was considering going on a Mormon mission, which would make him the first of the Wright boys to do so and would make Evelyn, especially, awfully proud.

A ranching axiom said that a family needed a hundred cows to make a living at it. Bill had grown his herd to about twice that, with Cody's help, but it needed to double, and keep doubling, to feed children and their children. As the Wrights grew exponentially, so must the herd.

"We want to get bigger," Bill said, "and it kind of depends on who's comin' in. We're just barely startin' to make some money in this."

Cody was in, and the other sons were coming behind him, slowly swept in the same direction, like dried leaves sucked forward by a passing truck. Calvin, Alex, Jake, Jesse, Spencer, and Stuart were still figuring out what came next, watching to see what Bill did, watching to see what Cody did, and figuring out whether they could turn rodeo into ranching.

"They're all interested," Evelyn said to someone on branding day, out of earshot of the boys, "but not all invested."

■ ■ ■

Evelyn was the glue that held everyone together, which was true of the women in most ranching and rodeo families. She was the heart of the family, if not the guts, always positive, persistently funny, quick with a bit of street wisdom. She was a ray of sunshine, even in the dark times. And her children knew what kind of dark times she'd pulled herself and them through.

Her family settled in Toquerville in the 1860s, part of the same Mormon migration that brought Bill's ancestors to nearby Virgin. Both their families worked on the Hurricane Canal, which took eleven years to complete and brought water seven miles from the Virgin Narrows into the valley, back in the early 1900s.

Evelyn spent her early years in California, but her parents split

when she was in grade school. She and her siblings came back to
Toquerville with her mother. It was only about six miles down to
Hurricane, and Evelyn would go to the old Eugene Theater there,
on the corner of State and Main, a block from where a rough boy
named Billy Wright grew up. He was a classmate of Evelyn's older
sister, and the sister teased Evelyn about the crush she had on Billy.

Bill's family knew the theater's owners, so when Bill was fifteen
he had a job there, selling popcorn and candy. Evelyn was twelve,
and she'd visit with him and they'd sit up in the balcony and watch
the ends of movies together. Before long, Bill rode his mare, Bunny,
from Hurricane to Toquerville to visit Evelyn. They went on horseback trips together, up into the barren hills and down to the swim-
ming hole in the Virgin River, where all the teenagers gathered.
When Bill turned sixteen he bought a 1957 Chevy, a black two-
door hardtop, and she could hear him heading to her house from a
mile away.

Bill and Evelyn married in Toquerville, at the Church of Jesus
Christ of Latter-day Saints, on November 9, 1973. Bill was nineteen. Evelyn was sixteen, and didn't yet know she was pregnant.

"Any time I do something good," Evelyn said forty years later,
"he says, 'Man, I did a good job raising you.'"

Their first baby, Selinda, came the next May. By then, Bill was
working at the Grand Canyon, and the little family lived at Yaki
Point on the South Rim, not far from the tourists at Grand Canyon
Village. Bill ran mule trains, loaded with supplies and city-slicker
tourists, down and up the Kaibab Trail. The route started at 7,260
feet and snaked steeply and sharply, dropping nearly a mile in elevation to Phantom Ranch, at the edge of the Colorado River. It was
where Bill learned how to handle horses in tough desert terrain,
where any misstep could be the last.

"We would pack the young mules for a while until they gentled down," Bill said. "Then the packers like me would ride 'em, then the guides would ride 'em. When we finally felt comfortable enough with 'em, we'd let the tourists ride 'em. But the pack mules were the least trained."

It was also where he learned to tell stories. When he got to telling them, he slowed down, mulling his thoughts along the way and adding tension in the right places, as if he was talking in front of a campfire.

"Tuesdays and Wednesdays were grocery day," he'd say. "We'd put supplies and food into Phantom, plus hay and grain and beer if there was room. This particular day, we had a string of mules with beer, forty-some cases. We went by a hiker who pulled off his backpack and dropped it on the ground with a thud. That spooked a mule. They were all tied together with pigtails on their pack saddles, this quarter-inch hemp rope that would break if they yanked too hard, to keep 'em all from going over the edge if one of 'em did. The spooked mule stirred all the rest of 'em, and they broke apart and started buckin'. They throwed every load off each mule. It took me an hour to gather all those mules, they was so spooked up. And out of forty cases of beer, there was one can that didn't get punctured."

He laughed at the thought of it and continued when he caught his breath.

"Once, we packed a river-raft boat motor. Another time, we had a bunch of toilet bowl cleaner, and the mule bucked and broke the jugs. It was an acid cleaner, and it spilled and scalded the mule. Burned the hair off and made these big blisters. We also packed cases of eggs. All the mules had different gaits, so you had to know which ones to put the eggs on. Some mules never broke a single egg. The ones that moved side to side, so its back just swayed, they could carry 'em. But the mules that rolled, with their backs that went up and down in a twisting motion, they would break the eggs.

"Near the bottom of the trail, you go through a tiny tunnel, right onto a suspension bridge over the river. It's six feet wide, with ropes hanging down to hold it up. We packed a three-foot-by-six-foot piece of glass to take down, and we put bales of hay on each side of the mule, and then laid the glass across the top. It barely made it onto the bridge. And then, as the bridge rocked, with each step, the one edge of the glass went between the ropes. It'd take another step, and the glass went between the ropes on the other side. We slithered across the bridge with no space to spare."

Bill still remembered the mules' names: Harry, Josie, Jackie, Marshall, Booger Red—that was the one that kicked and broke Bill's hand. Josephine and Geneva were the ones that Bill put the expensive supplies on. But if the mules were too good, too gentle, they were promoted from carrying packs to carrying guides. And once they showed that they were trusty enough, they carried the tourists.

"There was a guy named Wilbur, some kind of newspaper editor from back east," Bill said. "He and his wife would come every year from New York and we took them down to Phantom Ranch. Well, with mules, you wanted to keep them together so that they wouldn't trot to catch up. It's safer that way. But one mule, one named Croppy, kept lagging behind. This woman, the editor's wife, I'll never forget, she said that Croppy was tired.

"'No, he's not tired,' I told her. 'He's just lazy.' And she said, 'Young man, I'll tell you something. Anything that's been between my legs for eight hours is sure going to be tired.'"

Bill laughed when he told stories, sometimes before he reached the end, the kind of laugh that erupted from the chest and shook his shoulders and made it impossible to talk for a moment or two.

Summertime temperatures on the trail into the Grand Canyon could blast past a hundred degrees, and Bill sometimes left in the relative cool at two in the morning to beat the heat. He'd come across sleeping hikers, who usually heard the mules coming and stumbled out of the way. Sometimes Bill would have to yell at them, and sometimes even get off his mount and kick them awake.

"One guy didn't get up," Bill said. "I nudged him in the foot. His head was kind of behind a water break across the trail. But there was enough moonlight to see that he was puffed up. I thought I saw maggots on his face, but it was just June grass. I checked his pulse. There was nothin'. So I rode back up. I woke up Evelyn and I called the rangers. We went back down and I helped load the guy into a gurney from a helicopter. And I remember he was groaning as he moved. I thought, 'Is he still alive?' But I guess the air comes out of 'em when they die, so they make noises when you move 'em."

Bill came across another dead body once—smelled it before he saw it, and thought it was a dead mule deer in the brush. It was a hiker who had fallen over the edge from high above. He rescued a doctor who had hiked down to Phantom Canyon around Christmas but was afraid to face the cold and the uphill hike back to the rim. Bill carried him up by mule, thinking he might lose him in the freezing temperatures. Bill and Evelyn warmed him up in the mule barn. Some time later, when Booger Red broke Bill's hand, Bill walked into the doctor's office and found the same man. "Take care of this guy," the doctor said to the attendants. "He saved my life once."

■ ■ ■

After several years at the Grand Canyon and at a nearby ranch, and after Bill and Evelyn eternalized their marriage on November 11, 1975, at the temple in Manti, they settled back into Hurricane to raise a family. Cody was on the way, born two weeks before the family moved into a three-bedroom house on 100 West Street.

It all happened at about the same time that Bill's father got ill and decided to sell his modest farming and ranching operation at Smith

Mesa. At the time, Bill had $4,000 in savings, a wife, a growing family, and professional rodeo aspirations. He had gone to college at Dixie State over in St. George and competed on the rodeo team, but he got fed up when coaches wanted him to be a steer wrestler, not a bull or bronc rider, because that's where the team had a need.

He still thought rodeo could be a way to make a living for a time. He was headed to Wyoming to ride broncs when Evelyn was struck with appendicitis. Her illness wiped out much of their savings, and Bill reconsidered his career choices. He took on the small operation at Smith Mesa and went looking for other work to pay the bills.

"If things had went a little different," he'd say now and again, "I'd a been a rodeo bum, too."

Bill got on as a waterman, controlling the flow of irrigation for the farmers in the area. A stone marker off of Highway 9, just after it bent north to avoid the bluff with the town's H painted on it, provided a key bit of history should anyone ever pull off the road and read the small print: "Hurricane, August 6, 1904. After 11 years of work on the canal (1893–1904), 'they let out a big shout as the water gushed down the hill. Names for the new city-to-be were discussed and voted upon. We thank God for these pioneers of our valley.'"

The name became Hurricane, apparently for the fierce winds that whipped through, and Bill and Evelyn's growing family settled a couple of blocks from where Bill grew up on Main Street. The children kept coming, thirteen spread across twenty-three years. Selinda was born when Bill was twenty and Evelyn was seventeen. Then came Cody, then Laurelee, Calvin, Michaela, Monica, Alex, the dark-haired twins Jake and Jesse, red-headed Spencer, Kathryn, Becca, and Stuart.

Evelyn was seven months pregnant with Spencer when she helped fifteen-year-old Selinda deliver her first baby, which was how it was that Evelyn became a thirty-three-year-old grandmother. The last four children, starting with Spencer, were uncles and aunts before they were born. Bill said that the numbers grew fast once the grandchildren started to hit the ground. Evelyn shook her head at Bill's choice of words.

"Hit the ground?" she said. "He's always comparing children to calves."

The Wrights even took in another boy who was Cody's age for a time, a boy who was too much of a handful for his grandparents to raise. He and Cody slept in a camper outside. Calvin slept in a pantry that they called the fruit room. The girls slept in the living room. The four little boys—Alex, Jake, Jesse, and Spencer—slept on blankets laid out on the floor each night.

"We had kids stacked everywhere, like firewood," Evelyn said.

They were polite and precocious kids raised on the Book of Mormon and the Little Britches books. The boys were a little rough, but well-meaning, like their father, who once got in trouble for rolling tires down the hill from the painted H above Hurricane into people's backyards. They got in fights, and one father scolded his son for being dumb enough to pick on a Wright boy. You don't fight a kid who gets on two-thousand-pound bulls, the father said. They ain't scared of nothing. Bill laughed when he told that story.

But nothing stays the same, no matter how much you want it to, and Hurricane was at turns too small and too big, too familiar and too new. St. George, a few miles south along the interstate, had sprawled into a retirement community and a vacation destination filled with golf courses and chain restaurants. Hurricane, too, had changed from a nothing blip to a gateway to outdoor adventure and the national park that was getting more popular every year. There were stoplights and tourists and what counted as traffic on weekends in the summer.

With all the new construction going on, Bill left his job as a waterman and got into the concrete business, doing small jobs around the area—sidewalks, gutters, driveways, things like that. It's the work that really raised the Wrights. Concrete paid the bills, and most of the boys helped out with jobs, learning the value of hard work and an honest handshake.

But they always dabbled in livestock and farming at Smith Mesa. The Wrights had a few cattle and some pigs—ten sows and a boar—and Bill made money on the side breaking horses. The night Calvin was born, a sow had thirteen piglets. The next day, Bill told his friends all about the birth—of the piglets, not Calvin. "You forgot to tell 'em about Calvin?" Evelyn said.

Bill and Evelyn tried to build a bigger house, but one parcel they bought was zoned for commercial, not residential, use, and they couldn't get it changed. Then they bought land up the hill from Hurricane, not far from the dump, but it was declared a tortoise habitat and the city wouldn't let them build. They started thinking of leaving.

"I guess the Lord just wanted me out of there," Evelyn said.

But there was more to it than that. Bill had developed a habit of drinking. He disappeared for days at a time, doing God knows what, carousing in far-off places and leaving Evelyn alone with all the children. She couldn't depend on him anymore, never knew where he'd be or what he'd be doing or what kind of condition he'd be in, right at the time in life when she needed all the help she could get. It was definitely enough to chase Evelyn away and leave Hurricane behind.

"He broke me," she said, and her voice softened as she talked about it twenty years later. "I had to get out."

She had heard about a town named Milford, where the schools were good and the houses were cheap, about ninety minutes north of Hurricane and separated from most of the world by windy, wide-open spaces tied together by two-lane ribbons of empty blacktop. She packed all the possessions into a horse trailer and took her children, eleven of them at the time, along with her.

Selinda was just about out of the house by then, and Cody was in high school, and everyone could cram into the old Jefferson place that Evelyn rented on the main road outside of town, four to a bedroom. Alex, Jake, Jesse, and Spencer shared a room, with two pairs of bunks, and when Evelyn checked on them on the first morning there, she found the beds empty and the boys on blankets on the floor, like they were used to.

Evelyn was afraid she'd have to support herself and everyone else, so she took college classes in the small gaps of time she could find and became a teacher, and all the kids learned how to cook and help and do things for themselves. Evelyn told Bill he could come if and when he got his act together, which he eventually did, after a year by himself in Hurricane, when he finally traded whisky and beer for two new vices, Coke and Smarties.

He bid on, and won, a big concrete project on the pig farms outside Milford—so big that he had fifty-six people on the payroll for a time and Cody running crews, even though he was still a teenager. That's when Bill came and stayed, begging forgiveness, vowing to be a changed man. Along the way, he poured the foundation for a house on five acres at the north edge of town, and before the couple could start building on top of it, the man was transferred to Wyoming. The Wrights bought the land, changed the plans, and built their own house. And eventually, Bill built a rodeo arena out back.

And sometimes, so many years and heartbreaks later, when Bill and Evelyn found themselves sitting together somewhere quiet and peaceful, he would take her hand and look at her, and tell her softly, "I'm sorry for all the hell I put you through."

And when they were somewhere with all the kids and all the grandkids, somewhere like sitting next to a campfire at Smith Mesa or in the living room at home, he would look at her again and tell her, "And to think, I almost missed all this."

4

The Prayer

BILL BROUGHT THE HERD south from Beaver to Smith Mesa late each fall. By late spring, with the temperatures rising and the grasses thinning, most of the cattle had wandered off the mesa and down into the wash, looking for feed and shade. The cattle couldn't always be seen from the cliffs at the edge of the mesa, but when the wind was right, their conversational grunts and the hollow clang of the bells strapped to a few of the habitual wanderers floated up to the mesa. The trick each spring was to get them out. That took Bill and the boys a few days.

The wash was unremarkable on maps. If marked at all, it was a thin squiggle of blue dashes to indicate that water was an irregular presence. Topographic maps did the landscape more justice, with their waves of lines squeezed together to mark the canyon's steep edge. It was such a vast, sunken place that to survey its depths from the crumbling cliffs required the chin to be pressed to the chest and an absence of a fear of heights. Hawks and eagles, even the occasional condor, soared below the edge of the rim, above a messy jumble of giant boulders, piñon pines, and, mostly hidden from view above, a creek bed.

Water flowed only for a brief time during the spring runoff and after summer thunderstorms that doused the desert with irregularity. But the drought had been relentless for three years running, and the creek bed was little more than a dusty trail snaking through the depths of the canyon. It funneled south to North Creek, then on to the Virgin River—five miles as the crow flew, at least twice that as a cow walked.

Up on the mesa, the camp in the hollow percolated to life, the smell of eggs and bacon wafting into the clear sky. The boys chewed quietly on breakfast before shuffling up to the corral. Soon, they swung themselves on horseback and slinked over the canyon walls through a narrow perforation of crumbled rock. The mere journey into the wash was a daring rite of passage reserved for brave teenagers and young horsemen and, on occasion, one of the Wright sisters. Most of those a generation older and a generation younger stayed on the mesa, traveling miles of old dirt roads and rolling hills in search of stragglers from the herd. But the Wright boys threaded unmarked trails so steep that they had to double-check the cinches of their saddles and sometimes had to dismount and lead their nervous horses by the rein. One slip, one misstep, meant possible death for cowboy or horse, or maybe both.

Once to the canyon floor, the boys and their horses worked in small groups, combing upstream through the prickly landscape. They wandered into the deep side pockets of the wash, looking for flashes of movement and listening for the grunts and murmurs of cows or the metallic chime of their bells. Even once you found cattle and nudged them in the right direction, you could lose them fast in the thicket and rocks. The day before, Jesse tried to negotiate a tangle of thorny trees and got hung up on a thick overhanging branch as his horse walked on underneath without him. Jesse ended up on the ground. The brim of his straw cowboy hat, caught and twisted in twigs, was ripped away in a circle, separated like the lid of an opened can of beans.

Jesse worked in a pair with CoBurn, his brother-in-law. They lost sight of the other Wright boys soon after they got into the wash. By late afternoon, as the folds of the landscape got absorbed in shadow, they had herded a dozen cattle into a deep box canyon. To keep the procession moving in the twilight, Jesse used a language of interjections. He clicked his tongue and made kissing noises to get their attention, and shouted when he needed more immediate attention.

"Git!" he shouted. "Ha!"

CoBurn cracked a whip. The jolt echoed off the canyon walls and startled the cattle into movement. There was no obvious exit, but the cows and calves trekked up the steep, skinny trail, single file, as able-footed as mountain goats, up out of the trees and toward the canyon rim. They had found their way into the wash, and they were remarkably stable climbers coming out.

The trail reached a hairpin curve. It was a sharp, reversing left-hand corner that forced the cattle to momentarily turn straight up the steep slope for about ten feet before the path completed its arc. One by one, with little hesitation, the cattle scrambled up it, each one's hooves loosening a small cascade of dirt and rocks onto the one below it. They negotiated the stretch and kept plodding, higher and higher, toward the canyon rim.

The cattle safely up the corner, the boys dismounted. Jesse took his horse by the rein, and together they scrambled up the curve, boots and hooves pumping, sliding, pumping, as if climbing a greased stairway. After a few seconds, they were perched safely on the horizontal trail overhead, hearts and lungs pounding.

CoBurn followed. His horse heaved and jerked up the incline, desperate to find solid footing. It slid back and paddled wildly between its upward bursts, then fell back onto its hind legs and lost its balance. Its snout pointed to the sky. Its feet scrambled for a foothold. In irretrievable slow motion, the entire horse tipped backward.

"Watch out!" Jesse shouted. "He's coming!"

CoBurn leapt to his left and ducked behind an overhanging boulder. The horse, all spindly legs and braying head, tumbled past in a sliding, bouncing somersault. For fifty feet it rolled helplessly until it crashed into a stand of trees, shaking them furiously. A dust cloud rose from where the horse had passed. Everything went quiet.

"Is he dead?" Jesse finally asked from above. His voice carried a presumption of the answer. CoBurn stared down the slope, looking for signs.

"I think so," CoBurn replied.

The dust slowly settled. After a few silent moments, through the trees came a heavy wheeze.

"He's breathing!" CoBurn said. He scrambled and slid down the hill on the heels of his boots and found the horse on its side, against a pair of sturdy trunks. "I think he's OK!" he shouted up the hill.

The horse tried to stand after a minute or two. It wobbled and could not keep its balance in the loose rocks of the steep slope and fell again. It slid through the stand of trees like a pinball through bumpers, another twenty feet down the mountain.

The boys assumed that the horse had at least one broken leg and would have to be put down. Jesse had a pistol holstered to his belt. He tied his horse to the root ball of a juniper along the narrow path and scrambled down the loose slope to CoBurn.

CoBurn's horse, as if startled awake by the prospect, scrambled to its feet again and stood on all fours. The boys stared at it with wide-eyed surprise.

"I think he's OK," Jesse said, with an inflection of wonder. The saddle was ruined, broken like kindling on the inside, the hard, curved shape of the wooden saddletree mangled and limp beneath the smooth leather. CoBurn slung the rigging over his shoulder, hoping some of it could be salvaged. The boys tied the horse to a tree.

"I wish I would have been up ahead of him," CoBurn said. "I could have held him with my lead rope and at least tried to balance him."

"He's fine," Jesse said. "He's walking and everything. You want to wait like an hour and then go jump him up it again? I think you ought to leave him. I sure hate to see that son of a bitch go down twice."

The cattle were long gone, already atop the mesa. They were scattered among the trees and out of sight, like seeds in a breeze. The boys scrambled back up the loose slope, untied Jesse's horse, and hiked the remaining stretch of the skinny trail until they were out of the canyon. They decided to let CoBurn's horse stay overnight. Jesse offered to gather the cattle alone and push them the remaining few miles to the pasture next to camp, where the herd was being collected and held. It would take a couple of hours. CoBurn, without a horse, broke away toward the dirt road.

At camp in the hollow, dinner was ready and Bill and Evelyn were surrounded by a herd of Wrights. Bill took off his cowboy hat for the first time all day, but it left behind a crease in his buzz cut where it had been sitting. Everyone held hands and bowed heads. Bill squinted his eyes shut.

"Our heavenly Father, we come before you this day, we thank you for the blessings we enjoy," Bill said in his gravelly voice. "We thank you for the opportunity we have to come and enjoy one another's company and get the work done on the ranch. We're especially thankful for this free nation we live in and the opportunity we have to worship Thee in the manner we choose, and to choose our livelihoods, and for this great nation. And we thank you for this food that's been prepared, and ask you to bless it to give our bodies nourishment and strength that we might better serve Thee and others. These many blessings we only ask and thank you for in the name of Jesus Christ. Amen."

A line formed toward a table with a checked cloth, covered in Dutch ovens filled with chicken, others with peach cobbler. There were bowls of fruit salad and ears of corn. Most of the boys were still gathering cows in the dark while everyone else ate near the campfire. Over strawberry shortcake, Bill learned about CoBurn's falling horse. He barely stopped chewing.

"It ain't the first time that's happened," he said between bites. Just a year before, Spencer was atop a horse that tumbled. The horse was all right, but Spencer was thrown against a tree and knocked momentarily unconscious.

"When I was a boy, we lost a cow over the edge," Bill said. "And I did it again a few years ago, lower in the wash."

He explained that the rocks and dry dirt got loosened by all the hooves. He told himself that he needed to build some sort of wall to hold it all in place, because there was no other reasonable place to drive the cattle out of the wash.

Back in the dim canyon, Alex, the third of the boys, came up the trail with a half-dozen pairs of cows and calves and found a horse tied to a tree in the dusky light. He recognized it as CoBurn's and could only guess why it was there. It seemed fine. He untied it and coaxed it up the incline, and it came without hesitation. Alex tied it to his own horse as he drove his day's find back toward camp.

Ahead of him by about a mile, Jesse drove his batch along the canyon rim. He opened a gate and nudged the cattle into a vast pasture where the herd was being collected. A bit later, the land as dark as the sky, Cody came along on horseback, following a few more cows and calves that he had pulled from the wash. He passed through the same gate and closed it behind him. The cattle disappeared into the black field.

By the time Cody got back to camp, his children were asleep, the Dutch ovens were cold, and the coals in the campfire smoldered a dusty orange, like faded sunlight.

PART TWO

King of the Rodeo

5

The King

CODY PARKED HIS TRUCK out front of his house and checked to see that the horses were in the pen out back. The wind blew across the flat valley, kicking up a dust devil that danced in the barren field.

"I need to plant something really bad," Cody said as he looked to the west. "I'm tired of the dust blowing."

The house where Cody and ShaRee raised their five kids was on the south side of Milford, on nine acres in the flats, where the circular hay fields, shaped by center-pivot sprinklers, were crosshatched by narrow lanes. From the air, it looked like a bunch of circles fitted inside a bunch of squares, like game pieces on a checkerboard.

One of Cody's sisters married into a hay-farming family and lived in a majestic house across the highway. Jake and Loni lived about a mile away, not far from Jesse and Aubrey. Most everyone else lived in town. The house was a split-level, and over the stairs in the entry hung a large poster-board photograph of Cody at his first National Finals Rodeo, a vast sea of faces watching him ride a bronc named Mullin Hill. Cody won that round, the tenth and final one, with a 91, and he finished third in the world that year. The silver buckle that Cody received for the go-round win was on the belt he still wore nearly everywhere he went a decade later.

"Great horse," Cody said as he walked upstairs. "He's dead now."

A saddle lay on the bannister. Next to the sofa was a table lamp molded like a bronze cowboy boot. A dog had chewed a throw pillow to smithereens, the guts spread across the carpet. The boys were eating peanut butter and jelly sandwiches and vanilla Zingers. Stetson, now in his teens, stared into a computer screen, watching YouTube videos of his father's old rides. Cody looked over his shoulder.

"What's that one, Stetson?" Cody asked. "Sundance?"

"Yeah. You were 88 and a half on that ride," Stetson said. "That's my favorite ride."

Stetson watched his father kick in perfect rhythm with the horse, tighten and straighten, tighten and straighten, like pistons. The rein stayed taut in his left hand, his right arm stretched behind him to make himself a long diagonal plank atop the bronc. Some rodeo announcers, when they introduced Cody, said he was lifted from a textbook. His form was classically perfect. It was the form his brothers and sons imitated.

Cody flipped through the mail on the counter and wandered back outside, into a stiff breeze. A swing in the shape of a rocking horse hung from a cottonwood in the yard. The dirt drive held Cody's two Dodge trucks, his motor home, and an old Milford ambulance that Rusty and Ryder had bought with the hope of renovating the inside and using it to travel to rodeos. A metal shipping container, like those carried by freight trains, was planted in the dirt nearby, there long enough to grow weeds around it. It served as a tack room and was filled with rodeo gear like saddles and reins. A litter of kittens lived underneath it, and just then a mother cat came from the field, carrying a baby gopher in her mouth. Cody didn't notice. There were a few Australian cattle dogs that Cody bought from a breeder in Oklahoma and was trying to train, a couple of goats, and, in a nearby field behind the house, about ten horses. Lily Jo, Cody and ShaRee's five-year-old, named after a flower because ShaRee figured it would be the only girly thing about a girl with four older brothers, raced past atop a horse, like a jockey atop a thoroughbred, her blond ponytail bouncing behind her.

And on one edge of the drive, under the shade of a big cottonwood, was a mechanical bull. It was surrounded by an inflatable mat and hooked to a generator that whirred to life with the push of a button. The bull itself was covered in hide, but the hair was matted and worn off from use. Cody wished it was a bit narrower through its midsection, shaped more like a bronc than a bull, but it worked well enough. A bronc saddle was strapped to the machine's back.

Statler straddled it and Cody turned on the power, low. The thing hummed and heaved, and Statler, not yet a teen, bobbed up and down comfortably in the saddle. One hand clenched a thick rein, the other waved over his head.

"The only thing that needs to move is from your knees down, plus your hand as the horse bobs its head," Cody said. "But you have to keep the rein tight."

A bucking saddle was different than a riding saddle. There was no horn, and the stirrup leathers came out of the front, not straight off the side. It attached to the horse in two places. A wide, multi-roped cinch went under the horse's chest behind the front legs. It was connected to the saddle on each side by a thin, supple leather strap called a latigo, which was drawn tight through rings until it ran out of length and was tied off. A back cinch, snugged tight with buckles, wrapped just behind the low spot of the horse's belly. The thin end of a six-foot rein clipped to a halter on the horse's head.

The other end was a thick and loose weave, almost frayed, to give the rider something meaty and soft to hold inside a clenched fist.

The key calculation for every ride was how much rein to give. Too little, and a drop of the horse's head might pull the rider over. Too much, and the rider exited off the back or got jerked to the side.

The career of a bucking horse could last a decade or more, and it built a reputation for how it bucked, skipped, hesitated, spun, and tossed its head. Some broncs were rejects from ranches or racetracks, deemed too dangerous to ride. Others were bred to buck, the way fast horses were bred to run, and bloodlines were important. The top broncs weren't ridden often, maybe once a week, so that they didn't get too used to having something heavy on their backs.

The Wrights recorded all their rides in a worn ledger to tell future Wrights what a bronc's habits were and how much rein to give a particular bronc. With the rein pulled tight, one fist past the front edge of the saddle was "a little." A fist and an extended thumb was average, what the cowboys called X. An "X and five" meant a fist with an extended thumb, plus the width of five fingers of the other hand. A 2X meant two fists, with the thumbs extended. Cody kept the book in his truck, but more and more he typed notes into his phone, his contacts list full of horses. When his brothers were at a different rodeo and they drew a particular horse, they called and asked for the recommended rein to give and any advice from Cody's memory bank about how the bronc came out of the chute or the direction it liked to turn in the ring.

When the gate swung open, the horse bounded out sideways. Cowboys had to be prepared for that initial burst, like an engine starting with the gas pedal floored, and for the ninety-degree twist into the arena. Someone behind the chutes held a flank strap, thick with padding, that wrapped around the bronc's belly against its back legs. The rope was let go as soon as the bronc pulled it tight with its first bounce or two. Bucking horses bucked naturally, but the flank strap got them kicking.

The best kicked their back feet high, higher than their front shoulders and over the head of the cowboy, while their chins dropped nearly to the ground. They had a natural tendency to jump persistently high and hard—not to run across the arena, not to hesitate between bucks, not to thrash their head or twist and jerk like a bull. The hope was for a dependable, smooth performance, up and down, the bronc arching its back with all four feet off the ground, then landing and recoiling and doing it again, ten or twelve times over eight seconds. Power and height and consistency were virtues more revered than unpredictability.

The goal for the cowboy was to find a rhythm instantly and sustain it in a charade of effortlessness. It was an eight-second partnership of choreography in which the bronc was an angry participant. The rider's lower legs were supposed to cock back as the horse bucked into the air and snap forward just as the bronc landed on its front hooves.

"When the front feet hit the ground and the back feet are kicked up, your feet should be forward, so it's like you're standing," Cody told Statler as the machine dipped and lunged. Cody controlled the joystick and the boy found his groove. When Statler's older brothers were at the control, they'd turn the dial up high just to watch him get thrown onto the thin, worn pad and have a good laugh. Cody let Statler ride, trying to build memory into the boy's muscles.

Rider and animal each got half the score, on a scale that added to 100. A score above 90 was rare. Anything above 80 was usually in the money. The bronc was judged for how high, hard, and consistently it bucked. The cowboy was judged by how well he stayed in control above the chaos. The rein should be tight, the seat in the saddle, the legs churned together in time with the ups and downs of the horse below. The higher the cowboy's dulled spurs stroked up on the horse's neck, the better, all the way to the mane. Keeping the toes pointed out, spurs against the animal, was point-adding showmanship. Clinging for dear life excited the crowd, but not the judges.

There were only a few hard rules. There was no touching the horse with the off hand. As in bull riding and bareback riding, the cowboy had to stay on for eight seconds to receive a score. A rider's feet had to be above the break of the horse's shoulders when the horse landed on its front feet the first time out of the chute. That was the "mark out" rule, and breaking it meant instant disqualification.

No points meant no money. Even staying on didn't guarantee anything. At most rodeos, only the top six scores were in the money, leaving most of the riders empty-handed. There was an insult-to-injury quality to the exercise. Riders that rode smoothly and safely usually got rewarded with the best scores. The ones left broken in the dirt got nothing.

Cody turned off the machine and Statler stepped down and jogged back into the warmth of the house. The sun had fallen behind the hills across the valley and the wind was cold now. Cody had chores to get done, and he didn't have much time before dark. He had been helping Bill out the past few days, down at Smith Mesa, and he had to leave in the morning for a stretch of rodeos. Coming and going like he did always got him thinking.

The herd was growing and Bill was getting older, and every year Cody took on more responsibility from his father. His oldest boy, Rusty, had finished high school and moved out, and the others were growing up fast. Life felt like it was in transition, and Cody wasn't sure which way to lean. Just a few days before, he and ShaRee were talking about all of it. Maybe it was Cody's growing list of rodeo injuries that got them thinking, or Bill's rising anxiety over where everything was headed, but Cody wanted to get it out into the open.

"What do you think about ranching when I'm done?" Cody asked ShaRee. She figured that was where things were headed. Cody had bought all those cattle for his dad's herd, and he'd been going with his dad lately to look at ranches to buy should they ever sell Smith Mesa.

"Would you go with me?" he asked.

"No, I want to live in Milford all my life," she said sarcastically.

And now here he was, teaching another of his sons how to ride a bucking horse, feeling the tug of the future and the past, wondering just how a man is supposed to know when the big moments of life are at hand.

"I can't figure out for sure if I could stop rodeoing and just do ranching," Cody said, the wind whipping dirt off his pasture. "I don't know if I could quit doing it and not take away from Dad. He enjoys it, and I like seeing him enjoy it."

His father was one reason to keep at it. His sons were another.

"I never gave it a thought that I'd still be riding when Rusty was riding," Cody said.

Rusty had turned pro, and Ryder was only a year or two away and looked to be as good as Rusty. And behind him was Stetson, already a junior high champion, and then Statler, plenty comfortable atop the mechanical bucking horse.

No, this had to be done. Cody would help Bill as much as he could. But he needed to—wanted to—be there for Rusty, and maybe the others, God willing, because being among the best in the world at something was one thing, but doing it alongside your son, and maybe your next son in a couple more years, and maybe the one after that and the one after that, might be about the rarest thing in the world.

Besides, summer was coming, and Cody was in first place in the world saddle bronc standings.

■ ■ ■

Cody pulled his Dodge into the dusty contestants' lot, behind the livestock chutes opposite the grandstand, about thirty minutes before the rodeo started and parked it among the sea of pickups and horse trailers. He stepped into the heat wearing what he wore to drive: a black T-shirt tucked into his Wranglers, cowboy boots, a straw cowboy hat, and sunglasses. His arms and face were tan. His belt was still pulled tight on his narrow waist, cinched by a silver buckle that reflected the sun. He was feeling good, healthy, and cruising comfortably into the heat of the summer.

"Can I have your autograph?" a belt-high young girl asked Cody at the urging of her mother, who prodded her forward by the shoulder. The girl handed Cody a rodeo program, and he knelt down and signed it and handed it back. Cody smiled and thanked the girl and her mother with a tip of his hat.

He was still the king, drawing nods from competitors and cattlemen, reverential handshakes from young cowboys, and autograph requests from children, encouraged by parents who thought their kids someday would appreciate having Cody Wright's signature.

It had been a stellar spring, and Cody dominated the Texas swing. He won in Fort Worth, barely beating out Rusty, who had finished high school a semester early so that he could turn pro and start traveling with his father. Cody took a go-round and finished second in the finals in San Antonio. He won in Bay City, was runner-up to Jake in San Angelo, won in Mercedes and Lubbock, and took second in Beaumont. He went up to Oklahoma and dominated the circuit finals, winning two go-rounds and the final, which they called the short round or the short go. He grabbed more than $20,000 for the weekend.

Then the circuit shifted to California, as it did every spring. One morning, when Rusty got in the truck back in Milford, he carried just a small bag.

"You know we're going to be gone all week?" Cody said.

"I thought we were just gone two days," Rusty replied. He didn't know where they were going, exactly, or when they'd return. He hustled into the house and scooped up a few more days' worth of clothes. They pulled into Red Bluff about forty minutes before the start of the rodeo, the sun already behind the big grandstand to the west.

Plans didn't always work out. Flat tires and blown radiators had caused plenty of misses. Jesse missed Lewiston because he missed a flight—"Cody was madder'n hell at me for that," he said—and CoBurn hit a deer outside of Sheridan, so the crew missed Dodge City. A fatal wreck closed the two-lane road to Plains, and a truckload of Wrights sat for hours on a desolate road, thinking they would miss the performance. "I gotta admit, I wasn't too worried," Jesse said. "I had a piece-of-crap horse. But everyone else wanted to get there."

In Red Bluff, Cody filled out paperwork for the others on the back of the truck.

"Is your birthday the twentieth?" he asked Spencer.

"Twenty-first," Spencer said. He wore a T-shirt, tucked into his buckled jeans, and a mesh cap with a flat brim. He looked part cowboy, part skateboarder. The boys changed into their pressed, monochrome snap-button shirts.

"Let me see your hat," Rusty said to his dad. The front of Cody's brown felt cowboy hat didn't extend out and dip forward like an awning, the way the boys liked to wear them. Each had his individual style and color preference. Jake usually wore black and Jesse something closer to white. CoBurn liked his tan hat tall, like a proud sheriff, and Cody wore his relatively flat. They all avoided making the sides too deep and steep, like taco shells. Rusty massaged and bent his dad's hat with his hands, trying to mold it into a respectable shape.

"Stetson's already tried to fix it," Cody said.

"It's pretty soft," Rusty said.

"That's all right," Cody said. "So am I."

They carried saddles over one shoulder and duffel bags over the other from the parking lot to the chutes. Along the way, people Cody recognized—and some he didn't—went out of their way to say hello to him. He greeted everyone with a sheepish smile and a nod. He seemed embarrassed by attention, even though he had been getting it every time he neared a rodeo grandstand for twenty years.

"Mr. Wright," another bronc rider said.

Rusty stopped. "Goldang it," he said, "I forgot to call someone about my horse tonight."

He set his saddle down and reached into his bag for his phone, then held it to his mouth. "Call CoBurn Bradshaw," he said, with perfect diction, and the phone dialed. CoBurn had had the bronc in Walla Walla the year before.

Behind the chutes was a hive of activity and nervousness. The public-address announcer interrupted. The cowboys barely noticed. It was background noise.

"There are people in places in the world today that would rather not see it fly, that would rather see us die," the announcer said somberly over a recording of "Proud to Be an American." A parachutist dropped out of the sky at an angle. A flag was attached to him, too, and it fluttered behind him as he landed perfectly in the middle of the arena. The crowd cheered and the announcer led a prayer. He thanked Jesus Christ, and when fans cheered after a chorus of "amen," he added, "Bless you for that cheer." A woman sang the national anthem.

"I love you, too," Cody said into his cell phone, to someone back in Milford. One of the top bronc riders approached.

"Hey, Cody," Jacobs Crawley said. "Whaddya reckon on Hat Stomper? You been there a few times."

Cody scrolled through notes in his phone, seeing what he had on how much rein to give one of the era's great broncs. It'd been ridden only four times in five years, the horse's biography on the rodeo company website said. "Has thrown off every Wright brother," it added.

"Sounds like he wants to squat," Crawley said. "Whaddya think? Close to average?"

"I'd probably go a loose average," Cody said. "I missed him out in Santa Maria, and Jake had him in Reno. He was sittin' back, and sometimes he leans to the side. He's a cheatin' son of a bitch. If he'd stand up in the chute, then throw you off, that's just buckin'. But if he's leanin', that's cheatin'."

Cowboys hated leaners. They squeezed your leg against the chute to the point of excruciating pain. Sometimes they tripped the latch. Often, they came out off balance and sideways, even back end first.

Crawley thanked Cody, and Cody put his phone inside his duffel bag.

By then, the sky was the color of slate, except for the last embers of the sunset behind the grandstand. The arena lights were on. In the shadows behind the chutes, Cody and Rusty sat side by side, their arms crossed just alike, their legs stretched in their Wranglers in front of them, just the same. A nearby cowboy held a cigarette and a Pepsi. The dirt was littered with empty Red Bull cans.

A line of anxious broncs clanged into the chute behind them, and the riders picked up their saddles and searched for their assigned horses. Those in the first wave of contestants began to saddle them up as the crowd's attention was diverted to calf roping.

Cody plopped his saddle atop a horse, and Rusty used an old coat hanger, bent straight like a long stick but hooked at the end, to reach under the animal's belly to grab the straps on the other side and bring them within Cody's reach. He wrapped the straps and tightened them with a tug, buckled the back cinch snug, and clipped the rein to the halter on the animal's snout. Cody took off his jacket and handed it to Rusty.

He put on the thin protective vest that all the bronc riders wore, covered in dark leather and a few sponsor patches. He reached behind one leg and, with one hand and without looking, buckled the four small buckles of his chaps on one side. He did the same with the other. He spit into his palms and rubbed them together. He climbed on the horse and shimmied into position, as if trying to get a firm grip on the saddle with his backside. He pulled his hat off, put it back on, and pushed it down tight until his ears stuck out. He pulled the rein tight, leaned back, grimaced, and nodded. The gate opened. The horse stalled, then sprang to life. It took three jumps right in front of the chute, tossing dirt clods on those left behind, then hopped away meekly. Judges gave it a 75, a middling score that meant no money and might as well have been zero.

"Even horses have bad days," Cody told Rusty with a shrug. That's what Bill always told Cody.

It was a long way to come for a few seconds of forgettable bucking and no check, but that was part of the rodeo life. Cody didn't let his frustration show. He was just as polite afterward as he was before, as he carried his gear back to his truck and folks thanked him for coming. They told him they hoped to see him again next year.

■ ■ ■

There was no horizon. Through the cracked windshield, sky and desert were painted the same charcoal hue. Las Vegas was six hours of darkness away. The GPS attached to the dashboard said they would arrive at 3:35 a.m. The headlights reeled the black highway in and, like a treadmill disappearing underfoot, gobbled up the painted dashes on the pavement.

"Rusty?" Cody called through the truck's back window, into the camper. "You guys check in for your flight in the morning?"

The day had started at dawn, fifteen hours before. Cody, Rusty, Spencer, and another bronc rider from Utah drove three hours from Milford to Las Vegas, then another six hours through California's Mojave Desert, over the Tehachapi Mountains and into the flat and wide Central Valley, through Bakersfield and past Visalia and another hour to Fresno. Now and again they spotted a familiar pickup with an oversized camper riding piggyback. Inside were Jake and Jesse.

The two loads of Wrights arrived forty-five minutes before the Clovis Rodeo began, as the leaden sky poured a cold rain and turned the arena dirt to mud. Clovis had always been a solid springtime stop on the circuit, a medium-sized event smack in the middle of both the state and the California rodeo swing. But the rain dampened any sense of excitement. In front of a smattering of fans, Spencer scored an 84, good enough for second and a $4,281 check. Jesse's 78 earned him $744. Cody's 77 earned $93. Rusty's 74 was out of the money, and Jake bucked off.

Everyone returned to their trucks in the dirt lot, filled with puddles, and changed clothes. The wet gear was packed and the boys escaped before the rodeo ended, but the two trucks now headed in different directions. The twins drove to Lakeside, near San Diego, and slept in a parking lot for a rodeo the next night. Cody and the others stopped at an A&W for cheeseburgers, then rolled down Highway 99, six hours back to Vegas. Two of the cowboys were in the back, trying to sleep. The others were up front, in the cab, their faces lit only by passing headlights and the screens of the mobile phones, which they checked constantly, even when they drove. A movie played on a screen strapped to the dash, filling the cab with banal dialogue, but no one paid it much mind. There was little talking. They got gas at a truck stop near Barstow around midnight, and the cowboys scanned the aisles for jerky, chips, and pop. In the truck, they rotated positions, two up front and two sleeping in back.

The truck arrived in Las Vegas a little after three in the morning. The four men slept for a few hours in the airport parking lot, awoke and packed their bags with just what they needed, and flew to Houston. They didn't fly much, maybe a few times a year, but this stretch was wound too tight with time and too loose with space. They drove three hours in a rented minivan to a rodeo in Corpus Christi, where only Spencer earned any money—$2,940 for second. They drove back to Houston, slept the early-morning hours in the van near the airport, flew to Las Vegas at dawn, and retrieved Cody's truck in the parking lot. Then they drove five hours to Lakeside, passing Jake and Jesse, who had ridden the night before, coming the other direction somewhere along the way. Rusty made $1,518 for second in Lakeside, and Spencer got $231 for seventh. After the rodeo, they drove eight hours back to Milford, through Las Vegas for the fourth time in the weekend.

It was thirty-five hours of driving, two flights, three time zones, and three rodeos in three days. Between airfare, gas, entry fees, and food, never mind the time, Cody spent about a thousand bucks. He earned $93.

He was in the middle of a year in which he spent $11,040 on entry fees and about $20,000 on gas. He put ninety thousand miles on the truck and replaced all four tires twice.

These were things that Cody wanted to teach Rusty. There were costs involved. Some you could add up on a calculator. Others, like time from family or aches and pains, you never could fully measure. Rodeo was a lifestyle, but it was also a business. Competing for championships meant giving yourself over to the nomadic life of rodeo—maybe a hundred of them in a hundred dusty arenas in a hundred different towns, sometimes three or four on the same weekend, a thousand miles apart. The only guarantee was a chance.

It had never really occurred to Cody until a couple years before that they might be riding broncs together on the pro circuit. But then Rusty started winning national high school championships and Cody, good as ever, was still competing for world championships. And when Rusty turned eighteen last winter, he got his pro card and left high school early, having gotten all the requirements finished early for just this reason. He won in Denver and finished second to Cody in Fort Worth and was hitting 86s and 87s in Houston, and Cody and Rusty, father and son, were pictured together on the cover of *ProRodeo Sports News*.

So Rusty could have the best, most experienced saddle bronc rider in the business as a travel partner. And Cody could teach his boy about how to schedule four rodeos in one weekend, and how to weigh the costs and the prizes, and how a bronc rider, as much as anyone, can't get too down about a thousand-mile drive to a buck-off, and can't get too high about a $10,000 payout.

Bronc riding might be done in eight-second bursts, but rodeo was a cruel and lonely slog. The next ride might be a winner. Or it might be the last. Either way, it was always a long way back home.

■　■　■

Cody's boys chased eight bucking horses into a corral near the chutes behind Bill and Evelyn's house and changed into their riding clothes. They put shin guards under their Wranglers and hand-me-down chaps over them. The horses were a bunch of misfits, some of them old broncs retired from the rodeo circuit, some of them horses that never got broken all the way to be much use on the range.

Bill and Cody talked near the chutes. Ryder was better at this age than Rusty was two years ago, Cody said to his dad. Stetson already had a really good mark out, and his fast feet reminded a lot of people of Cody.

"They're all just in different stages," Bill said. "It ain't the ability. It's the drive and the work ethic."

Stetson climbed on top of a bronc named Rockin' Ronnie, the toughest of the bunch. The horse bounded from the gate, and Stetson, with Cody on horseback running alongside as a pickup man and shouting support, survived a long ride straight across the arena. But when Stetson tried to get off, his boot stuck in the stirrup. He tumbled, upside down, to the dirt and was dragged beneath the horse's feet as it bucked and ran. Cody desperately reached to rescue the boy as Stetson's face scraped the dirt, and he oofed and grunted loudly enough to be heard back at the chutes. The horse stepped on Stetson's arm along the way. Eventually untangled and dumped, Stetson returned to the chutes with a forearm that looked like road rash and a purple mark next to his eye. He didn't complain.

"He stepped right on your head," Cody said.

"He never lost his hat," Bill said with a shrug. "He's OK."

"Don't stop until the pickup man comes in," Cody said to his son. "That's the moral of that story."

Stuart, Bill's youngest son and Cody's youngest brother, was in the same grade as Ryder. He had missed most of the high school baseball season with an arm he broke at an Ogden rodeo, when he went over the top of a bronc and got stepped on. But he wanted to practice with the other boys. His horse bounced him across the arena in a straight line. Cody gave chase.

"That's the best ride I've ever seen!" he shouted to Stuart. "What'd ya think?"

"Don't think it's over," Stuart said, as he lurched and reached for Cody's help.

Stetson wanted to go again, on an unpredictable horse he'd never ridden.

"Think I oughta let him?" Cody asked Bill. Bill shrugged. Stetson begged.

"Why don't you let someone else test her out first?" Cody suggested. "Ryder, you take her."

Ryder got aboard, and when the gate opened, the horse froze. The boys hanging on the chutes pushed the bronc, shouted at it, and spanked it on the backside. Like a dead motor that finally caught, it bolted to life and carried Ryder away toward the middle of the arena.

Rusty took a turn. His ride was crisp, full of big, consistent bucks and synchronized kicks, the kind of ride that scored high. Evelyn stood on the back porch, watching.

"Good riding, Rusty!" she called to him.

"Doesn't get any prettier than that, does it, Ma?" Cody shouted from the pickup horse.

He turned to Rusty. "That was awesome," he said to the boy. "I couldn't top that ride at all."

"Still wasn't easy," Rusty said.

"I didn't say it would be easy," Cody replied. "I said it would be worth it."

6

Home on the Range

A SIGN ON THE TWO-LANE highway into town greeted arrivals:
"Welcome to Milford, Settled 1873." Another pronounced Milford as the home of Cody Wright, world champion saddle bronc
rider. Jesse's name was added after he won the world title, a strip
along the bottom that felt as much an afterthought as a Post-it Note
on a page. There wasn't much room to add any more, and you
couldn't help but think that might be a problem someday.

Framed between the forgotten hills to the west and the Mineral
Mountains to the east, amid an improbably flat plain, Milford, elevation 4,968 feet, was a windswept oasis of shade trees in an otherwise
shadeless landscape. It sat, mostly unnoticed, midway between Las
Vegas and Salt Lake City, but far from the busy interstate that connected them. It was the kind of place you lived in or passed through,
but didn't visit unless you knew someone there.

There were three ways into Milford, and all of them had signs
announcing it as the home of Cody, but two of them were like back

doors that hardly anyone used. One of those two warned travelers on the way out of town that the next services were eighty-three miles away, which was pretty much to the Nevada line. About the only people who left Milford that way worked at the copper ore mine a few miles outside of town. Beyond that was a ghost town with a ramshackle cemetery hidden in the brush.

The other backdoor highway cautioned travelers heading out that they'd have to go seventy-five miles before they found much of anything useful. Just outside of town, acres of solar panels tilted southward. More were being built every day, it seemed. Dozens of wind turbines, with giant propellers that turned slowly in the persistent wind of the valley, sprouted high into the sky and were spreading like weeds. At night, the synchronized red lights atop each turbine flashed eerie, silent beacons that could be seen from anywhere within reach of the horizon.

The main way into Milford was from the south, from Cedar City or Beaver, past Minersville and the hay fields and the hog farm that was one of the biggest in the West. When the road reached Milford, it suddenly swooped into the air on a curved overpass, high above the railroad tracks. The overpass was a welcome addition a few years back, because it put an end to the long waits for the coal trains that persistently crept in and out of town and blocked the road.

Main Street's commercial district, about eight blocks long, was lined with old memories and good intentions, like a lot of small towns around the West. The chances of a storefront having an open store behind it ran about fifty-fifty. The downtown district gave way to homes, small ones of brick or vinyl siding. It was an outpost of Wrights. Bill had always told the boys that they should buy a house before they started buying cattle or doing anything else, so that's what they did. Within a couple of years, Alex and Megan were living next to CoBurn and Becca. Another of the Wright sisters was a couple doors down, Spencer was across the street, and Rusty was around the corner. Any one of them could step out a door and holler to get help or start a gathering.

With Milford hemmed in by the railroad tracks to the east, it sprawled about ten blocks to the west, up a small rise toward a bulbous water tower that read "Milford" in faded paint. On top of the ridge was the Church of Jesus Christ of Latter-day Saints, next to the low-slung elementary school where Evelyn taught third and fourth grade and one of her daughters taught kindergarten.

Near the high school, home of the Milford Tigers, were ball fields and a rodeo ring. When the family first arrived, before Bill built the ring at home, Cody loaded broncs and calves into a trailer and hauled them over to the ring to practice his roping and riding skills. When he started winning big-time rodeos, they named the ring after him.

Bill and Evelyn's split-level house was off a gravel road on the north edge of town, where they could raise horses and an army of children and build a rodeo ring out of reach of city ordinances. A concrete water-storage tank was on a small, treeless rise nearby. It was covered in graffiti, including the dozen or two boys and girls graduating from Milford High in any particular year. Usually, there was a Wright or two.

The hospital was close, too, which was handy because the boys took turns over the years being hauled into the emergency room. A couple of boys sliced their hands open on the jagged top of the chain-link fence that surrounded the rodeo ring. That taught them all to never reach out for the wall while they were riding a bucking horse.

The worst injury was to Spencer, who was sixteen when he bucked off a horse and flew into a light pole. The pole was fine, but Spencer cracked the socket around his right eye and broke a bunch of bones in his face. When he woke up on the ground, his head on his knee, he was bleeding all over his chaps. Evelyn loaded him into the car and passed the little Milford hospital on her way to a bigger one in Beaver, thirty miles away. Spencer opened the car door to puke as they went, but he told his mom he was all right, even though he could see in the side mirror what looked like bone inside the deep cut to his eye. And when they got to Beaver, doctors took a look and airlifted the boy to Salt Lake City because he had a brain bleed.

Evelyn thought she might lose Spencer, but he got better and was out of the hospital and back on horses in a couple of months. Spencer didn't remember much about it, and it might have made him remember a little less of everything.

"It really affected my memory for a long time," he said one cold afternoon at Penny's Diner, a town hangout next to a motel built mostly for the railroad workers who stopped in Milford between shifts. "I have a hard time remembering things."

He shrugged and took a bite of his BLT on white bread and chased it with black coffee. They called him Red. He had strawberry-blond hair.

"I make it sound a lot worse than it was," he said.

Bill and Evelyn's house had a gravel drive. Horses were usually in a corral to one side, and the area near the garage was home to a hodgepodge of concrete mixers, rusted farm equipment, cars, a camper or two, and a sprawling mound of big metal tools that looked like they'd gotten comfortable there. Evelyn complained that there were gophers living in the junk pile, but corrected herself. "Sorry," she said, sarcastically. "The spare-parts pile."

Inside the upstairs living room was an upright piano and a painting of the Mormon temple in Salt Lake City. There was a big sofa and a big kitchen table with benches for seats. The refrigerator was covered in photographs and sayings that sounded like they could have been spoken by Evelyn.

"Behind every good rancher is a wife who works in town," one read. "If stress is a good way to lose weight, I should be a size 2," read another. Sliding doors led to a deck that overlooked the rodeo ring and framed the dusky Mineral Mountains.

The house was once filled with more than a dozen Wrights, several to a room, squeezed into every corner. One by one, they moved out on their own, though usually not too far. Evelyn missed the commotion. Now the house held just Bill and Evelyn and Stuart, their youngest, except when everyone crowded in at Christmas or some other holiday. Downstairs, the hall and a family room were lined with photos of everyone else, from school shots to wide portraits taken at some family gathering, usually a wedding, where the girls wore some combination of leather, denim, and fringe, and the boys wore boots, jeans, pressed shirts, cowboy hats, and large belt buckles. It could be hard for the family to take a photograph without at least one person flashing a discreet middle finger. Evelyn called it the "California salute."

■ ■ ■

Bill was gone a good many nights in winter and spring, leaving Evelyn and Milford to live in the camp trailer at Smith Mesa, about two hours south, to take care of the herd. He went to bed early and rose before the sun, when the sky softened from black to the darkest of blues with the coming of dawn.

Bill emerged through the trailer's screen door wearing a smudged suede cowboy hat. A pair of old Australian shepherds, one with three legs and one without a tail, rose to attention and followed him. Dog—that was one's name—lost a leg in a coyote trap. The other, Hoss, had been chained to the truck bed once when Bill was driving on Smith Mesa. It bounced out of the truck bed from a bump and dangled for a moment from a leash that was too long. Its tail slipped under the wheel and was crushed, and Bill stopped and cut it off with his knife. Now Hoss was Bill's best friend on the range, an old and fearless herder, and Dog was surely the fastest three-legged dog this side of the Wasatch.

Bill climbed into the old pickup. The dashboard was so dusty that notes could be written on it with a finger. The steel of the truck's right side was creased hard from when one of his daughters jackknifed on the highway while pulling an empty trailer. She was unhurt, but the passenger door no longer latched. A leather belt kept it cinched to the frame at the top of the open window. A high-pitched beep persistently called for the seatbelts to be fastened. It went ignored or unheard. Bill pulled a sleeve of Smarties from his jacket pocket and pawed them into his mouth.

The truck rumbled and squeaked on the two-track dirt road that passed the corral and ended at the gate. Bill stopped, got out, swung the gate open, got back in, moved the truck through the opening, got out, closed the gate, and returned to the truck. He turned left onto Smith Mesa Road, dusty from drought, which cleaved the rangeland in a drunken serpentine. It loosely followed the contours of the wash to the left.

Bill stopped the truck on the side of the road, got out, and walked west, weaving through the junipers, shrub live oak, Mormon tea, yucca, prickly pear, and cow pies. It was the start of spring, and the air was warm, not hot. Cactus flowers had begun to bloom in purple and yellow. Bill's pointed boots sunk into the sandy red soil, leaving a string of meandering arrows behind him. The boys were off riding broncs on the rodeo circuit's Texas swing, somewhere between Austin, Nacogdoches, and Lubbock—Bill could never keep up.

His cell phone sang a tinny tune, breaking the day's silent void, and Bill fumbled to fetch it from the holster on his belt. He poked at it with thick, callused fingers. Bill's callers were usually greeted with a few inadvertent beeps, the moo of nearby cows, and, eventually, a drawling "Hello?" that stalled in the middle, as if struggling to get past the tall hurdles that divided the syllables. He had dropped a few phones over the years and either lost them in the dirt or had them stepped on by his horse. Evelyn didn't want to get him a good one because he'd lose it or break it.

A man's voice said he had found one of Bill's cows. Sometimes the calls came from park rangers who said that a cow had wandered in, spotted by hikers or campers, and the ranger would kindly wonder if Bill could come get it out. This time it was a neighboring rancher, and the men used the occasion to make small talk. They discussed the weather and the lack of rain, the state of the vegetation, and the latest trouble from coyotes.

Bill told the man he'd be by in a day or two. He thanked him, pressed a button, holstered his phone, and began walking again. He pinched the brush as he passed, like a tailor feeling fabric. There was gooseberry and rabbit brush, June grass and foxtail.

"The only thing they don't eat is this juniper and piñon pine," Bill said, still moving. "But they eat the oak. And this service berry here, and this browse."

He had walked this land for decades, and he knew all the plants, even if he only knew them by the nicknames he'd heard them called by his father and grandfather. He had never seen it this sparse. The West had gone dry for four years running. Bill trudged through the junipers, and his voice conveyed worry.

"We usually have three times as much feed as now," he said with a shake of his head. The herd was starting to feel it. Fewer cows were ovulating. The percentage of cows giving birth was declining, and their schedules were out of sync. Bill used to be able to orchestrate the calendar with precision. He would introduce his ten bulls into the herd and know that, nine months and ten days later, give or take, ninety-some percent of his cows would give birth. He wanted them born in the spring, just as the area usually burst into green.

Now everything was off. The feed wasn't greening as early as before. Births were scattered through the season, and with less to eat, the calves weren't growing as quickly.

"Good cows do three things, in order of their own priorities," Bill always told his boys. "One, they maintain their own body. Two, they give milk to their calf. And three, they ovulate and conceive. With a drought, you have less cows conceiving. Plus, you sell less pounds of meat."

Bill stepped through the last of the junipers, where the sand gave way to blocks of rubble, like ancient ruins, and the last step dropped off several hundred feet. He stared down into the void, past the toes of his boots. It was the same view he used to share with his late father, the same timeless landscape that his grandparents and great-grandparents and all those before had absorbed over 150 years. It hadn't changed. The horizon was the same, the rocks were the same, the dirt the same, the plants the same, the sun the same. Only the people and livestock had changed.

Bill never wore sunglasses, and his blue eyes were in a perpetual squint under the brim of his hat. Years had trained them to see specks of black and brown moving, almost imperceptibly, among the red dirt and dry brush far below. There's a pair there, he said to himself with a casual nod. And another there. Some had gathered in a patch of grass greened by a natural spring. But cattle, given the chance, spread out. Bill's were spread over thirty square miles of high desert and winding arroyos.

"My dad and I talked about it a lot," Bill said. "We always said if we could better ourselves, we wouldn't be sentimental. Things have changed so much. This ground seems to be worth more as scenic land than agricultural land."

■ ■ ■

Most of the land that Bill could see did not belong to him. In this way, Bill was like most other ranchers out west, especially in wide-open states like Utah. Most ranchland was leased from either the Bureau of Land Management or the United States Forest Service. That was especially true in Utah, where almost two-thirds of the land was owned by the federal government, about the same percentage as Alaska and a bigger proportion than anywhere but Nevada.

Down the Virgin River a ways, after it carved through the Virgin Canyon in the northwest corner of Arizona and snaked into the Nevada desert, trouble was brewing between the feds and a cattle rancher named Cliven Bundy. A simmering spat had blown into a national story, the kind that made the network news and all the big newspapers. It put a spotlight on the longtime anxiety, distrust, and occasional animosity between ranchers and the feds.

The conflict went back two decades, to when the BLM designated hundreds of thousands of acres for conservation, not far from Las Vegas. The government wanted to protect the threatened desert tortoise. It restricted off-road vehicles and bought back grazing permits from area ranchers.

But Bundy didn't budge. His family wasn't that much different from the Wrights. It had been running cattle in these parts since the 1870s, since Mormon ancestors homesteaded in the area, and Bundy wasn't about to move out of the way for something like the desert tortoise. It was a question of who came first, and whether the federal government had authority over the land and rights over state and local governments.

Bundy called it a land grab and refused to sell his permits back, so the feds revoked them. Bundy kept running his cattle as if nothing had changed. The government tried to keep a count of his herd, sometimes from helicopters, to assess fees and fines that Bundy and his family never intended to pay.

The debate simmered for years, and it was far from the only one. There were lawsuits from counties across the West, arguing that they had jurisdiction, not the federal government. Ranchers went to court to make their cases. Bundy was one of them. After a judge ordered him to remove his cattle, he took his case to the Ninth Circuit Court of Appeals. He lost. To some ranchers, it was part of a revolution, and they portrayed themselves as American colonists against the tyrannical forces of an overreaching government far away and far out of order. In some courtrooms, people dressed in white wigs, like American revolutionaries. In one, a banner read, "Has the West been won, or has the fight just begun?"

Bombs went off in Forest Service and BLM offices. Fences and gates erected to keep cattle off of protected areas were mowed down. Signs warning against grazing were shot up with bullet holes or chopped down with chainsaws. Forest Service and BLM rangers traveled in pairs and made sure they had constant communication with officials in case they confronted trouble in the form of a frustrated rancher or an angry mob.

After twenty years, the BLM told Bundy that it planned to round up his cattle. But it abandoned those plans after it received several threats of violence. So the BLM went to court, and the court ordered the cattle off the land within forty-five days. The BLM sent Bundy a letter saying that it planned to round up his cattle, and it closed off more than 300,000 acres of range. It said that Bundy owed $1 million in fines, and would be responsible for the estimated $1 million it would cost for the round up, expected to last several weeks.

Bundy bunkered at his ranch with his fourteen children and fifty-two grandchildren. He filed a notice with the county sheriff called "Range War Emergency Notice." He got support from local officials, including a county commissioner who said that the United States government "has perpetrated a bigger fraud on people over these tortoises than Al Capone did selling swampland in Miami." A vast army of armed supporters from around the country made their way to an Interstate 15 overpass outside of Mesquite. They called themselves a militia and waved guns and copies of the Constitution. The BLM established a couple of "First Amendment" areas for protests. Bundy supporters surrounded an auction house to prevent any of Bundy's captured cattle from being sold off.

Bundy became a celebrity, especially among those whose politics swung hard to the right, and he entertained reporters as tensions mounted. "Hey, the tortoise is a fine creature," he said. "I like him. I have no problem with him. But taking another man's cattle? It just doesn't seem right."

After a few days, the BLM backed off. "Based on information about conditions on the ground, and in consultation with law enforcement, we have made a decision to conclude the cattle gather because of our serious concern about the safety of employees and members of the public." Bundy and his supporters called it a victory. The feds said they'd be back.

As Bill overlooked his own herd at Smith Mesa, the Bundy standoff was taking place downriver, over the desert horizon. Bill and his family didn't join it, but he paid close attention. He knew Bundy a bit and considered him a smart rancher. Bill thought Bundy was being bullied by the feds. The thought of a man's ranching operation being yanked away because of an animal like the desert tortoise irked him. He thought about the possibility of that happening at Smith Mesa.

"What about them black gnats?" Bill joked. "You don't want to protect them black gnats?"

About a year later, Bundy's sons and several others took control of a federal wildlife refuge in Oregon. A standoff lasted forty-one days. One of Bill's cousins was among those arrested. One of the group's leaders, LaVoy Finicum, was shot and killed by Oregon state troopers after his car crashed into a snowbank, trying to evade a roadblock, and Finicum got out and reached into his jacket. About a thousand people went to his funeral in Kanab, Utah, down by the Arizona border, on the other side of Zion.

Bill stayed out of it and mostly kept his thoughts to himself. He wasn't much of an activist. But he knew the landscape was changing beneath him. He knew that there was an emerging battle over federal lands all over the West. It was getting political, sometimes pitting cattlemen against conservationists, sometimes putting them on the same side. In the shifting sands of the West, Bill wondered if the rancher was the one slowly getting buried.

Most of the federal land around him was used for several purposes—recreation, livestock grazing, conservation—and Bill worried about getting squeezed out. Down past Virgin, over the sandstone slabs and red-soiled hills, was some of the best mountainbiking territory in Utah. The bikers just added to the hunters, hikers, four-wheelers, and conservationists who wanted access and preferred that their views and their movements not be impeded by cows, cow pies, and fences.

"There's a conflict with sportsmen," Bill said. "Elk and deer take a lot of feed, and they're really hard on the fences and the haystacks. Some people want to cut the cows out, give more of it to wildlife. And I know with the drought, there'll be more stipulations."

Bill had occasional arguments with BLM and Forest Service officials about things like fencing and water. At Beavers, as the summer
range was called in Wright shorthand, he was told he couldn't run
his cattle above the timberline in early summer because there was a
poisonous scrub plant that seemed to affect cows, but not horses or
sheep. Bill explained that his cattle didn't make their way up that
high until late summer, anyway, and that by that time in the growing season, the plant didn't appear to have any harmful effects. That
didn't seem to matter to the rangers, who called now and again to
tell Bill that his cattle were in places they shouldn't be. Bill coun-
tered that there was an old fence line that hadn't been maintained for
years before he ever got hold of the permit.

"I apologize," he said. "I forgot to tell my cattle not to go where
there's no fence."

Certain subjects got him animated, and it was the only time he
talked fast. He usually concluded with an apology for getting riled up.

"I just think the Creator, or whoever put this all here, is a better
manager of the land than the BLM or the Forest Service," he said.
He stepped away from the edge and followed his footprints back to
his truck.

■ ■ ■

Bill's goal was to feed the herd without supplemental hay. That was
the biggest expense for many cattle ranchers. And it drove deci-
sions that were made when it came to rangeland: to buy or lease
smaller plots of land and feed with hay, or have enough land to
feed the herd naturally. To Bill, raising cattle with natural feed was
preferred, a matter of cost, convenience, and tradition. Besides,
when it came time to sell, he could tout his cattle as "grass-fed," a
trendy term in the beef market. But it meant he needed more land

to grow the herd. And that was just it: he was boxed in and priced out at Smith Mesa.

The BLM controlled most of the land around Smith Mesa, among its 155 million acres of grazing land around the country. Ranchers paid at least $1.35 per head, per month, to use the land. The feds set the price. Some years, it spiked over two dollars. For Bill, that added up to a few hundred dollars a month. It wasn't much.

The real cost of ranching was up front, in a patchwork of purchased permits that gave a rancher, or several ranchers, a right to particular parcels approved for grazing. Bill did not know exactly how many acres he leased—twenty thousand around Smith Mesa, maybe—because ranchers did not think in acres. They thought in terms of capacity and sustainability.

Not all parcels had the same amount of vegetation and water. In the high desert, with low brush spread across hard soil, a cow might need to roam tens of acres to sustain itself for one month. Someplace else, someplace lush, thick with grass, an acre might be enough.

The government decided how many animal units per month, or AUMs, a parcel could withstand without long-term damage to the ecology. A permit might cost $100 per AUM, provide for four months of use during the year, and allow for up to two hundred cattle. Multiplying those factors—two hundred cattle over four months would be 800 AUM, at $100 each—the permit might cost $80,000. When you started combining horses and sheep and hogs, or sharing parcels with other ranchers, or figuring out what times of year certain parcels were available, the math got complicated in a hurry.

One of Bill's permits was one that his father and uncle got in the aftermath of the Taylor Grazing Act of 1934, a huge piece of legislation meant to bring order and prevent overgrazing across the West. Now he had five around Smith Mesa, and he was always looking for someone willing to give theirs up, because access to more land was the only way to grow the herd. He paid for his early permits with hefty bank loans. He or the boys paid cash for the more recent ones.

Permits came with rules. You could be fined for running too much livestock on a permit, or for using it during the wrong dates. That wasn't a smart thing for a rancher to do in the long run, anyway—you wanted to keep the land healthy for your herd. Bill thought lots of conservationists and environmentalists didn't understand that no one had more to lose than the rancher when it came to abusing the land.

AUM limits were reevaluated every ten years, and they were only educated guesses as to what a particular parcel could withstand. If the feds decided that a parcel was overburdened, they lowered the AUMs. If they decided that the parcel had a better use, maybe for more recreational space for humans, or for the extraction of something of value from the ground, or to help save an endangered species like the desert tortoise, Bill could be forced to sell them back.

"They look at the permits as a privilege," Bill said, his voice gaining speed. "We look at them as a right—because we buy 'em."

Evaluations every decade couldn't account for the vagaries of drought and disease, or the rising numbers of wildfires scorching the West. They couldn't predict a heavier-than-usual snowpack that covered the winter feed, or a flooded creek that might cut off access to the other side, just long enough to starve young calves.

■ ■ ■

The cascading effects of the worst drought in decades had reached the herd. Most years, Bill sold his yearlings in September, when they were sixteen months old—all the steers, certainly, and most of the heifers, except about twenty that he rotated into the herd to replace the aging cows. They usually weighed more than eight hundred pounds and fetched $1,200 or so.

More than ever, all this was guesswork. It was spring, but creek beds were dry. Feed was sparse. The yearlings might not make it to eight hundred pounds by September. On the other side of the equation, the number of cattle in the United States was at its lowest since 1951. A winter freeze in the Dakotas killed off thousands of cattle, and beef prices were at record highs, a factor of supply and demand. Bill did the imprecise math, equations built on hunches and worry. He cashed in. He sold 102 yearlings, months earlier than he ever had.

"I sold a steer for $2.53 a pound," Bill said. It was a price he had never seen. "When I was a boy, my dad bought cattle for twenty-two cents a pound. I remember we bought it once for thirty-three cents, then had to sell it at twenty-two cents. We lost $20,000 on a hundred head of yearlings."

Bill wasn't a big-time rancher. By raw numbers, owning two-hundred-some head of cattle put him in about the top ten percent of ranchers, which sounded impressive, but ranching had become a game of haves and have-nots. Like a lot of the American economy, it was hollowed out in the middle. The only categories that were growing were operations with five thousand head or more, and those with fewer than ten head. The haves were the big corporations with thousands and thousands of cattle, and the biggest one percent of them were responsible for almost half of beef sales in the country. The have-nots were those with just a few cows, enough to make cattle a hobby but not a career, and certainly not something to pass to the next generation.

Bill was in the middle, nowhere close to the top. He knew all the market forces and trends that were against him. He knew that the number of cattle in the United States was falling and that the average age of a rancher was rising. It was not a good combination.

But he also knew that beef prices were rising, and that there was more money to be made in ranching than ever before, even if the money was being made by fewer and fewer people. Bill figured he had advantages that others didn't. He had valuable land and a patchwork of permits that he might be able to parlay into something bigger. And he had boys, a lot of boys, who might want to help, and those boys were starting to come into some money. He'd keep working and see how it played out. That's all he figured he could do.

For now, though, he had to get these cows up north. He wanted the cows off of Smith Mesa a few weeks earlier than normal, because the natural forage that fed and fattened the herd was already thinned and brown. He got back into his truck and drove back down the hill off the mesa, through the corner of Zion, and down the paved squiggly line that headed toward Virgin. At the lower end of the wash, in the corral made of crooked logs, Bill loaded a dozen cattle he had gathered the day before through a chute and into an old trailer hitched to his truck. It was afternoon now. The sun rested on a nearby cliff and the shadows were long. Bill clanged the trailer gate closed.

In the dimming light, Bill climbed into his truck and pulled the rattling trailer onto the road toward Virgin. The dogs were in the bed of the truck, and the taillights of the trailer did not work. Bill figured he wouldn't get pulled over, or that he'd talk his way out of it if he did. It was a two-hour drive past Beaver to the foothills of the Tushar Mountains, just getting green with spring runoff, where he emptied the cows into a dark meadow.

He came out of the hills and through Beaver, passed under the interstate and pointed the headlights of his old truck another 30 miles toward Milford, where Evelyn was waiting.

7

Born Into It

ALL OF THE MOTELS around Rock Springs, Wyoming, were full, even thirty miles away in Green River, because of the National High School Finals Rodeo. Hundreds of campers and RVs over- ran vast swaths of the Sweetwater Events Complex on the north edge of town, against the flat-topped mesas to the west. They were assigned, according to the home states of their inhabitants, to make- shift campgrounds that were covered in truckloads of gravel to keep the dust down.

In the middle of it all were the Wrights of Utah. Cody's thirty- foot motor home was squeezed between two others, the weeklong home to Bill, Evelyn, Cody, and ShaRee. Rusty and Ryder shared a room at the Motel 6 off the highway, but Stetson, Statler, and Lily stayed in the motor home. The canopy above the side door gave shade to camp chairs, a big folding table, and a two-burner stove hooked to a propane tank. A dog was tied with a chain near the front wheel.

July was the critical part of the pro rodeo circuit, the busiest time of the year with the most money at stake. Jesse, Jake, Spencer, and CoBurn raced between Nampa, Idaho, and Salinas, California, driving eleven hours between them for four nights in a row. Jesse swept all the rounds in Salinas, and he and Spencer and CoBurn all came away with thousands of dollars in winnings.

Cody, meanwhile, sat in a lawn chair in the shade of a gravel campground, comfortably in second place in the standings. Spencer, Jake, and Jesse were in the top twenty, too, and a buzz was building over whether all four of them would make it to Las Vegas in December. There had never been four brothers competing in the same event at the National Finals before.

For the moment, Cody was more concerned about Rusty. Rusty's fast start to his rookie season had given way to a procession of unspectacular results the past month. He was slumping through the doldrums of summer and the incessant schedule was chewing him up with injuries. He fell off a pickup man in Prescott and could barely walk because of his sore hip. He broke a finger in Red Lodge.

Rusty never complained about injuries. He'd been raised to be unafraid of the next buck. He broke his right wrist in eighth grade riding a bull, and shattered his left arm in tenth grade falling off a bronc. His left forearm bore a scar from a chainsaw cut when he was fourteen and cutting trails—such a clean cut it didn't even bleed, Rusty remembered with a bit of wonder. At the beginning of this season, in Texas, when things were going so well, he thought he had hurt his knee on a ride. The next day, the knee felt fine, but Rusty couldn't walk because his foot ached so badly. Cody said they'd have it checked out back in Utah, so Rusty kept riding. Two weeks later, the doctor found that the foot was broken. It was too late to do too much about it then, and Rusty still had a bump on it under his boot and it still hurt when he rode, but no one needed to know anything about it.

It was his head that was the problem with his riding lately. He kept missing his mark outs. That happened to everyone sometimes, when a horse tricked you out of the chute with an unexpected shimmy or got you off balance before the gate even opened. But when it happened a lot, such incidents could not be blamed on the horse—they were sloppy mistakes of the rider's own making. Rusty knew that. The odds of him joining his dad and uncles in Las Vegas slipped every week. He was sitting thirty-seventh.

"If he does it right, he's got a chance," Cody said. "There's a lot of money left."

Cody was frustrated with Rusty, and that was something he didn't show much. Like Bill, only the quickened pace of his words, a tilt of his head, a tightening of his gaze, or a few swear words revealed Cody's frustration or concern. You had to know him to notice the nuance in his manner.

Cody worried about Rusty's standing, but not enough to have him go chasing paychecks this particular week. Rodeos in Salinas and Nampa came along every year, but there were only so many chances to win a high school national championship. Jake and Spencer had each won one. Cody, an all-around champion in Utah, never did. He was hurt as a senior. As a junior, he led going into the final round—in rodeo, called the short round or the short go—but scored low on a bum horse.

"Even good horses have bad days," Bill said. He reserved his frustration for people, not horses.

Rusty was the first Wright to win nationals two years in a row, and everyone came to see if he could make it three. His biggest threat among the contestants was Ryder, who had just finished his sophomore year. Back in Heber City, Rusty won the Utah state high school saddle bronc title. Ryder placed second in saddle bronc and won the bull riding. That got the boys into the national championships in Rock Springs.

It started well. Rusty led the first round with an 83, and Ryder was second, with 76.

"I hope I get 76 and Ryder gets 83 in the second round," Rusty said. "And then we tie in the short round."

■ ■ ■

The rodeo on Thursday morning began with a cool breeze and a prayer. The emcee asked the smattering of souls in the bleachers to bless all contestants and stock. ShaRee sat with other family members, across from the chutes. She didn't get nervous watching Cody ride, but watching the kids was something different. She wanted them to win. She mostly wanted them to walk.

"Let's go to Milford, Utah," the public-address announcer said through the speaker system. ShaRee aimed her iPad's camera toward Rusty, who was in a chute on an angry horse. Cody and Ryder leaned over him, double-checking the cinch and the saddle. Long before the gate opened, the bronc bucked wildly. Its front hooves got caught over the top rung of the steel fencing, six feet off the ground, and the horse somehow got itself turned backward.

The upbeat announcer blurted out the usual between-ride preamble, part of the banter that linked the episodic chaos of rodeo— Rusty Wright, one of the Utah Wrights, a two-time high school national champion, his brother here competing, his dad a two-time world champion, his uncle a world champion . . .

A judge motioned to the announcer.

"They're going to move on," ShaRee said.

"Why the hell didn't they have him tied in?" Bill said.

"Hopefully, that doesn't bust his saddle up," Stetson said.

As another boy and another horse burst out of a gate, Rusty's horse continued to rear up, fully unhinged.

"What a disaster," ShaRee said to herself.

Finally, the horse settled and Rusty scooted into the saddle. He held the rein in his left hand and raised his right hand high over his shoulder, his arm bent in an arc around the brim of his hat, which he pulled low over his ears. He clenched his jaw and bit hard on his mouth guard. He nodded his head with a jerk.

"C'mon, Rusty," ShaRee said from behind the camera.

The gate swung open. Rusty leaned back and flung his feet forward as the horse leapt out of the confines of the metal fencing. It landed on its front feet, then its back feet, then jumped again, all the hooves up, as if the ground was afire. Rusty's left fist held the rope as it slacked and jerked with every leap. His right hand waved in the air like a banner in the wind. His boots rocked from the horse's front shoulders to its side flank. The horse twisted and arced and whipped, trying to toss its rider.

"Go! Go! Go!" Bill shouted from the bleachers. "Good one!"

A man in the arena wearing black and white stripes and holding a clipboard dropped a yellow handkerchief to the ground.

"He threw the flag!" Bill shouted in disgust.

"We've got some bad news here," the announcer said mournfully over the applause. "No score for the young man who led the first round."

Rusty disappeared behind the chutes, leaned against a livestock pen, and hung his head low. In the bleachers, the family fell into shoulder-sagged silence. No one spoke for a couple of minutes. ShaRee, fighting the sun's glare, tried to watch the replay on her small screen. The rodeo continued. It did not pause for heartache.

"You threw away a frickin' title because you can't hold your damn feet," ShaRee finally said. She excused herself, stepped down the aluminum benches, and lit a cigarette.

Evelyn sighed and smiled. "I think we'll leave them alone at camp for a little while," she said.

An hour later, Rusty tried to take his mind off his lost opportunity by playing video games inside the motor home. Cody grilled hamburgers outside. His disappointment sizzled, like beef patties over hot coals. Bill tried to be encouraging. Over the years, he had been so mad at calls that had gone against his sons that he sometimes lost his temper. He once chased down judges to berate them. Cody was cooler-headed. Bill told Cody that it looked like the left foot hit the mark all right, but he did not see the right.

"I thought the right was pretty low," Cody said. "I wouldn't have argued it. I wish I could stand here and be on his side, but I can't."

Only four boys recorded scores during the morning's round, and none of the rides were memorable. Had Rusty merely marked out, he would have won the round and put himself in perfect position to win a third straight national title.

"My thing is, he knows better," Cody said. "Why make it so difficult? When there's a 66 winning the round, why does he have to put so much pressure on himself?"

Maybe Ryder could win the title instead. Bill had always thought that Ryder had as much natural talent as Rusty, maybe even more. Ryder, though, was more fascinated by bulls than broncs. There was a certain allure to them—the danger, the unpredictability, the glamour of the event, the lure of big payouts and big markets of the Professional Bull Riders tour. It was probably a passing phase. All the Wright boys rode bulls for a time, just as they roped calves and wrestled steers and tried other rodeo events. Mothers hated it. The bulls had an element of danger that didn't exist with broncs. Cody might have a twenty-year career in saddle bronc, but no one had that on bulls. There were no old bull riders. You just hoped your boys outgrew the thrill and prestige of bulls and saw the sense in broncs before it was too late.

In the motor home, Ryder was asked which he hoped to ride professionally, bulls or broncs.

"Be honest," ShaRee said, "because I want to know, too."

"I don't know," Ryder said. He was quieter than Rusty.

"You're so full of it," his mother said. "Be honest."

"I really don't know," Ryder said.

He sat silent for a few moments. Stetson sat next to him. He was two years younger, but he rode broncs and bulls, too, and had just been at the national junior high championships. He liked the idea of joining the Professional Bull Riders tour. Twenty years before, some of the best bull riders in rodeo had broken away from the Pro Rodeo Cowboys Association and started the tour, and the best of them measured their annual prize money in seven figures, not six.

"I like the bulls because you get more money," Ryder said.

"I'll do the PBR if Ryder does it," Stetson said. "When you stay on the bulls, it's a lot funner than the broncs."

"The adrenaline rush—it's awesome," Ryder said.

Even a serious injury hadn't dampened his enthusiasm. The previous fall, Ryder had been on a bull at a rodeo in St. George when he was flung off. The bull stepped on his back. When Ryder sat up, the bull stepped on his right leg. The pickup men could hear the femur crack. Ryder had a rod in the leg now, screwed into place.

There would be no national title. On Friday morning, Ryder's bull spun flat for several rotations, then popped its backside into the air like an ejection seat. Ryder flew over its horns, landed in the dirt, and was slow to stand.

"You OK, ShaRee?" Bill asked in the bleachers.

"I'm OK," she said, putting her camera down. "He got up and walked out."

■ ■ ■

With the week wasting and time to kill, Rusty and Ryder looked for better luck at a different rodeo on Friday night. There was one in Evanston, a hundred miles west down I-80. Carrying his gear out of the Motel 6, Rusty slid into the front seat of the twenty-year-old Lincoln he'd bought two years before from an old lady in Milford.

The dashboard was decorated with a Wrangler sticker, a springy hula dancer, and a computerized navigation system. Fast-food wrappers littered the back, and massive drinks with straws filled the cup holders. Rusty's longtime girlfriend, Morgan, with bleached-blonde hair and a job at Dairy Queen in Beaver, sat in the passenger seat. Ryder, the quiet and brooding type, slinked in the back.

"I'm not doing so hot lately," Rusty said as he steered the Lincoln toward the setting sun. He was chattier than his dad. "I keep missing my mark out. It's kind of a mental thing now. I did it once, and now I keep thinking about it. It's in my head. I'm making it harder than it is."

The rodeo had begun by the time they got to Evanston. Rusty pulled the car into a dirt lot at the fairgrounds, next to a small office. Warm evening air and an announcer's muffled voice greeted them when they opened the doors. Rusty and Ryder looked at a sheet of paper taped to the office wall. Rusty swore. "I didn't want that horse," he said of Party Rocker. "He bucks, but he's hard to ride. I scored 88 on him once, but it's all or nothin'."

They signed in and each paid the $75 entry fee in cash. Two young cowboys looked at each other as Rusty and Ryder stepped past.

"Them Wright boys are here," one whispered to the other.

They opened their bags and changed clothes—their dress jeans and boots replaced with grungier versions, soccer pads on their shins, worn leather chaps on their legs. They sat in their saddles, adjusted straps and buckles, and rocked in the shadows behind the chutes.

"How many of you have heard of the Wright family from Utah that flat-out win everything in bronc riding?" the announcer asked, and Ryder's solid ride quickly took the lead with a 76. With little expression, he returned to the chutes and climbed onto the fencing, leaning over Rusty to help him get ready.

"Here's another of the Wright brothers," the announcer said, and the gate opened. Rusty's feet flipped high on Party Rocker's shoulders, staying until long after the horse landed its initial buck. Horse and rider were one, bucking and leaping and rocking across the arena dirt. The eight-second buzzer sounded. Judges awarded Rusty an 83.

"Rusty, that was awesome," said the announcer. He knew what had happened in Rock Springs. "Yeah, I believe you got robbed in the second round, but I'm not a judge. I wasn't there."

Rusty returned to the chutes, out of breath and smiling.

"It felt great," he said. "I haven't felt that good in a long time. I should have been doing that forever."

Bulls were shoved into the chutes. Ryder removed his gray felt cowboy hat and pulled on a hard plastic helmet he carried in his bag. Behind the bull he was assigned, Ryder stood in place, swaying nervously from side to side. The announcer said it was time for bull riding, on "1,800 pounds of live leather." Rusty held his cell phone between his ear and shoulder, talking to Cody, a hundred miles away. A man interrupted with a smile and shook Rusty's hand.

"You're not supposed to make it look easy, like your dad," he said.

"I promise you, it wasn't easy," Rusty said.

In the chute, Ryder climbed aboard a horned bull named Tapout.
It spun out of the open gate like an off-balance merry-go-round.
Ryder never had a chance. He quickly slid from its back and onto
the dirt in a heap. That didn't deter the bull. It kept gyrating and
trampled Ryder before the bullfighters, their faces streaked in clown
makeup, could rush in and try to shoo the animal away. Ryder sat up
on all fours, dazed and slow, and the bull smashed into him again.
The clack of hooves banged against his plastic helmet loudly enough
to be heard across the arena. Amid the swirl, a horn caught Ryder
under the jaw, and he fell to the dirt, momentarily unconscious. A
bullfighter jumped on top of him, like a hero on a grenade.

Ryder lay on the ground for two minutes. Medics hovered over
him and helped him up, and Ryder wobbled to an open gate. A
patch of blood dripped from his jaw. Rusty was concerned, but tried
not to show it.

"Man, that's scary," he said. "I hate bull riding."

"Me, too," Ryder said, smiling weakly.

But it was obvious from Ryder's blank look that something was
not right. Rusty recognized it in his little brother's glazed eyes.

"My bronc kinda quit me at the end. You remember that?" he
asked Ryder.

Ryder absently shook his head side to side.

"You remember my ride?"

Another no.

"You remember *your* ride?" Rusty asked.

Ryder shook his head again.

"I'm not a doctor, but I don't think that's good," Rusty said.

Ryder knew his name, and he knew he was in Evanston. He did
not remember his ride in Rock Springs that morning, and did not
know his saddle bronc score from an hour before. Rusty called their
father. Cody said to check Ryder's eyes and see if the pupils were

dilated. Rusty shone a light from his iPhone into his brother's eyes, one at a time. The pupils shrunk in the light and expanded in the dark. A man stopped, looked over Rusty's shoulder, and said that it was a good sign. It is when they do not work in sync that you should be concerned, he said.

"He'll be all right," the man said. He smiled, thanked the boys for coming, and walked away.

It was the first night of a two-night rodeo, so Rusty and Ryder didn't know if their one-two placing in saddle bronc would hold up. If it did, they would receive a check in the mail a few weeks later. The boys packed their gear and hauled their saddles and duffels back to the trunk of the Lincoln, where they found Morgan, who had watched the rodeo from the grandstand. A stream of headlights snaked out of the fairgrounds around them. Ryder slid into the front seat.

"You done with bull riding now?" Rusty asked his little brother next to him.

Ryder grunted.

"You done?" Rusty asked, raising his voice. "You done with bulls?"

"I don't know," Ryder replied in a whisper.

"You should be," Rusty said. "You're a good bull rider. But you're a better saddle bronc rider."

■　■　■

The campground in Rock Springs was dark and quiet when the Lincoln rolled in a couple of hours later, its tires crunching the deep gravel. It was nearly midnight. A light glowed from inside the motor home, and the boys swung open the screen door to find Bill, Stetson, Statler, and Lily sitting on the benches at the kitchen table, watching a small television that sat on a shelf. Evelyn was asleep on a mattress in the shadows a few feet away. Cody and ShaRee were in the back bedroom, awake, waiting for the boys to return.

Bill asked Ryder how he felt. There was a red welt on his jaw, but his mood and memory had improved dramatically during the car ride.

"Pretty good," he said.

Ryder and Rusty slid down the narrow hallway and crawled onto the bed with their parents. The four of them crowded to watch the small screen of Morgan's phone, reviewing the rides that she had recorded from the bleachers. Ryder was scheduled for his second high school go-round in saddle bronc at nine in the morning. There was no discussion about whether he would ride.

The coolness of the next day's dawn gave way to dry heat. The bareback competition had ended, and the saddle bronc horses were funneled, single file, into the chutes. Ryder, a dime-sized spot of red on the curve of his jaw, climbed atop the fence and stroked the horse he was assigned. He placed a saddle on its back. The saddle was one of Cody's old ones. On the back of the seat, burned into the leather, were the crossed sevens of Cody's cattle brand and the names of his children: Rusty, Ryder, Stetson, Statler, Lily. Most of the boys' equipment was handed down from Cody and their uncles.

Ryder climbed aboard. Others leaned over him, like technicians checking an astronaut before takeoff, tugging on loose leather ends and buckles. The announcer said something about Milford and the Wright family. Ryder raised one arm and nodded his sore jaw. The gate opened. The horse leapt and spun left, then bucked out of rhythm on the half beat. It threw its head to the right and kicked its feet the same way, curling like a fish pulled on a hook out of water. Sunfished, the cowboys called it. Ryder toppled off its back and hit the dirt, carrying the last of the Wrights' title hopes with him. He stood, climbed over the fence in a beat, and speed-walked, head down, through the dust and mingling cowboys. He collapsed against a fence and dropped his gray hat over his face.

Cody followed and Rusty trailed him like a shadow. Cody kneeled and leaned in, to get under Ryder's brim and look into his son's eyes. He whispered that every ride was a new chance. He'd have plenty more if he kept his head up. Cody stood and, with increasing animation, gave his son a lesson in technique, as if teaching a dance—arm up, twist the torso, repeat.

"If this was easy, everyone could do it," he said. "You go from champ to chump in a jump."

Rusty and Ryder still had the two best scores among about two hundred rides, an 83 and a 76, but each scored zero in the second round. Their point totals after the two rounds were still enough to get them into the finals—the short round—on Saturday night. The overall winner, the national champion, would be the one with the highest average over three rides. Buckoffs and missed marks were killers. To have any chance, Rusty and Ryder probably needed the ten boys who had received scores twice to get bucked off or get no score in the short round. It was possible, but not likely.

Hours later, when the sun had spun to the other side of the wide sky and rested on the buttes to the west, the big lights in the arena were turned on. The bleachers were jammed with thousands of fans. Rusty and Ryder were back at their spot in the shadows behind the chutes.

"Hey, bud, how'd you ride this morning?" a teenaged boy said to Ryder.

"Got bucked," Ryder said, barely looking up. Ryder was polite, but only the boy talking to him failed to recognize that he was not in the mood for conversation.

"You still sitting OK?" the boy asked.

"Sixth or seventh, I think," Ryder said.

The boy nodded. He introduced himself as a bull rider from Tennessee.

"You ride bulls, too, don't you?" he asked, and Ryder nodded. "I thought about riding broncs, but I don't know." He looked around, then back at Ryder. "You was kinda born into it, wasn't you?"

Ryder gave him the slightest of smiles. "Yeah," he said. "I suppose I was."

Ryder was up first. Rusty gave him a pep talk in the chute. "Bear down, Ryder! Lift!" he shouted to his brother, sitting atop an impatient horse.

"Let's go to Utah!" the announcer shouted. "One of the sons of two-time world champion Cody Wright!"

The gate opened. The horse took off. A yellow flag dropped. Cody swallowed his frustration with a grimace and slid along the top rung of the chutes toward Rusty, now positioned on his horse. Rusty clamped down on his mouth guard. His fist clenched, his arm raised, his chin nodded.

It was a clean ride, scored an 80. Rusty, with 163 on two rides, was in first place for the moment. In the end, three boys completed three successful rides, though only one had more total points than Rusty scored on two head. The missed mark out in the second round cost him an unprecedented third national title.

"That's the first time I kind of wished someone bucked off," Rusty admitted as he changed into his dress jeans and shirt. He thought for a moment. "That's ridiculous that I beat them on two."

He turned to Ryder, thinking maybe video games would cheer up his quiet brother. "Wanna go kill some zombies?" Rusty asked.

Ryder smiled. He sat atop the metal fence that penned a cluster of bulls. Rusty stuffed his chaps and dusty clothes into his duffel bag and zipped it.

"I just wanna redo this week," he said.

"Me, too," Ryder said.

"Well, you got two more years to win it," Rusty said.

They walked around the arena, just beyond the glow of the lights, and climbed to where the rest of the Wrights sat, high in the bleachers. They accepted hugs and watched the replays on ShaRee's iPad. She wore a black hooded sweatshirt that read "Rodeo Mom" in silver studs on the back, with a bucking bronc in silhouette. Morgan sat quietly next to Rusty, wearing an oversized leather jacket that Rusty had won in Rock Springs almost exactly a year before, declaring him the national high school champion.

There was little chatter. The air was cool and the atmosphere deflated. The Wrights shared tired expressions as they silently watched the bull riders in the finals end a week's worth of rodeos. The announcer thanked everyone for coming, and people descended the bleachers and flowed into the dark shadows.

Rusty checked his phone.

"Hey," he said, cheerfully. "I won that rodeo in Evanston. Ryder got second."

8

Open Gates

THE TUSHAR MOUNTAINS rose quickly east of Beaver, a town on the interstate surrounded on the other three sides by farms. With his rodeo earnings, Jesse had bought a permit the year before, a wide chute called Bone Hollow. The lower end of it started at a cattle guard not far from the town water tank and angled like a ramp into a treeless valley covered in sagebrush, headed straight for the snow-capped mountains.

Bone Hollow connected to another Wright permit, and another, a patchwork of summer range that hopscotched for miles uphill, all the way to a ski resort. Starting in late spring, after Bill had moved them from Smith Mesa, the cattle would start at Bone Hollow. Slowly enticed by open gates and the promise of cooler temperatures and fresher grass, they made their way into the mountains through the summer. Dictated by the rules of each permit, gates opened in front of them and closed behind them, like a series of locks for a fleet of boats.

By late summer, the cattle would be sprinkled around the summit of 12,174-foot Delano Peak, the highest point in the range. As fall arrived, the cool temperatures and a lot of nudging and steering slowly brought the cattle back to where they started. Bill had to get them out before the big early storms hit and left them stranded. The year before, he lost a calf that he found alone and nearly frozen. He brought it home, into the living room, and the grandchildren wrapped it in a blanket, warmed it by the fire, and nursed it from a bottle. It died after a few days.

"Sometimes we lose cattle on the mountain to quick pneumonia," Bill said. "Find 'em eaten by bears. They're smart, those bears. They sometimes will just eat the maggots and leave the cow, because then there are more maggots, and then even more maggots."

Bill liked Beavers. It was different than Smith Mesa, and not just because of its varied terrain, rising from flat farmlands, through rugged foothills to pine-covered forests smothered in deep snow all winter. It was closer to Milford than Smith Mesa. Bill could work all day and return home at night, rather than camping out for days at a time.

But its easy access attracted a lot of other users. Hunters on four-wheelers and teenagers on dirt bikes kept leaving gates open behind them. Bill would leave for home in the late afternoon and return in the early morning to find his cows scattered across meadows that had been empty the day before. The feds agreed to let him install a few extra cattle guards to help keep the cattle in and out of various parcels, regardless of the gates. He and Cody put in one that was narrower than usual, to keep cars and four-wheelers out. They returned to find that something wider than the opening had driven right over one of the posts. When they fixed it, it happened again.

Higher up, thrill seekers ran their vehicles over the landscape, crushing the vegetation, causing erosion, and sometimes cracking the plastic pipes of the above-ground water system that Bill and the boys installed. Bill sometimes found the fences split open with wire cutters, places where hunters wanted to get through but couldn't spend the time looking for the nearest gate or the effort to crawl between the barbed wires. A few times, he had come across one of his cows, shot dead by a bullet.

Fencing was part of what the cost of the permit was supposed to pay for, but a rancher couldn't always depend on a quick response to getting problems fixed. Rules for fences were different everywhere, depending on who had jurisdiction, who owned the adjacent land, and what special circumstances had to be addressed. At Smith Mesa, most of the fences had to be at least five feet tall, with four horizontal wires starting just above the ground, held together tightly by vertical wires. Posts couldn't be more than twenty feet apart. At Beavers, the Forest Service wanted forty-two-inch fences, short enough that deer could safely jump over. Sometimes cattle thought they could jump over these, too, and they got sliced up by the barbed wire and tore down a section of fence with their weight.

And when public land came against private land, it was usually the private landowner's responsibility to put up a fence to keep unwanted people and animals out. For a time down at Smith Mesa, Bill couldn't understand how his cows kept getting into the national park. It turned out that one of his neighbors had taken down his fence. When the cows came onto the man's land, he opened the gates on the other end, leading to the park. The park service caught him letting Bill's cows through by setting up a hidden camera.

Bill could handle cattle. People were his problem. That was why Bill spent so much time each summer riding the range on horseback. He checked fences and fixed the leaks and broken sections of the water supply. He policed the lower gates, most afternoons and on weekends, to follow fresh tracks of motor bikes and four-wheelers to make sure they didn't leave the cows with a way out.

A couple years before, a few miles up the property, Bill came across a huddle of ashen-faced teenagers surrounding the dead body of a friend who had just crashed on his motorbike. The boy's skull was crushed. He was due to leave overseas for his two-year Mormon mission a couple of weeks later.

■ ■ ■

Water was less an issue at Beavers than it was in the desert of Smith Mesa, mostly because of the runoff from the winter snowpack. The problem was diverting it to all the right places, which was why Bill and Cody were there on a mild summer day with two workers from the Forest Service.

Ten coils of black, flexible plastic pipe, each of them five hundred feet long and four inches in diameter, were wound tight and tied off so that they could be loaded onto a flatbed pickup. When released from their ties, they sprang and bounced into a rolling corkscrew, like an outstretched Slinky. Once pulled tight, straightened, and connected, they would divert water from a high creek of snow runoff to a series of water basins hidden in a forest of junipers. It was how Bill got water to his herd through the summer.

Bill and Cody were on horseback. One Forest Service worker had brought the coils of pipe on a truck, and another followed on a four-wheeler. They brought one coil to a water tub, connected it to the valves just below the ground, and pulled the pipe through the landscape with the four-wheeler, unwinding and stretching the coils so that the pipe lay tight against the ground. The pipe sometimes dragged rocks and logs or got caught and needed to be rerouted. Sometimes it twisted almost to a tangle, so tight that it suddenly sprang dangerously like a whip when it released. When the men got it straightened out, they attached it to another tank. On and on it went.

Bill was frustrated with their pace. They had a mile of pipe to connect, and Bill didn't want the work to spread to the next day, when Cody and the boys were off to some rodeos. The men took a long lunch break and sat in the cab of the truck while Bill fidgeted with impatience. A year before, he'd done this with no one but Rusty, and they'd finished the work in less time than this was taking.

In the early afternoon, Bill politely excused the workers, telling them that he and Cody could handle the rest. The men were glad to go. Their truck and four-wheeler rumbled downhill, out of sight, leaving only quiet behind.

Coil by coil, Bill and Cody connected one end to a water basin and tied the other to Cody's horse, which pulled it through the forest to the next tank. They didn't bury the pipe underground, because that would be both too hard and too permanent, and the permits didn't allow anything permanent. So it ran above ground like a snake through the forest, occasionally held in place by a pile of rocks. Cattle and wildlife sometimes stepped on the pipes and broke through the plastic. One of Bill's constant chores through summer was to check on the water basins to make sure they were full, and to decipher where in the pipes the leaks were and fixing them.

He and Cody made good time. They didn't say much to each other, because that wasn't their way. Neither of them minded long silences. Cody didn't feel great, but he didn't say anything about his compounding injuries—the pinched nerve in his neck, the herniated disc in his spine. They hadn't kept him out of rodeos, but they affected his riding. The goal on a bronc was to stare down the horse's neck, but Cody couldn't keep his chin tucked, making every ride a jerking bout of whiplash. Cody said he felt like one of those bobblehead dolls, and he started riding with a neck brace, the kind the bareback riders wore. He was plenty secure to make it to Las Vegas, but had started to slip in the standings.

Bill and Cody were on their knees, side by side, digging into the hard dirt and connecting pipe to the basins, when the subject of ranchland came up. Bill told Cody that someone had called, asking about buying Smith Mesa, but they'd lowballed him, and Bill knew it. Some real estate people around Hurricane thought he could get $10,000 an acre for his land, and he was reluctant to consider much else.

A conservation group had called, too, offering $2,500 an acre and a chance to stay. They wanted to keep Smith Mesa away from developers, and Bill could still use it for agricultural purposes, with restrictions. But he was leery of more rules, even if it meant staying at Smith Mesa, even if it meant collecting money that he could use to buy land somewhere else. He kept finding reasons to say no.

Bill insisted that he wasn't the sentimental type, although Evelyn thought he was, more than he realized. The idea of selling property that had been in the family for 150 years, land that had been worked by seven generations of Wrights, wasn't a decision of the heart, but the head.

"When you work on things like that, you grow quite attached, because you have a lot of blood, sweat, and tears invested in it," Bill said. "But I personally figure if you can better yourselves, then I'm not goin' to let that hold me back. I'll have the same blood, sweat, and tears somewhere else."

Cody didn't say anything. He knew his father wouldn't sell Smith Mesa until he found a replacement for it. That might be the hardest part. Bill would have loved to find one place big enough to keep his herd year round, so he didn't have to move it every spring and fall. Maybe something up against the mountains, to keep the cattle low in the winter and higher in the summer. It would be ideal to have private land, to deaden the impact of outside forces as much as possible, but permits and leases, for all their headaches and uncertainties, were still less expensive in a West where land was gobbled up by fewer and fewer interests.

"Most of the private land isn't cost-efficient any more," Bill said. "I heard that South Dakota still was, and I was talkin' to some guys that way, and it sounds like it was gettin' that way there, too. I've got some equity and things, and I think I can find things that's more efficient than what I've got. Just hypothetical, but let's say I run ten cows per acre. It'd be nice to find something I could run fifteen cows per acre. Something that's producing more."

Now and again, Bill took long drives to places in southern Utah and Nevada to look at huge swaths of available ranchland, tens of thousands of acres. Cody went along when he was home. He listened as Bill asked questions about water and feed and permits and put pencil to paper to figure out the numbers. To have land that he controlled, that he could irrigate the way he wanted, that he could move cattle across the way he thought best, that he could work in the summer and the winter without having to haul cows up and down the highway twice a year, was all too enticing to consider if the timing, place, and cost were right.

Bill looked at a place near Moab, close to the Colorado line, and it had farmland and ranchland and water rights. Still, he'd probably have to give up all of Smith Mesa to get it, the family property and the permits, and something held him back.

There was a place near Escalante, on the other side of Zion, that he thought seriously about. The Wrights considered moving there years ago, before they ended up in Milford, and now there was a big piece of property that would suit Bill for years to come. But it had no good road access, so every trip into it required two days on horseback.

That area made him nervous, too. Twenty years before, President Bill Clinton had turned a lot of the land around there, a chunk about the size of Delaware, into Grand Staircase–Escalante National Monument. And that designation put restrictions on the ranchers who grazed cattle there, limiting things like roads and erosion controls in the washes. They couldn't extend or move water lines in their allotments, the way Bill and Cody were doing at Beavers. It had run some longtime ranchers out of the area, Bill had been told. Now a huge chunk of federal land west of there, called Bears Ears, was being turned into a national monument, too, by President Barack Obama. If Bill was trying to get away from the feds, that direction didn't seem like the way to go.

There was a ranch over in Nevada that Bill had explored. It was a good chunk of land, and the boys would like it for hunting in their spare time. Bill had looked at it years before but lost out on a bid to someone else. He'd since heard that the man who bought it was struggling to make payments. Bill was leery because he'd talked to another man who was hired to run the place, who said he could find only half as many cattle there as he had been told, so he left for another job. Bill wasn't sure if he could trust the sellers. He asked about water rights and leases and permits and how many head he could run. He didn't get very clear answers. Something didn't seem right.

Every time he went looking at places, he went home to Smith Mesa without a deal. Bill knew the value of Smith Mesa would rise with time, probably faster than the places he was looking at to replace it. And the longer he waited, the longer he gave his boys to figure out what they wanted to do in the long haul, and the longer he gave them to make good money in rodeo to get there.

Only Bill and Evelyn would decide if Smith Mesa should be the cost of building for future generations. Maybe doing it right meant doing it now. Maybe it meant waiting a bit longer. It was hard to build for the future when you didn't know when that future would arrive.

"It's coming," Bill said a couple of months later. "I know it's coming. Cody's not that far off."

■ ■ ■

It was always good to have Cody around, but he was gone the next day. The boys might be home for ten days between Memorial Day and Labor Day. Sometimes they scrambled hardest in September, trying to squeeze dollars out of little weekend rodeos to make the top fifteen in the standings by the October 1 cutoff for the National Finals.

The herd had grown to about 240 cows, but it had been a tough summer. Fifty of the cows were dry, by far a higher number than ever. Years of drought had knocked other cows off their cycles, and calves were coming deep through the summer, which never used to happen. At Beavers, Bill couldn't put the herd on the parcels that were being reseeded by the Forest Service for a couple of years, and a section where he'd normally be able to put ninety head for two months was available for only ten days this year. Some adjacent private ranchland he had been leasing for years was gone, too. When the old rancher who owned it died a few years back, his will split the property among five kids. There was a sibling spat, and one of the boys fenced off his parcel and rented it to Bill. But after three years, the family made amends and rented it out to other ranchers.

"That's what happens on those rented pastures all the time," Bill said. "Someone else comes and offers more money or they decided they're going to sell it off."

Bill and Cody sold dozens of yearlings months before they usually would, because they didn't have the room to put them and because beef prices were still so high. They trucked another 125 yearlings to a feedlot out in Kansas to fatten them up. As always, Bill had to guess when the cost of feed and transportation no longer made up for the price he'd get for a bigger animal. Part of it, too, was about taxes, trying to stay under certain triggers and even out the revenues from one year to the next. Last thing he wanted to do was pay more taxes. Everything was more complicated than before.

"I can't just have a plan, and I can't run it by a calendar or anything else anymore," Bill said. "I have to roll with the punches. When they took that pasture away from me that I was runnin' those yearlings on, I wasn't too concerned, because I had this other. But then they come in and reseeded that, and it will be better eventually. I looked around for feed around here, but no one was lettin' feed go. I just figured I've done well feedin' cattle in the feedlots, so that's what I done. I'm not gonna do that all the time. I might do it again, because it appears it's working pretty good. They're gainin' three and a half pounds a day, they figure. I've had some gain four pounds in a day."

As the days shortened, Bill gathered the herd to move south for the winter. Snow came early to the Tushars, traces here and there, and Bill liked to go riding on those days immediately after, because he could track the cattle more easily by their tracks.

But Bill didn't know the land that well, certainly not the way he knew Smith Mesa. There were miles to cover and a hundred different gullies to trace. It required guesswork and experience. He talked to old-timers for advice. The trick was to coerce the animals down the mountains over the course of many weeks at the pace of the coming season, and the cattle themselves did a lot of the work for him. It was instinct, but instinct only told them to move downhill, not exactly where to go.

"That's the way God made them, the Creator made them," Bill said. "It's amazing to me to watch them in that country. They work downhill, but they get ledged out, get hung up, because snow has moved in behind them."

One big storm could strand them high and starve them, so he had to time it right. So Bill spent the shortening days of fall coaxing bunches of cattle downhill, steering them away from cliffs and box canyons, keeping an eye on the forecasts and the elevations where rain turned to snow, and where snow piled up.

When he had most of the herd down at Bone Hollow, he called for the truck, and they hauled load after load, about fifty cows at a time, two hours down to Smith Mesa. He hoped to have them all found by the time he had to go to Las Vegas, but that usually didn't happen. Cows weren't always that cooperative, and he'd probably get a call telling him that some of them had been found wandering around town, having slipped through a gate that someone had left open.

9

The Quiet One

THE CONVERSATION SLOWED and the buzz from the beers wore off. Everyone got quiet. The second hand of the clock on the wall ticked, ticked, ticked, between roars of the sellout crowd that funneled through the hard bends in the arena hallway like wind through a canyon. The cheers swirled into the room and faded. Tension rose.

The fifteen best saddle bronc riders in the world, four of them brothers named Wright, grabbed their saddles and reins and shuffled quietly out of the locker room. They were mostly in their twenties, lean and tan, rugged like men unafraid of sun and injury. Their footsteps were deadened by carpet, the procession announced only by the jangle of spurs.

Out in the arena, eighteen thousand people surrounded a brightly lit ring of dirt. Rodeo didn't get any bigger than the National Finals Rodeo. Bill leaned against a gate next to the chutes, peering between the rails under the brim of his clean felt hat. He wore a new jean jacket with a big NFR logo on the back. A red neckerchief was tied around his neck because he had been asked to wear it. He looked a bit like someone at a dude ranch who might sing "Ghost Riders in the Sky" as tourists ate beans from a tin plate.

For years, Bill had volunteered to work a gate that riders walked through after coming undone from their bull or bronc. When a cowboy approached, Bill slid the gate open a crack, closed it behind them, and resumed his solemn stance against the rail. It gave him a prime view of the rides. When one of the cowboys was one of his sons, they sometimes stopped to share a few words, staring up together at replays on the overhead video board while waiting for the scores from the judges to come in.

Evelyn was in the stands, a face among thousands, though the arena cameras sometimes zoomed in on her and showed her on the big video boards. She'd missed Cody's tenth and winning ride the second time he won the world title. That's what rodeo called you, the world champion, even though almost all of the participants were from the American West and the event where you won the world title was called the National Finals. She had waited at the hotel for one of her daughters, who came late, and they got stuck in traffic on Tropicana Avenue, right in front of Hooters. Becca, the youngest of the Wright sisters, was in the arena, on the phone with Evelyn to relay the unfolding scene. When Evelyn arrived, a woman stopped her and told her how sweet it was that she was crying, but she was mostly crying because she'd missed it.

When the National Finals opened on the first Thursday night in December, Spencer, Jake, and Jesse put up big scores and were, for a few minutes, one-two-three on the scoreboard. Then some of the generation's other top riders, men like Taos Muncy, Cort Scheer, Jacobs Crawley, and Wade Sundell, leapfrogged the Wright boys into the night's standings. Spencer, in fifth, was the only one in the money.

Cody finished out of the money on the second night, and again on the third. He was scoring points but not winning money, standing still while others passed him in the rankings, which wasn't hard to do when the first-place prize each night was more than $19,000. It wasn't until Round 4 that Cody earned a check, for third place.

That was the night that Spencer boarded a dark mare named Mata Fact. It reared up when the gate opened and looked like it might flip over backward before it slammed down on its front hooves at the same time that Spencer kicked his spurs to the bronc's mane. It was a powerful horse and a cool ride, and Spencer won the round with a score of 84.

It was his fourth night in a row in the money, but Spencer was the least known of the Wrights in Las Vegas. He had no history of big wins and was in his first National Finals, and no one paid much attention to him, even though Spencer had climbed from thirteenth place to seventh in the standings. Cody slipped to fourth.

They stayed that way for a couple more nights, through the sixth round, which Jake won. The Wright brothers were sprinkled across the standings—Cody fourth, Spencer seventh, Jake tenth, and Jesse fourteenth. But that was just raw money. When the computer figured in the average, rewarding those who got the highest average scores with bonuses reaching almost $50,000 at the end of the rodeo, the projected rankings had Cody in second and Spencer in third. Scheer, a confident and chatty cowboy from Nebraska, was at the top with four nights to go.

"Cody is getting screwed," Bill said in the hallway before Round 7. He was in the night's work clothes, a pressed shirt with an NFR logo, a bandana, and his best hat. "He shoulda won two nights ago. And Jesse is getting screwed every night. I don't know why they won't score him. Evelyn always thinks they take advantage of the boys. I tell her that every mother thinks the same thing."

113

He studied a list of the standings in his hands and did the math in his head. He knew which cowboys had a chance in the end, because he knew which ones would get the bonus for the average and which ones would not.

"Cody's right there," Bill said. "And no one's even thinking about Spencer."

Bill scooted out into the bowl of the arena, darkened for introductions and the laser show and the grand entry—all the cowboys and cowgirls introduced by state, galloping into the arena. "And UTAHHHHH!" the announcer shouted, and Cody rode in with the Utah flag on his hip, followed by his brothers and about a dozen others from the Beehive State. Dust rose into a cloud in the rafters. The preshow bombast only slowed and quieted for the nightly prayer.

"Rodeo is an American sport," the announcer said solemnly, and everyone stood hushed, and the men took off their hats. "And one of America's greatest freedoms is to pray to the god of our choice at the time of our choice. And while we are a diverse nation with many different faiths, and we have a deep respect for all of them, tonight I want to offer this prayer, in the name of my lord and savior, Jesus Christ."

There was a chorus of amens and cheers, and then the national anthem, treated with equal reverence. Then the lights, energy, and volume were turned up and the events rolled by, moving quickly, more efficiently than at any hometown rodeo. Bareback bronc riding always came first. When that ended, the saddle bronc contestants solemnly and nervously left their locker room for the chutes, which were being loaded with broncs pushed through arena tunnels under the stands from the corrals out in the parking lot. The cowboys saddled up the horses during calf roping and steer wrestling, which came out of the chutes at the other end of the arena. Then came saddle bronc, always fourth of the seven events.

Spencer churned atop a roan gelding called Pretty Boy, the two perfectly timed like dance partners, and the announcer's voice rose above the cheers and his syllables were drawn out for emphasis. "The red-headed Wright brother!" he shouted as Spencer shuffled across the dirt and waited for his score. "He has ridden sevvvven of sevvvven. He has been perfect alllll week. And look at this number on this Wednesday night! Eighty-five!"

Three cowboys in a row bucked off. Then came Cody's turn. ShaRee and Rusty and Ryder and a bunch of other Wrights were in Section 112, and Bill was leaning against the gate next to Chute 7, hands folded over a rung. Cody, another world title in his grasp with four rides to go, climbed atop a bronc named Camp Fire. He marked it out as it lumbered out of the chute and faded like a toy with a pull string. Cody rode it hard to the buzzer. He got a score of 65 and a re-ride option from the judges, because his horse hadn't lived up to its billing.

But before Cody knew all that, and before the pickup men arrived to help Cody off, with most people looking up at the replay on the overhead video board, Camp Fire suddenly sped along the rail and zoomed out from under Cody. Cody fell off the back end, as helpless as a man pushed backward into a pool. He twisted in the air to brace for the landing, but didn't make it all the way around. He crashed clumsily on his left shoulder, and the pain shot through him like electricity. He knew instantly that it was serious. His expression and his casual walk across the dirt kept the pain a secret, but he held his left arm across his chest, like a running back holding an imaginary football, as he headed for Bill's gate.

"Shit," ShaRee said. Even from halfway up the arena, she could tell. So could Rusty. So could Bill. Bill opened the gate and Cody passed his father with just a glance. Bill knew from his son's eyes. Bill closed the gate and leaned against the rail, and hardly anybody else in the arena knew that Cody's championship hopes were gone.

■　■　■

ShaRee excused herself past all the others in her row. She walked up to the concourse, where you could buy Coors Light and ten-dollar slushed drinks, and cowboys and cowgirls and ranchers and farmers—and people who wanted to look like cowboys and cowgirls and ranchers and farmers—strolled aimlessly, like a Friday night on Main Street. She weaved through them and took an elevator down to the floor level, into the maze of concrete hallways and rooms in the bowels of the arena. Spencer had the best ride of the night, and he was the hottest bronc rider of the week, and he was about to be interviewed on live television.

Cody was around the corner and two doors down in the medical room. It was filled with medics and trainers in cowboy hats and matching shirts, as if they had arrived that night together on horseback. There were examination tables and a few chairs where hurt cowboys were treated, massaged, stretched, and taped. Cody was on a table behind a black curtain that shielded badly hurt cowboys from view. ShaRee joined him. Jesse went in for a look and came back out to the hallway a minute later.

"He's all right," Jesse said. "They're just poppin' his shoulder back in. I'll bet he's a sore sucker tomorrow. I wouldn't be surprised if he rides with his other hand."

Doctors tried to wrangle Cody's arm back into its shoulder socket, but it was like stretching an elastic band already pulled taut. They inserted an IV and fed him a sedative, loosening his muscles, and they twisted and tugged his arm and twice thought they had snapped it into place. But Cody's body kept tensing up at the last moment, and the thing wouldn't go into place. A doctor told Sha-Ree that Cody needed to be knocked out. That meant taking him to the hospital.

Medics came in with a gurney, and Cody stood, shirtless, his left arm taped to his body in a sling. His jeans and belt buckle were undone. His eyes had the look of a happy drunk. He was helped onto the gurney, his back propped up at an angle and a tube coming out of his arm. Jesse carried Cody's chaps, hat, and spurs, and ShaRee walked alongside her husband as he was carted out the door, into the hall, up an elevator, and out the glass doors into the cool night.

The rodeo was just ending, and the ambulance was parked where the fans came out of the arena. The men were decked out in their hats and pressed shirts and the women in denim and leather, everyone in cowboy boots and holding plastic cups. Cody was steered through the crowd by paramedics. Fans stared at him the way they would a zoo animal. The back doors to the ambulance swung open.

"That's probably the bronc rider," said a man after swallowing a mouthful of beer. People stepped out of the way, and a few took photographs with their phones. Someone whispered that it might be Cody Wright.

ShaRee gave Cody a kiss as he was lifted into the ambulance. Her eyes were filled with worry, his with dopey confusion. The doors clanged shut and the ambulance drove off, wiggling through a jam of brake lights, leaving ShaRee alone in the parking lot, holding Cody's things, wondering where the rest of the family was.

Deep in her mind, she wondered if this was how a champion rodeo career would come to a close, without ceremony or cheers, because you never really know how things will end until they actually do.

■ ■ ■

The South Point Hotel, Casino, and Spa was a twenty-five-story hiccup in the low sprawl on the southern end of Las Vegas, several miles from the hubbub of the Strip. For ten days each December, as a culture clash of boots and brash smothered Las Vegas casinos, the South Point was smothered more than most. It was filled with men in jeans and cowboy hats drinking longneck beers, and women wearing lace and leather and too much makeup drinking slushy, colorful concoctions from boot-shaped plastic cups.

Each night at eleven, the winners of that evening's rodeo events were called on stage, one by one, and handed an enormous belt buckle and a bottle of whisky. Bill had never missed a buckle ceremony for his boys. He'd probably been to more than anyone other than the emcees—even more than Evelyn, who sometimes missed parts of the rodeo because she was back in Milford, teaching school.

Bill had been there the night before, when Jake won, and Jake was handed the bottle of Pendleton Whisky and tore off the top and threw it into the crowd. He took a swig of whisky and did a dance, and the fans cheered and laughed. Jake was the most gregarious of the bronc-riding Wrights, a well-known favorite. The year before, he had been in perfect position to become the third brother to win a world title in a four-year span before he was flagged for missing his mark out on the ninth night—the same costly no-score fate that befell Cody when he seemed destined to win *his* first title. Jake couldn't make up the difference on the tenth and final night, and he was stuck forever in the record book in second place.

Spencer stood alone in the dimly lit black hallway behind the stage, among the winning contestants of other events and their families, sipping on a longneck Coors Light. He nervously called his parents, who were inside the casino, eating at Steak 'n Shake. They knew how long these ceremonies took, and even though it started at eleven, you had to wait for the bareback ceremony, and then the team-roping ceremony, and then the steer-wrestling ceremony. There was time. Bill knew that. He ate his hamburger slowly, Evelyn at his side, Jake and Loni and CoBurn at the table, too, while Spencer paced in the hallway across the casino, calling their phones but getting no answer.

Over burgers and shakes, there wasn't much worry for Cody.

"Cody's fine," Evelyn said. "He'll ride."

"This is rodeo," Bill said. "It ain't football."

They finished eating and took their time walking through the crowded casino. Spencer was relieved to see them appear with about five minutes to spare. He pulled a dip of chewing tobacco from his lip and flicked it into a trash can. He looked around with his hound-dog eyes, his head down. Evelyn watched him from across the hall and laughed.

"He always looks a little embarrassed," she said.

A woman with a headset gave them all a nod and tugged at their elbows, ushering the Wrights, about ten of them, through a gauzy curtain and onto a huge stage. It was lit with spotlights so bright that it was hard to see the thousand or so fans at their feet.

"Poor Spencer," said Flint Rasmussen, a longtime barrelman and rodeo clown who was one of the two emcees. "He just hates this."

"Your dad just said that you can't dance, but you can sing," said the other emcee, rodeo announcer Randy Corley. Spencer smirked and stayed silent. Corley turned to the crowd and shrugged.

They showed the replay of the winning ride on a big screen behind them and asked Spencer to take them through those eight seconds. "Any point in that ride you thought you were in trouble?" Corley asked.

"Not really."

"You're leading the average. You feeling good?"

"Yeah, but I'm just taking it one ride at a time."

Corley turned to the crowd. "As you can tell, Spencer shows a lot of emotion. How old are you?"

"Twenty-three."

"He's twenty-three," Rasmussen said. "We just told him that he's won sixty-eight grand this week and he does this," and Rasmussen shrugged.

They presented Spencer with his buckle and his whisky, and Spencer and the Wrights shuffled off stage. Spencer spotted Kathryn, his sister, and his face lit up for the first time. Like a lot of the siblings, they tried to get to NFR when they could, but work, travel, and family plans made it hard. Kathryn had arrived too late to make it on stage. "I didn't know you were coming," Spencer said. He gave her a hug, but his hands were full—one with whisky, one with a buckle. A longneck beer poked out of his Wrangler pocket.

■　■　■

Cody was in a hospital room, muscle relaxant dripping into his arm. He started to count and didn't make it past three, but he was still alert enough to pull back his arm whenever the doctor tried to snap it back into his shoulder. The flow through the tube was increased. Cody's glazed eyes closed, but his body still flinched with each pull. Finally, there was a muffled pop, like a firecracker under a blanket. Cody came to about fifteen minutes later. He was asked if he was all right, and he said he was. He was given two painkillers, and ShaRee drove him back to the rented house and guided him to bed.

By mid-morning, Cody and ShaRee were back at the arena, now empty and quiet. They headed straight downstairs to the medical room. The doctor iced Cody's shoulder and gave it electrical stimulation. Cody wanted to see if he could ride.

They walked down the hall to the saddle bronc locker room. Cody sat in his saddle on the floor, his feet stretched before him. He held the reins in his left hand while others kneeled and held the saddle, and Cody tugged and jerked to see what his shoulder could handle. He winced with pain, and his left shoulder, loose and weak and wrapped against his body in a sling, could not hold firmly in place. He tried holding the rein in his right hand, which to a cowboy felt like writing cursive with the wrong hand. Cody could ride like that, and he had, but doing so at the National Finals meant he would have to raise his left arm over his shoulder during the ride. He couldn't lift it that far.

He grabbed the rein with his left hand again, and pulled and twisted, trying to simulate a ride. Then the shoulder popped, loudly enough for everyone to hear, and that was what clinched it for Cody. Another year chasing a world title, and just when it was in his grasp, in the final weekend of the year, he had to drop out. Officially, he doctored out, which under the rules meant he had to sit out at least two rounds. It was noon in an empty arena when the decision was made, ending a streak of 117 consecutive National Finals rounds, dating back twelve years.

A statement was released to the media a couple of hours before that night's show. "Shoulder injury sidelines Cody Wright for at least two rounds," the headline read. In the dusk outside the arena, in the parking lot, backdropped by the lights of the Strip a few blocks west, Cody stood at his camper. His brothers and his father were already inside, getting ready, but his sons stayed nearby. Stetson and Statler tossed a football. Ryder and Rusty leaned on the hood of Cody's truck. Already that week in Las Vegas, away from the prime-time event of the National Finals, Rusty had been named rookie of the year and won a pair of two-round rodeos for ascending young bronc riders. He had gone to the College of Southern Idaho in the fall and won two college rodeos he entered, but didn't think he'd return in the spring. He wanted to rodeo full time with Cody, except now Cody's own career was in jeopardy.

"I felt it go out when I was sliding off," Cody said. "I fell backward on my shoulder. It was going to be that or my head."

"You've got a hard head," Rusty said. "You shoulda done that."

"Hindsight being 20/20, I would've done it. I coulda just worn a helmet tonight."

When the show opened that night, Jesse carried the Utah flag. During the competition, in succession, Spencer scored 82.5, Jake had an 80.5, and Jesse an 83.

"Look at that board!" the announcer shouted. "Look at that board! Jesse, Spencer, Jake! It's a Wright brothers family reunion! Somebody take a picture of that and send it to the Wrights' mom!"

■ ■ ■

There were two nights to go. Spencer was in second place. The Wright brothers took over their corner of the room, and Spencer compared the brim of his hat with the others'.

"I got this stiffened," he said, twirling the hat and gliding his fingers on his brim. "It's a lot stiffer than it was. It used to flip around."

About half of the men sipped on cheap beers, supplied by the previous night's winner and dumped, with ice, into the shower and the sinks of the locker room. Some sat in folding chairs, mindlessly putting baby powder on their saddle straps or taking a steel brush to the worn, slick inner thighs of their leather chaps. Others sat in their saddles, on the stained carpet, stretching and adjusting stirrups.

A few cowboys kept to themselves or whispered in small circles.

Most were part of the broader conversation, talking about every-thing except the world standings and that night's rides. One told a story about whacking a rooster that he thought was dead until it sprang to life, another about punching an ostrich. The men laughed and swore and fended off nerves. A few of the most extroverted, like Jake, shouted out punch lines that wouldn't make sense to anyone outside the walls.

"I was like, 'You don't ride with a riding heel,'" one cowboy said. "And he is like, 'I ride with a walking heel!'"

The others broke into laughter and knowing smirks.

The rodeo started with the bareback riding, the first event, and the saddle bronc riders watched it unfold on televisions bolted high on the wall. Jesse paced. Jake and Spencer rocked in their saddles, legs shaking with nervous energy.

A veteran bronc rider named Chad Ferley walked in. He had won the title twice, including the year before, when Jake no-scored on the second-to-last night.

"Champ, will you sign this please?" Spencer asked, with his usual sheepish manner. He held out a Sharpie marker and a piece of aluminum with the NFR logo on it, shaped like the red, white, and blue highway signs seen on the interstate. He wanted to get the autographs of all fourteen other saddle bronc riders. Ferley smiled and signed, and Spencer smiled back with the fake teeth he got after he lost his real ones when a pickup man ran over him in Walla Walla back in the summer. Spencer slid the memento back into a bag to protect it.

Cody walked in. "Mr. Wright," someone said. The left sleeve of his jacket had no hand coming out its end. His arm was tucked underneath, in a sling. Scheer was clinging to first place in the pro-jections. He stood and gave Cody a fake punch.

"Ho, ho! That was a close one!" he said, and Cody smiled.

He sat in a metal folding chair near his brothers. Side by side, Jake, Jesse, and Spencer changed out of one pair of jeans into their riding pair—dingier Wranglers carrying the dirt of a hundred rodeos. They wore big buckles won at big rodeos. Jesse's came from his NFR title two years before, because he figured something with such sentimental value didn't belong in the duffel bag. They wrapped their fringed chaps around them and cinched them with small buckles on the side of each thigh.

They unfolded the straps of their saddles and sprinkled them with baby powder to keep them soft. They rolled them back up and tied the end into a rectangular buckle. They sat in their saddles and rocked back and forth, pausing to press a couple of pebble-sized chunks of black rosin onto the saddle where the insides of the thighs would go. They pressed it with their fingers, the heat softening the rosin into a tacky smear, and then squeezed the saddle with their thighs until the soft leather of their chaps grabbed the hard leather of their saddles. Every time they released their legs, it sounded like Velcro being undone.

Spencer stood on one end of the rein, tugged it tight with his rein hand, and held the pose for eight seconds. His face contorted, then loosened. He repeated it a few times and sat down on a folding chair. He took his hat off and crossed his legs, idly spinning a spur on the heel of his boot with his fingers. He was matched with Pony Man, which had bucked Jake four nights earlier. Cody had scored 82 on it back in Cheyenne. He scooted close to Spencer and pulled out his phone, and in a minute they were watching the ride on video. Spencer wondered if he should shorten his stirrups.

"I wouldn't mess with it," Cody whispered, and Spencer left his rigging alone.

Cody turned to Jesse, who was talking about Chicken Dance. He'd had it in Amarillo. Give it a lot of rein, Cody said, and he helped Jesse wrap his sore abdomen with athletic tape. Jake had Let 'Er Rip. Cody had had it once in Corpus Christi, and as they started talking, they heard a noise from the bathroom stall.

"Who's pukin'?" someone asked. "Is someone pukin'?"

"It's Red, man," Jake said. Spencer's chair was empty. "He does it every fuckin' night."

Spencer came back to his chair. He didn't say anything or look at anyone. His eyes were watery and red. A few seats over, a cowboy casually gouged chunks of dried dirt from the heel of his boots with a knife.

"You all right, Spence?" one of the men asked. "You have a puke?"

"I puke every night," Spencer said, and he got a cup of water from the cooler to wash the taste out.

It was time. The cowboys slipped out, silent except for their spurs, carrying their saddles and dragging their leathers on the carpet behind them. They left behind the detritus of empty duffels, beer cans, polished boots, jackets, chew cups, baby powder, and empty tins of Copenhagen and cans of Red Bull.

Cody was suddenly alone. He wore his brown cowboy hat and the letterman-style NFR jacket given to all contestants. He leaned back in the metal folding chair and watched the competition on the television mounted to the wall. There was no sound coming from the TV, but the music, cheers, and unintelligible voices of the announcers snaked around a couple of bends in the hallway from the arena. Cody stood now and again and looked at the night's order and matchups on the wall.

A ride would end, the announcer would exalt or encourage, the fans would applaud, and the rider would disappear from the TV screen, only to reappear back in the locker room. Most were expressionless. A few were angry. A couple were hurt enough to drop their things and head straight to the medical room.

The first cowboy back into the room had bucked off, and he set his saddle down by his chair.

"That horse come in flat?" Cody asked.

"That thing slid out and I couldn't hold my rein," he said. "I don't know why that keeps happening."

Cody nodded and kept watching. Spencer was up, and he held on to Pony Man, cocking and releasing like a cylinder. But Cody fixated on something he saw wrong with Spencer's rigging.

"That saddle is loose," he said to himself. "Looks like it might slide off its back. Look at the frickin' saddle."

Spencer scored an 81.5, the top score to that point. Jake beat it with an 82, but as soon as the buzzer sounded, Let 'Er Rip ejected him like a dart from a toy gun. Jake flew off forward, arced, and landed on top of his head. He bounced like a pogo stick and was slow to move off the dirt. He finally hobbled away.

Scheer went last. But his horse jerked and lurched like a misfiring car, and Scheer did all he could to simply clench his feet and hang on until the buzzer. The 68.5 score cost him the top spot in the projected overall standings, now flipped with Spencer.

"Fuck, that was a fuckin' spur bath," Scheer said as he returned and tossed down his saddle in frustration. He sat down and cracked a Keystone Light.

Spencer came in behind him, dragging his saddle and straps. He was unhappy, too, even if he had the night's third-best score and the year's top spot with one round to go.

"He was soakin' wet," he said to Cody. It was raining outside and the horses came into the arena dripping. "My saddle was wet, too. I thought I had it on. I pulled it tight. Kept hitting my back cinch."

The stock contractor who owned the bronc walked in and patted Spencer on the shoulder. "I thought he rode good," Spencer said politely, "but I couldn't get that saddle right."

The room refilled with cowboys and chatter, and the heaviness of the mood lifted. Beers were cracked. Cigarettes were lit. Talk loosened. Even Scheer smiled and laughed.

"I'm going to go check on Jake," Cody said, and he left. In the medical room, Sundell was on his stomach, with a cooler's worth of ice packs on his aching back. He was the night's winner. Next to him was Jake, who was second. His shirt was off and he was on his stomach, too. Ice packs were stacked on his shoulders and neck. Jake was quiet, which meant he was in pain.

"Been fifteen minutes yet?" he asked Cody with a wince.

"No," Cody said, and he laughed at his brother. "About two. You got frostbite yet?"

A stock contractor spotted Cody.

"You gonna ride tomorrow?" the man asked.

"I'm tryin' to decide," Cody said. "I ain't as tough as you."

"If you ain't right, don't do it," the man said. "You got too many rodeos ahead."

"It makes me sick to be standin' here," Cody said, "because the shoulder doesn't bother me too much. But I know it's hanging by a string."

■ ■ ■

By noon on Saturday, the last day of the National Finals, all the brothers were behind a table, signing autographs at Cowboy Christmas, a sprawling daily trade show at the Las Vegas Convention Center. Hundreds of booths offered clothes, boots, hat, saddles, jewelry, home décor, campers, horse trailers—anything that could be considered Western. There were stages for performers, temporary rodeo arenas for demonstrations, and a food court selling Angus burgers.

People gawked at the Wrights. Men mostly stayed back, taking pictures from a distance. Young women approached and made small talk and asked to join the boys for photos. Children in cowboy hats had the same wide-eyed wonder and apprehension as those meeting Santa Claus at the mall. Each brother had a box of glossy photographs of himself. Cody used just his right arm, keeping his left tucked tight against him, but his smile made it seem that he was feeling just fine.

Evelyn loitered on the edge of the crowd, wearing a sweatshirt that read, "Doin' it the Wright Way," along with each of the four boys' names. She had called Spencer's hotel room at ten thirty and woken him up to see how he was doing. "Mom, I don't appreciate being riddled with questions first thing in the morning," he told her. That made her laugh.

Evelyn went to the end of the line, because she wanted autographs, too, but the security guard told her the line had been cut off and she was out of luck.

"But I'm their mother," she said with a smile, and the security guard didn't know if she was serious. He told her no. Evelyn laughed and waited until the end, when she slipped past, unnoticed, and got the autographs of her sons. Bill stood to the side and talked to CoBurn about the night's matchups. He had already done the math.

"Spencer's got Lunatic from Hell," Bill said. "It's a buckin' son of a bitch. I think it's enough horse to win. I don't think Cort's got as good a horse. I don't know if Spencer'll win the round tonight, but I think he'll be right up there and it'll be enough."

Bill hadn't said a word to Spencer. The Wrights went out of their way to try to make everything seem as normal as ever, like teammates of a baseball pitcher working on a no-hitter.

"He knows what he's gotta do," Bill said. "He's been handling it in fine fashion. I wanted to say something to him yesterday, because I think his mark out the night before was weak. But I didn't, and his mark out was super."

By one thirty, Spencer was back in his room at the Aria to take a nap, and most of the rest of the Wrights killed time in Bill and Evelyn's room across the Strip at the Venetian. It was a two-level room, complimentary because of Bill's work with the rodeo, and if you lifted one of the overpriced bottles of booze or any of the snacks that the hotel wanted to sell you off the countertop, a sensor inside knew it and charged it to your room bill.

"Don't touch anything," Evelyn said.

By twilight, Cody was at his truck in the arena lot, talking to his longtime doctor from Cedar City, who could have made a decent living just tending to the injuries of the Wrights. They stepped into the back of the camper, where Cody was fitted with a brace to secure his left arm and shoulder. He had decided to ride, and was matched with Spring Planting, a two-time saddle bronc horse of the year. ShaRee tried to look calm.

"I have to admit, I'm pretty nervous," she said. "I'm not sure I've ever been this nervous."

A couple of hours later, Cody and Spring Planting came out of Chute 2, and Cody grimaced as he held his right arm high and kicked his feet and held tight with his battered left arm. It looked like a solid ride, but he was flagged for a missed mark out. He was so worried about his shoulder that he didn't concentrate on his feet, and as he walked through the gate, he stopped and talked to Bill.

"You missed it, over the forearm," Bill said, and he felt for Cody, because he thought everything was lined up for him that year. Just a few days before, Cody had been positioned to win a world championship. But now he needed surgery to repair his shoulder, and rehabilitation was expected to take at least three months. It was reasonable to wonder if he would ever return to the National Finals and get that chance to ride alongside his sons.

Jake was next. The X-ray that morning showed a compression fracture in his back, and he would have to miss the start of the next year, too, but he lasted eight seconds on Stampede Warrior and scored a painful 78. "After about the third jump, I thought I was going to piss down my leg," he said.

Jesse boarded Son of Sadie, which ran and bucked diagonally across the arena and, at the buzzer, dumped him against the fence. He scored an 81.5.

The real anticipation was directed toward Chute 1. Spencer cinched his saddle atop Lunatic from Hell, a paint horse with chocolate splotches on his face and neck. It was one of three in the round from the same bronc family, along with Lunatic Fringe and Lunatic Party, among the nastiest and most intimidating broncs in the game. Spencer, dressed in his black Wrangler shirt and his coffee-brown hat, flipped a leg over the horse and poked his toes into the stirrups. He grabbed the fluffy rein with his left hand, just as Bill had taught him, giving a finger of extra rope for the wild lurching he expected. A couple of men down in the dirt pulled the gate open, and another behind the chute held the flank strap until Lunatic from Hell lurched out sideways and the rope tightened and was let go.

The horse landed on its front hooves with its hind legs kicked out and his body at a forty-five-degree angle to the dirt. Spencer's spurs were tight on the bronc's neck, just below the mane, a perfect mark out. The horse lunged and rose, lunged and rose, and Spencer twice missed a pump to clamp his heels in the animal's side to hang on. It was a decent ride, not a great one, and earned him 79 points, good for fourth place in the round.

Scheer needed to finish two spots ahead to leapfrog ahead of

Spencer in the final world standings. He never had a chance. Big Fork came out, stuttered and leapt and stuttered again, and Scheer was forced to dig his feet in on about half the jumps. He got 71. Spencer clinched the world title.

When he walked into the hallway leading to the locker room, Jake tackled him on the carpet. In the room, Spencer got high fives and hugs from the other cowboys, including Scheer. Someone had sneaked in a pony keg, and some took turns taking tap hits and spraying foam at the others. A wrestling match broke out, and the place filled with the stench of beer and sweat and the noise of relief and laughter. Spencer was escorted back to the arena, where the seven world champions in the seven events were introduced amid a spectacle of lasers, spotlights, and fog.

In about a hundred other rodeos over the past year, Spencer had won $60,265. In ten December nights in Las Vegas, he won another $145,122. It was one of the best NFR performances in history. Spencer was the first bronc rider to leap from thirteenth in the standings to number one.

"I'm speechless," Spencer said when the microphone and the spotlight reached him and eighteen thousand people went quiet to hear what he had to say. "I'm glad to have brothers. I love them. And I love my parents."

He was led to a room full of reporters, and he stood in front of the cameras with his hands tucked into the front pockets of his jeans. His boots were dusty and his hat was tipped back on his head. His sweaty strawberry hair was matted against his forehead. Someone handed him a water bottle. "Thank you," he said.

One by one, high-energy interviewers stepped in front of a camera and asked Spencer to put into words the emotion of winning a world title. Spencer mostly stammered and grinned.

"I'm happy," he said. "I'm proud. And happy."

A reporter, hoping for more, asked Spencer to take him through the ten nights.

"I think I did outdraw everyone all week," Spencer said. "I drew pretty rider-friendly horses all week. Enough to place on and win some." He laughed. "I couldn't a done a better job of drawin'."

Reporters approached Bill and Evelyn and figured out quickly that Evelyn had a comfort in front of the camera that Spencer didn't inherit. She told a story about Spencer being rookie of the year two years before, and her asking him if he could see himself at the National Finals someday.

"He said, 'Mom, I'm gonna win it,'" she said. "You just want what makes them happy. But what makes them happy doesn't always work out. It's hard on moms, watching them do this stuff."

Evelyn wrapped Spencer in a hug. He threw his arm around Bill, who couldn't stop smiling. Under the brim of his hat, pulled low, were tears in his eyes. The three posed for photographs in front of the world championship saddle. Spencer held the world championship gold buckle, framed in a box.

Just a few days before, Cody had been in line to win a world title. But Spencer got it instead, and he carried his huge saddle outside to the parking lot to stash in his camper. Then he piled into a limousine filled with brothers and sisters for a party on the Strip that lasted all night.

Cody wasn't among them. He and ShaRee and the kids headed home to Milford, and on Monday, Cody had surgery on his shoulder in Cedar City. The doctor figured he'd be out at least three months, maybe more, if he came back at all.

PART THREE

Cowbells in the Fog

10

Bent Out of Shape

FROM THE START of the year to the first of May, the almanacs said, there were usually six or seven inches of precipitation, but Smith Mesa hadn't seen that in years. There was nothing in January this time, no flakes or drops, just cool sunlight and gusty winds. Bill wasn't sure about all the talk of climate change—"I heard that was all a bunch of bullshit," he said—but he did see a trend. The springs were definitely drier than they used to be.

Years of drought had slowly turned the fragile high-desert landscape to dust, and the rising temperatures and slim prospects for rain made Bill nervous. It wasn't just the short-term worry over whether the herd would have water one week or the next, or whether the plants would thrive long enough in the warming heat of spring to nourish the new calves. Drought had a way of altering the cycles of the entire herd.

"Drought is harder on the cow business than low prices," Bill said. "Drought impacts you for years to come."

Bill usually introduced his ten bulls to the herd on May 15. Since a cow's gestation period was about nine months and ten days, it meant that the calves would arrive about March 1 of the next year. When it worked just right, they'd be born about three weeks before everything greened up on Smith Mesa. It was a strategic window, the calves born late enough to avoid the extremes of winter, but early enough that, by late May, when they were about three months old, they would be strong enough to brand and move up north. They spent the summer at Beavers, paired with their mothers, growing bigger and stronger in the mountains.

But the string of dry years took its toll. Normally, more than ninety percent of the cows got pregnant in May, the kind of rate any successful operation needed. That number was dropping. Last May, when the amount of feed at Smith Mesa was a third of normal, the month came and went with fifty cows not pregnant. The predictable cycle of the herd—calves born in spring, sold at eighteen months, the two-hundred-some cows in sync with the seasons and the sell-offs—was splintering into something more unwieldy, and certainly less profitable. A cow without a calf was costing money, not making it.

To fight back, Bill planted a few hundred acres at Smith Mesa, as he had done years before, just as his father and his grandfather and great-grandparents had done. It was mostly various types of alfalfa on the relatively flat areas near camp, but Bill wanted to keep the herd off of it for a season to let it take root. The dry spring did not help. He had water in the ponds, but not a lot of feed.

He needed to get the herd off the mesa and into the mountains. He normally waited until after the family roundup and branding day, every Memorial Day, and moved the cattle in June, when his permits above Beaver allowed. But now Jesse had the permit at Bone Hollow, and it gave Bill the flexibility to use it as a holding area between seasons. Bill decided to move the herd in May, not

June, and hold the roundup at Beavers, not Smith Mesa. No one in the family complained. Beavers was closer to Milford, and not so hot, and there wouldn't be any no-see-ums, the black gnats, to test everyone's nerves.

"Where: Beaver Mountains at the Bone Hollow Cow Permit," Evelyn wrote in an invitation she mailed to her children. "Bring your camping equipment, food, water, warm clothes and shades. There aren't many trees where we will be. There is a little ditch with water in it for the kids to play in close by."

Bill spent most of the month camped at Smith Mesa, nudging the herd up and out of the wash and onto the more manageable range atop the flat land at the base of the Zion cliffs. The boys helped when they could, especially Alex, back from working his in-laws' ranch in Oregon and living with his wife and children in Milford, near the rest. Alex, a year older than the twins, was a state champion saddle bronc rider in high school and a top rider in college. He joined the pro circuit and just missed making the National Finals Rodeo a couple of times. He once finished twenty-first on the money list, with $45,000 in winnings.

But Alex fell into a string of bad luck with injuries, and he had bills to pay. Last year, a promising return to competition ended with a broken ankle. Another fall from a bronc broke his collarbone at Thanksgiving. He spent the winter waiting for it to heal, but doctors finally decided that the separation between the broken pieces of bone was too much, so he had surgery. He hoped to be competing again by summer.

In the meantime, he had taken a lot of Bill's old concrete equipment and begun rebuilding Bill's old business, mostly doing sidewalks and curbs around Milford. And since he was not on the rodeo circuit that pulled the other Wright boys to Texas in March and California in April and May, he had time to help his dad.

Bill ordered the cattle pot from the man he knew in Colorado City to haul the herd north. The enormous double-decker trailer held about eighty head and cost $400 a load, and Bill figured he needed at least five trips from Smith Mesa to Beaver.

But then the rains came in May, two inches of it over the month in Beaver, and about the same on Smith Mesa. It felt like more. When it wasn't raining, it was threatening to, and the dirt never totally dried. Mud caked in the gap at the front of the cowboy boots' heels and through the treads of their truck tires.

The road to Smith Mesa was a rain-slicked mess. Ruts were deep enough for small cars to scrape bottom, but they were the only things keeping them on the road and preventing them from plunging over the cliffs. Now many tons of cattle were crammed into trailers, and the trailers pushed the trucks, in their lowest gear, down the road, around the muddy corners, and over the rutted straightaways, with the majestic cliffs of Zion on one side and the prospect of death of man and cattle on the other. Sometimes Bill put two wheels into the ditch on the side away from the drop just to make sure he didn't go off the edge.

The road was a ten-mile squiggly loop around the wash, loosely shaped like a horseshoe. Once it wiggled past the Wright property, it circled the top edge of the canyon and came back down the west side, as wickedly precarious as the east. It eventually spit out down near Virgin, too.

"Once, on New Year's Eve, I helped a friend on the other side of the wash get some cows," Bill said. "We got about ten in the trailer, and we were goin' down the road on that side. I lost control of the trailer, and there's a bigger drop-off on that side than there is on this one. I jackknifed, and the trailer pushed the truck sideways down the road. I basically conceded that I was goin' over the edge. It was just about to go off when it stopped. I don't really know what stopped it. The trailer broke the back window and crushed the side of the truck. But as soon as it stopped, the guy says, 'I don't know about you, but I was pretty happy to see that thing come to a rest.'"

The cattle pot made it, moving in a low, grinding gear no faster than a cow could walk, and returned for four more trips over a couple of days. Bill and Alex loaded horses into Bill's old trailer and got the load past the trickier parts. They could feel the weight of the horses pushing the pickup down, fighting against the low gear and the brakes. Blacktop came as a relief, and the stripe of pavement over and down the hogback to Virgin gave way to a wider road to Hurricane and a wider one still to the interstate. And soon the whole operation was moved from south to north, through Cedar City and then Beaver, and then into the relative cool at the foot of the Tushar Mountains, where the annual reunion of Wrights was a few days away. It rained some more, and the property was so muddy that Bill got his truck stuck for a time on Friday.

"Dad won't be home until dark," Evelyn wrote in a group text message to her daughters and daughters-in-law. "So we won't pull the camp trailer over until in the morning. That would have been nice to know since some of us left work early to get there on time and nobody is there. But I could never get him to really say for sure and couldn't get ahold of him. I guess it is difficult when you are working with livestock and the variable of weather and help. Thanks to everyone who has been helping this spring taking time to be there. Sorry for any inconvenience all of this may have caused you. Love ya."

"He who remains flexible will never get bent out of shape," Evelyn wrote a short time later. She had a million adages like that, a lot of them learned from her mother and grandmother, and she sprinkled them throughout her language as the situations dictated, which seemed to be plenty often. "People don't care how much you know until they know how much you care" was another one. She could recite all of "When You Get to Know a Fellow," the Edgar Guest poem. She considered it a family creed.

Rain kept coming on Saturday, waves of it. Only Selinda came to set up camp with her husband. They slept in tents in the sloppy meadow. Others stayed away, waiting for sunnier skies and the beacon of Evelyn's messages.

■ ■ ■

The boys had a rodeo to go to on Saturday night, a couple of hours north, and plenty of Wrights wanted to go. The arena in Eagle Mountain, west of Provo, sat by itself on the prairie, up against some dusty hills, just out of reach of suburban sprawl. Dark clouds bullied the horizon, but a rainbow and dashes of sunbeam tickled the valley.

Cars snaked into the dirt lot, directed by attendants on horseback. Smoke curled into the late-day sky from vendors selling barbecue. Rodeo queens handed pink rubber bracelets to young girls and Boy Scouts sold candy bars from boxes for a dollar. Between events, the rodeo clown, talking through a wireless microphone from the middle of the dirt arena, pretended to light a barbecue, then put it out, only to have the lid blow a hundred feet into the air, a bit of crowd-pleasing pyrotechnics.

There was a "cash calf" contest, featuring a young calf that had Ziploc bags filled mostly with trinkets and prize vouchers for drinks at a local gas station taped to its hide. The calf ran most of the length of the ring as a swarm of fifty children gave chase, then turned wide to reverse course. The swarm was slow to react and snaked back, and then the procession turned again, slowing, and again, slowing more, until the calf tired and was cornered. Children converged and pulled the bags from the still animal, and the sticky side of the tape was dirtied with strands of thick, coarse hair.

The grandstand was sprinkled with three generations of Wrights. Becca, CoBurn's wife, held their newborn daughter in a bundle. CoBurn grew up in Beaver and knew Rusty through rodeo. It was Rusty who set him up with his aunt Becca, the youngest of the Wright girls, but only about six months older than Rusty. CoBurn invited her to the prom by parking a donkey in front of Bill and Evelyn's house while they were away and putting a sign on it that read, "I'd like to take your ass to prom." He proposed to her at a Cedar City rodeo by having the rodeo clown pull her from the crowd and blindfold her. When the clown removed the blindfold, CoBurn was waiting there, on one knee.

They married when they were eighteen, and CoBurn studied to be an electrical lineman. Now rodeo looked to be his living, and he was having a breakout season. Their first child was born while CoBurn was with the Wright boys on the Texas swing, where CoBurn wasn't the only hot young rider. In San Antonio, Rusty won $14,476 in the short round, part of a $22,246 payday there.

"This is my first pro rodeo buckle that I've ever won, so this buckle is coming out of the case and going on my belt tonight," Rusty told reporters afterward. "I won the rookie-of-the-year buckle last year, and also won some rodeos, but this is the first rodeo I've won that gave out a buckle."

Aubrey, Jesse's wife, sat with Spencer's girlfriend, Kallie, not far from Becca. Cody's family sat in a cluster high off to one end. Bill and Evelyn arrived just as the performance began and scooted in with ShaRee and the kids.

It was the middle night of a three-night rodeo, and the saddle bronc contest was deep in Wrights. Jesse, Jake, Spencer, Rusty, and CoBurn were among the night's eight contestants. So was Cody. Shoulder sur-

gery back in December had been a success, but it had taken him longer to heal than he expected. He made the swing through Texas, to
the big rodeos in Houston, San Antonio, and Austin, but he wasn't
right. He won a small rodeo in Mercedes, but the shoulder was forever
sore and his neck still bobbleheaded with every big lurch.

Cody came home after the Texas stretch and decided to sit out
most of April and May. Summer was coming, and he needed to get
right. He started to feel better and took a stab at a small rodeo outside Las Vegas in mid-May. He had a 78-point ride, good for third
place, and the shoulder and neck held up. That was good enough.
Cody returned to Milford and signed up for rodeos throughout the
summer, beginning with Eagle Mountain.

The rodeo announcer extolled the riding virtues of the Wrights—
"Utah's own." Everyone got a score, on a pen of broncs without
much buck.

"Welcome to the future of saddle bronc!" the announcer shouted
as the gate opened for Rusty. His 76 beat CoBurn's 75. Spencer
scored 77, and then Jake trumped them all with an 81. He was late
to the circuit after breaking his back at the National Finals. Doctors
had told him to rest for eight weeks, but two weeks into his rehabilitation he broke both hands when he dumped a four-wheeler in
the snow while pulling a sled of children behind him. He got back
in the saddle in February, and soon pulled checks at most every stop.

Then it was Cody's turn, and everyone in the stands and behind
the chutes tensed up a bit.

"Cody Wright has drawn a horse they call Mirror Man," the
announcer said, stalling as Cody wriggled into the saddle. "What a
résumé. He is the oldest, the first one to win a gold buckle. If you
watch his riding style versus the other boys you've seen, then you
can tell that they believe in teamwork, and iron sharpens iron."

The gate on Chute 5 opened and Mirror Man bounded out,

ducked its head right, and leapt twice with great distance, as if crossing a two-forked creek while trying not to get its feet wet. Cody
kept his right hand raised and his spurs moving as the horse stutter-
stepped and bounded again toward the far corner of the arena.

"C'mon, Cody, c'mon!" the announcer shouted. "Yes! Yes! Ha ha!"

The buzzer sounded and Cody leaned onto the pickup man who
came astride. "Wooooo! Welcome a future Hall of Famer, Cody
Wright, from Milford, Utah!"

His 81 tied for the lead, until Jesse beat them all with an 85. The
result pushed Cody past $10,000 in season earnings, his slowest start
in a decade.

The rodeo was only halfway over, but saddle bronc was done,
and the Wrights in the stands instinctively moved down the bleachers and slipped through an opening in the chain-link fence. The
road was rarely a place for the Wrights to congregate, with the boys
divided into two trucks and the rest of the family left behind. But
there was a reunion now, in the dark of the contestant parking lot,
pocked with deep puddles. Bill held his latest grandchild, the eight-
week-old daughter of Becca and CoBurn. The conversation with
Cody turned to scoring, as it often did.

A van pulled to a stop, and Jake rolled down the window of the
passenger seat. CoBurn sat in the back, and another rider, Tab, who
had been bucked off minutes before, was at the wheel.

"We're going to Marysville," Jake said. "See y'all on Monday for
the brandin'."

Marysville, near Sacramento, was 663 miles west. The three
bronc riders would arrive in mid-morning, sleep in the van in the
parking lot, ride late in the afternoon, and drive overnight back to
Utah in time for branding. Jake's 78 would win and earn him $1,147.
CoBurn would get third and a $430 prize. Tab got no score and no
money. The others filled his van with gas.

At Beavers, the next day's dawn broke cool and the sky was a jumble of menace. Any swath of blue was quickly wiped away by clouds that could not be trusted, moving in directions that could not be predicted. Bill and some grandchildren loaded the cattle trailer at home in Milford with twenty-seven panels of fencing, each about six feet long and six tubular-steel rungs tall. The panels, like an Erector set, were designed to connect together to make a pen. Three grandchildren climbed into the trailer, with all the fencing. They sat close to the front to avoid the chill wind, as well as detection by passing cars and state troopers on the thirty-mile trip down the two-lane highway to Beaver.

They reached the lower end of the property by mid-morning. Evelyn was in the camper, set in a low spot in the gentle scoop of the treeless valley, just short of the cattle guard. She made tuna sandwiches, wet with mayonnaise and filled with cubes of cheese.

Bill pulled the truck over the cattle guard. There was a chute next to it, a funnel lined with logs, where cows could be loaded into a trailer. It was similar to the one down at Smith Mesa, at the lower end of the wash, but there, in the high desert, the logs were from scraggly piñons, and they were bent drunkenly. At Beavers, the logs were from firs in the mountains, and they were straight and thick.

The permit did not allow for permanent structures. If the rangers complained, Bill reasoned that he would tell them it wasn't permanent, because it had been built by Bill and CoBurn in a day, and anything built in a day could be taken down in less, which sounded temporary enough.

Things were already behind Bill's internal schedule because of the rain and the rodeo, and Bill wanted the fencing panels assembled into a large pen for the next day's branding. Now there were six boys, including Bill's youngest, Stuart, notably taller and leaner and more confident than he had been just months before. He could carry a panel by himself. Younger boys shared the duty, one on each end. Bill directed his workforce on where to bring the panels, and he wrestled the ends together and connected them with a pin. He soon had a crooked smile of fencing in the scattered brush that expanded from the chute. Bill eyeballed it, thinking about how wide he wanted to make the corral, to make sure he had enough room for three branding stations and a couple of fires and a few dozen calves at a time.

He needed horses and he needed more fencing. He got back in the truck, and the smaller boys climbed into the trailer for the ride back to Milford. Bill told them to stay down, especially when he stopped at a gas station, where he refueled the truck and bought the boys each a root beer. He was back in ninety minutes with a cab full of boys and a trailer full of horses. Jesse followed, pulling a flatbed of fence panels and another trailer of horses. Cody pulled in, and he had horses, too.

By midafternoon, the corral was built, the cows and their calves grazed in the meadow, and the day settled into one of leisure and catching up, like a reunion. The campsite was a jumble of trailers, cars, tents, and camp chairs. Children, some as young as two, took turns on horseback. A gaggle played at the edge of the irrigation canal that hugged a nearby hill. They climbed a tree along the bank. A few girls found an animal skeleton, a skull and a backbone still intact, and brought it to the growing assembly at the campsite, which determined that it was once a coyote. In the middle distance, cows sprinkled the gentle slope. The mountains beyond were smudged with the last traces of spring snow.

One Dutch oven was filled with beef from the Wright's own cattle. Another was filled with pork, simmering in a sauce made partly of Dr Pepper. Another oven held potatoes that the teenaged boys had sliced, and another was filled with peach cobbler. Everyone gathered near the fire. Bill took off his hat and crossed his arms. Evelyn stood to his left. Bill closed his eyes and gave the prayer.

Jake and Spencer arrived sometime in the night, straight from Marysville, and over French toast, sausage, and bacon, more Wrights and in-laws and friends arrived. Calvin came with cherries he got from Evelyn's sister Sylvia, down in Toquerville. The cattle were moved toward the makeshift pen for branding. Cody got the fires ready. The grandchildren helped with the roping. Bill had taught them all to rope calves at the heels, not the head, so as not to damage airways. Over several hours, calves were branded, tagged, and inoculated. The young steers were castrated. There was less dust than in Smith Mesa because the rocky corral was filled with more grass and sagebrush than bare dirt.

The little ones stayed around camp, played in the irrigation ditch up on the hill, and rode horses up on the opposite ridge. That was where six-year-old Lily Jo, all ponytail and sass, was aboard Judd, a trusted brown horse with an even temperament. Kruz, Jesse's three-year-old, followed on a little yellow pony named Darla.

Neither horse ever moved too quickly, which made them perfect for children. But Judd did not see the rusted coil of barbed wire hidden in the brush. It scraped the horse's leg, and Judd flinched and sidestepped into Darla. Lily held on, but Darla spooked. She skittered forward and sent Kruz tumbling sideways. He fell several feet to the ground and landed face first.

The commotion on the ridge caught the attention of those at the corral. Jesse sprinted up the hill, his boots digging through the soft sand. Kruz had lost a couple of teeth, and there was blood dripping from his chin and his ear. Jesse carried his son downhill the few hundred yards to camp, lifted him into the truck, and drove fast down the dirt road to the clinic in Beaver, thankful that it was only a few minutes away.

The boy had a jaw broken in three places and a concussion. Fluid filled his lungs, and doctors ordered a helicopter to get Kruz to a bigger facility in Salt Lake City. He was induced into a coma, placed on a breathing machine, and fed through a tube. Aubrey flew with her son in the helicopter. Jesse trailed in his truck, and by the time he got to the hospital, his son had had scans that found no serious damage to his brain and back. The next night, he had surgery on the breaks, one on his chin and the others near the ear on either side. Surgeons sewed up the holes where his small teeth had come through his lip, inserted a plate that had to be removed in a few months, and wired his jaw shut.

Kruz remained intubated for most of a week and was fed through a tube. The wires were taken out a week after the accident, and doctors worried that the fractures to Kruz's growth plates might keep his jaw from growing right, but he got out of the hospital as feisty and fearless as ever. Within a week, he was on his pony, but only when Jesse led it behind his own horse.

■ ■ ■

Staying on horses that wanted to buck you off was the Wrights' business, but falling off the ones you trusted was part of life, too. No one was immune. On a weekday in mid-June, Bill was alone at Beavers on an undisciplined horse they called Tiger, one that Spencer usually rode around the ranch. It had been known to buck off its riders, and Cody thought the horse wasn't worth anyone's time to turn it into a ranch horse.

"You're trying to make something out of nothing," he told his father. "That thing's mother's a mustang, you know that?"

The Wrights were looking for more horses—Cody had recently put his stud out to pasture with six mares. Meanwhile, Bill had traded his old mule, a black one he called Satan, while it was still worth something. He had a penchant for mules, from the years of running trains of them into and out of the Grand Canyon. But when he had serious work to do around cows, he preferred a horse. So Bill traded Satan to the government trapper for a horse. But that horse was still new to Bill, so Bill chose Tiger to go with him to check on the herd. The boys were scattered somewhere on the rodeo circuit.

Bill found a calf, close to its mother, that had been missed on branding day. He steered the pair down the valley, toward the corral and his branding tools. The calf at least needed a tag in its ear to identify it as belonging to the Wrights, in case it got out. The summer solstice stretched the day into night, and Bill figured there might be enough time to get the job done by dark.

But the cow backed into a fence and flinched, enough to spook Tiger. Without warning, the horse dropped its head, nearly dumping Bill over the top of its mane. Bill had hold of nothing but the rein, lightly between his fingertips, and he squeezed the horse tight with his thighs, desperate to hold on. Tiger's back hips jerked up, then fell again, and Bill rode the crazed animal for a few bucks until he was launched into the air and fell hard to the ground on his shoulder. He broke his right collarbone on impact.

The pain shot through Bill as he lay in the dirt. He stood, dusty and stunned. His right arm was limp and useless, but there was no bone sticking out of his shoulder—just a raised bump where the bone poked against the skin. But with just one arm, and with the pain shooting through his shoulder, Bill could not pull himself back aboard Tiger, who was probably headed for the bucking pen back in Milford.

In the deepening dark, Bill walked alongside Tiger, and they were able to keep the cow and her calf moving downhill, toward the truck and the trailer. Bill shooed them inside, tied Tiger in there, too, and closed the gate behind them. Bill drove west, through Beaver, under the interstate and thirty dark minutes home to Milford. He unloaded the animals into the pen out back.

And when he walked in the door, his face ashen and his clothes dirtier than usual, Evelyn knew immediately that something was wrong. He didn't say much, but just getting to bed was a chore. There was not much chance of sleep.

"If you'd a been knocked out, the only way we would have found you was by following the buzzards," she said.

Bill and Evelyn drove to Cedar City the next morning to see the same doctor who had performed countless surgeries on his boys. "If it's a compound fracture, we fix it," the doctor told Bill. "Or if you're an overhead athlete—someone who throws a ball or has to raise an arm overhead to compete—we fix it."

Bill thought about that.

"Well, I am an overhead athlete," he finally said. "I rope cows."

He had surgery on his collarbone the next day. His arm was in a sling, and he was instructed to spend a few weeks off of horses. It would be inconvenient and boring, but he always told his sons to let things heal before risking something worse. The boys frustrated Bill with their impatience. He still couldn't believe that Jake had broken his back and then broken his hand fooling around in the snow two weeks later. And Alex should have just had the collarbone surgery up front instead of wasting a few precious months of the rodeo season, hoping it would get better. Once he got it done, he was riding again in two months.

But the timing for Bill couldn't have been much worse. The herd was moving higher into the mountains in search of cool weather and fresh water. The fences always needed mending and the water lines always needed fixing. And the boys couldn't be much help. It was late June, and the busiest part of the rodeo calendar, the part called Cowboy Christmas that straddled the July 4 holiday, was on the way.

Bill was back on a different horse in a few days.

11

Out of the Money

THE ROADS AND RODEOS were strung like Christmas lights, few brighter than the rest, all tangled into nonsense until you pulled apart the knots and figured out their order. Cody did it almost by heart, year in and year out, but Rusty couldn't name a place he was headed beyond the next one.

And now the Wrights had three trucks crossing the West—one with Cody and Rusty, one with Jake and Jesse, one with Spencer and CoBurn. All of them took in orphans—increasingly, Alex, but sometimes other Utah cowboys—to fill the cab and share the bills. They swapped occupants at rodeos or off-ramps to get cowboys to certain places at certain times. Sometimes they passed on the interstate, in the dead of night, moving in opposite directions for the same prizes, nothing but another set of headlights.

The Fourth of July holiday was a week away, and the midday temperatures in central Oregon were already in the nineties. Rusty sat in Spencer's truck, waiting for Cody to arrive from Reno. Cody competed there the night before, got fourth in the short round and fourth in the three-head average, made about 2,700 bucks, and left town alone. He drove a few hours, slept on the side of the road somewhere near Klamath Falls, and set out north toward Prineville in the morning.

Spencer was supposed to be in Reno for the short round, too, but he hurt his groin at the rodeo before and pulled out to rest for the thicker stretch of rodeos to come. No one was sure if he'd torn something or just sored it up, as Cody put it. Spencer caught a ride home to Utah, and Rusty brought Spencer's truck to Prineville.

Rusty got out and leaned against the back of the truck, in a sliver of midday shade. He wore a black long-sleeved riding shirt, with "Wrangler" stitched down the side. Black seemed to be his color, just as tan was his father's, blue was Jesse's, white was Jake's, and red was Spencer's. Wrangler sent Rusty all different colors, but he usually grabbed a black one. With the heat, he wished he hadn't that day.

Now nineteen, he was making money nearly every ride and sat in fourth place in the world standings, pushing close to $50,000. Rusty tried not to pay attention to the standings, because that just added pressure. But he knew where he stood. You couldn't help but know. The announcer at every rodeo told the crowd. Small-town newspapers liked to write about the Wrights.

Cody's rank was deep into the twenties, probably the lowest position he'd ever been in this far into summer. Usually, by now, Cody was in the top two or three, coasting toward fall but building a cushion for December. This time, he would have to come from behind, rodeo by rodeo, dollar by dollar, mile by mile. Cody had wondered what it would be like to compete at the National Finals with Rusty, but now Rusty might be headed there on his own.

"I root for him so hard it makes my teeth hurt," Rusty said of his dad.

Cowboy Christmas could change things in a hurry. The calendar was clogged with rodeos. Small towns made them part of the holiday festivities, along with parades, carnivals, and fireworks. Contestants tried to jam as many rodeos as they could into the stretch, seeing it like one of those wind-tunnel phone booths with paper money flying around. You had to grab it while you had the chance.

Rusty wasn't sure about the next few stops on the itinerary. He knew that after that afternoon's performance, he would jump back in with his dad and they would drive more than a thousand miles overnight, down the length of desolate Nevada and deep into Arizona to Prescott, home of the "world's oldest rodeo" and a pretty good payout. Cody knew it from there. He was the master of logistics. He knew which rodeos to weave together through the calculus of distance, cost, and available prize money.

"He's really good at knowing where we should be," Rusty said. "I might need to pay attention a little closer. Or when he's done, I'll have to pay him to do it for me."

After Prescott, it would be back the way they had come, twenty hours toward Portland to Molalla and St. Paul for same-day rodeos in Oregon. Then east to Red Lodge, Montana, for a six o'clock performance, and south to Cody, Wyoming, for an eight o'clock show, and then back into the truck for a drive north to Alberta for the prestigious Calgary Stampede, where five of the invited saddle bronc riders were named Wright.

From Sunday night to Friday morning, there would be more than 4,300 miles and about seventy hours of driving. Cody and Rusty competed for four days in Calgary, with Cody winning the first go-round and Rusty the next three, which qualified them for the finals a few days later. In between, they went to rodeos in Casper, Sheridan, Vernal, and Wolf Point, stopped in Rock Springs to see Ryder compete in the high school national finals, and then headed back to Calgary for a disappointing final. It added another three thousand miles to the truck and subtracted another forty-five hours from their lives, just in driving. They got a little money out of it, not enough to make much of a dent in the standings, but it was better than sitting home and watching everyone else win rodeos that you might have won yourself.

■ ■ ■

No one understood the algorithm of the rodeo schedule like Cody, but even he had only a vague idea of where the others were from day to day. Jesse handled the schedules for himself and Jake, but he hadn't been returning Cody's messages for several days now. They were in Mountain Home, Idaho, and they'd tried to get into Prineville for the same Sunday afternoon performance as Cody and Rusty, but couldn't get a spot. Even the Wrights weren't guaranteed a place to ride whenever they wanted. And they sometimes stayed away from the same rodeos, because when another truck of Wrights showed up, the competition for everyone else just got tougher.

When Cody first started as a professional cowboy, the PRCA allowed 125 rodeos to count toward the standings for the National Finals Rodeo. Rodeo organizers liked it, because it meant that more of them got the top cowboys, but cowboys complained that the load was too big. It felt like too many. A few years later, about the time that Jake and Jesse turned pro, the number was reduced to seventy. That felt like too few. The number settled at 100, which felt about right to the Wrights. It was enough to weed out those who weren't fully committed.

The Wrights chose their rodeos using an unquantifiable set of factors—payout and geography, mostly. They didn't bother with many rodeos that didn't pay at least $1,000 to the saddle bronc winner, unless it was close to home or on the way to somewhere else. History and the strength of the relationships with various rodeo organizers played a role, too. Cody built his schedule around plenty of midsized rodeos that others might have skipped, simply because he was friends with the people who put the rodeo on, or because he had been coming for years, liked the way he was treated, and didn't want to let them down.

By tradition, most rodeos stuck to the same part of the schedule year after year. It might always be the first weekend in June or the third weekend of August or on the Fourth of July. That kept the schedule pretty consistent. There might be a million different routes to compete in a hundred rodeos, but the majority were the same ones for the Wrights from one year to the next.

Still, planning was a complex, constant, and time-sucking undertaking, and no one had figured out a way to apply a Moneyball approach, using a computer model that could show the best way to optimize the rodeos and the routes between. Scheduling was left mostly to tradition and intuition, sketched out on a calendar.

The boys requested rodeos months in advance, at least the big ones. They entered as a group, up to four at a time, so that every-one in the truck would get into the same rodeos on the same days or nights. Big rodeos filled their rosters first, and the smaller ones waited and filled the gaps between. Cowboys found out if they'd been accepted about five weeks ahead of time, then started building their schedule around the places they'd prioritized.

Rodeos came in varying lengths, too. Most medium-sized rodeos, the ones that made up the bulk of the summer calendar, were on weekends, spread across Friday, Saturday, and a Sunday matinee. A few were one-day events. Others, like Cheyenne Frontier Days or the Calgary Stampede, lasted a week or more. For some of those, cowboys stayed in town for the duration, part of a tournament-style event with a series of rides over several days that winnowed the field toward a finale. For others, the cowboys were assigned a day or two or four to compete, and if things went well enough, their scores qualified them to come back for the finals on the weekend. They filled the days between with whatever nearby rodeos they could find, and they usually found them.

As their calendars filled, they had to make more specific requests. In late June, Cody knew he might be in Reno on Friday and Saturday night, if everything went right, so he requested Sunday in Prineville. His name was drawn. Jake and Jesse made the same request for Sunday, but didn't get it. So they went home instead, a rare day off, but a wasted chance to make money on a Sunday in the middle of summer.

Cowboys sometimes traded their dates, looking to wedge another rodeo somewhere else into a weekend. They might give up a Sunday slot for a Saturday slot if they thought they could get into a Sunday rodeo somewhere else. Cody had long grown weary of that desperation. He didn't like to plead with others and be left feeling like he owed someone a favor. He figured there were enough rodeos to find another option if he had to. Besides, with four cowboys in a truck, you'd need to find four other cowboys to make a trade, and that wasn't worth the effort.

The other part of the equation was drawing horses. The rodeos matched broncs and riders, supposedly at random, and usually announced the assignments a few days ahead of time. When Cody learned that he'd drawn a paint horse called Risky Business in Prineville, he thought about turning out and saving himself the trip. The bronc had been good once with Jesse, and been part of a few winning rides with others, but was a bit of a dud for Cody, Rusty, and CoBurn the past couple of years. Cody skipped a chance on Risky Business back in April, during the California swing, not feeling healthy and not wanting to go that far for an inconsistent horse. By a karmic coincidence, Cody drew the horse again a few weeks later. He showed up and finished out of the money.

Cody had no good reason to skip Prineville, especially in light of his place in the standings. The horse came out halfhearted, like an athlete going through warm-ups, keeping its belly close to the ground. Cody pumped and spurred to try to make up for the bronc's uninspired scamper. Judges scored the ride a 73.

"I mighta headed the other direction if I'd a known that's how it was goin' to go," Cody said afterward. He unbuckled his chaps and took a swig from a water bottle. "But if you do that, you wouldn't get on half of 'em. I've won a lot on horses I thought I might turn out."

Cody was in no real hurry to get back inside and drive deep into the night. He talked about how horses bucked different in different arenas, depending on the size and shape of the ring or the location of the chutes. The size of the crowd, the heat, day or night, its appetite, its spent energy from the latest travel—all those elements might make a difference to a horse. The same horse that was a dud in Prineville might be a winner in Cheyenne. Horses had good days and bad days, just like the men who rode them. You could only hope that your best eight seconds matched their best eight seconds, and that the judges saw it from the right angle and scored it right. There were enough variables to make it interesting, and too many to control.

Rusty scored an 80, good enough for a paycheck of $657. He carried his saddle back into the dirt contestants' parking lot and loaded it into the back of Cody's truck. He grabbed a duffel bag out of Spencer's truck and moved it to his father's. Another bronc rider got into the driver's seat of Spencer's truck and pointed it toward Utah.

Cody and Rusty, traveling together again, got into the truck, the rodeo still going on behind them, the fans still in their sunbaked seats, and headed a thousand miles and eighteen hours overnight to Arizona. Neither of them won anything there.

■ ■ ■

Cody's motor home was in Rock Springs with ShaRee, Bill, and Evelyn. Ryder, now a junior in high school, had won the Utah state championship the month before, in Heber City. And his uncle Stuart, the last of Bill and Evelyn's thirteen, in the same grade as Ryder, finished third at state and made the nationals, too.

Bill sat under the awning in a lawn chair. His shoulder was still sore from collarbone surgery, and the insides of his thighs were black and blue from the bucking he took before he was dumped to the ground, a ride that probably didn't last eight seconds. Bill had been back on a horse, just not the one that threw him.

"He's in the buckin' pen," Bill said. "The boys tried buckin' him the other day. Cody says he's tryin' to make somethin' out of nothin'."

Bill had been doing some work at Beavers on a different horse about a week after the accident. But for reasons that only a horse could understand, it just lay down and quit against a fence, pinning Bill and his lame arm in motionless pain. He had to squirm out. "Like John Wayne," he said, "when he had to climb out from under a dead horse."

Stuart came out of the trailer, buttoning his shirt and buckling the buckle on his jeans. His face, soft and peach-fuzzed, was in adolescent transition and wore a worried look. He had gone over to the arena to see the horse he'd drawn that night. He didn't know anything about it and couldn't get a scouting report from anyone who knew. He told his dad that it looked old.

"Talk to Cody about it," Bill said. "He might call the contractor for you and ask him. Or get hold of Jesse."

"I did," Stuart said. "He told me to talk to Spencer."

But time was running out before the rodeo, and Spencer, wherever he was, wasn't answering. Bill sensed Stuart's apprehension and spoke to him calmly. If you don't know anything about the horse, he told his youngest son, you have to play it down the middle with your rein. And just make sure you mark him out.

Stuart brought out his saddle, one of Cody's old ones, and set it on the gravel outside the motor home. He sat down and wiggled his boots into the stirrups. He clenched the rein in one hand and pulled high and tight in front of him. Just like that, Bill said. He knew the secret to winning nationals. He'd been coming for twenty years and seen Jake, Spencer, and Rusty win it, and seen just about all of them lose it, including Rusty the year before, even when they were the best bronc riders in the field. Ride two head to get to the finals. Ride all three, hitting your mark and not bucking off, and you'll probably win it, or come close.

Among the Wright brothers, Stuart showed the least affinity for bronc riding. He did it well by any standard, but he had a broad range of high school interests.

He also wanted to go on a two-year Latter-day Saints mission when he graduated the next year. He'd be the first in the family. The other boys talked about going on missions when they were young, but rodeo eventually won out over religion. By their late teens, they all tried to make their living on bucking horses, and most of them had. They had all gone to college, too, at least for a bit, to learn trades that involved working with your hands. Jake and Jesse got welding certificates. Alex did welding, equine science, and was just short of his diesel mechanic's certificate. Cody and Calvin had studied equine science, and Calvin had studied welding, too.

Bill and Evelyn wondered if Stuart, twenty years younger than Cody, was part of a different generation of Wrights, headed for different kinds of adventures. None of the Wright children were pressured to do what they did, including the boys. They just rode broncs, first and foremost, as if it was in their DNA. It was not a sense of duty that put them there, but some hidden lure of tradition, habit, and desire. They all prepared for other kinds of work, knowing that riding broncs wasn't a long-range plan, even though the longer they went, the more they figured they probably wouldn't become welders and diesel mechanics, but ranchers and horsemen, or something like them.

Whatever tradition of bronc riding Bill had instilled in his boys carried through Cody to his boys, too, and you had to wonder if it would be the same way with Calvin's boys, or Alex's boys, or Jesse's and all the others still to come. What started as something between brothers might soon multiply into something between cousins. As Bill said, once the babies start to hit the ground, they add up fast.

Stuart disappeared into the sea of motor homes and headed to the arena to be with the other saddle bronc riders. When it came to his turn, Bill and Evelyn were in the same bleachers in the same place they were the year before, quietly and nervously watching.

Stuart had a good ride going, surviving a couple of big opening bucks. But he got a little loose in the saddle and couldn't keep up. Before the clock hit six seconds, Stuart was on the ground, then on his feet and scampering to the gate, out of the horse's way. He finished the week out of the top twenty.

It was his nephew Ryder, five nights later, with Cody and Rusty back from Calgary and everyone in the stands together again, who undid the frustration of the year before. He rode the third of his horses, outclassing the field for a 232-point aggregate. Now the first two of Cody's boys had high school national championships. Four Wright boys had won five of the past nine titles, and Ryder's victory was celebrated in the family like all the others—quietly and modestly, not as though it was the end of something, but as the start of something, which it was.

■ ■ ■

For most of the summer, Cody couldn't squeeze into the top twenty-five, let alone the top fifteen, unable to make up for the shoulder surgery over the winter. He got stronger as he went, and good results started to kick in over the final month. He won in Hastings, Nebraska, and in Plains, Montana. He made money at nearly every stop—$857 in Evanston, Wyoming; $583 in Blackfoot, Idaho; $767 in Fort Madison, Iowa; and $538 in Salt Lake City, all in a week. He crept up the standings.

Then Cody won in Pasadena, Texas, and took second in Pendleton, Oregon. He got first in Tyler and Amarillo, Texas, and spent $3,500 to charter a plane to make it to the rodeo near home in St. George, even though the top payout was about a third of that. You had to spend money to make money in rodeo, and sometimes you spent a lot just for a chance to get to Las Vegas.

It all came down to Omaha, the season's big-money finish. To give himself a chance, Cody had to win a round or two. He had done it before. But not this time. A couple of dud rides left him out of the National Finals for the first time in thirteen years. Cody finished the season with $53,349 in official prize money. It was about the same amount of money he had won thirteen years earlier, when he just missed out on his first National Finals. Then, he was in sixteenth place; this time, he was twentieth. He kept whatever disappointment he might be feeling swallowed behind a smile, prouder than ever of Rusty making it for the first time.

The end of the regular season could be a wringer for rodeo contestants. The Wrights knew the squeeze better than anyone. With a few weeks left, Jesse was in thirteenth place in the standings, cruising to a spot in the National Finals for the fifth year in a row. He was in Ellensburg, Washington, for a rodeo over Labor Day weekend, and scored an 83 in the first round. In the short round, though, he bucked off and landed hard enough to go unconscious for a few moments. By the time he was helped off the dirt, his shoulder felt out of joint. He tried to ride again. The shoulder hurt like hell.

He took a few days off and missed the big rodeo in Salt Lake City. An exam discovered a torn labrum in his right shoulder. It probably needed surgery, but Jesse needed more winnings first. He started to ride with his opposite hand, clenching the rein with his left and throwing his busted right arm into the air. It was just as awkward as a pitcher trying to strike out a batter with his opposite arm.

"After ten years of riding right-handed, it feels like I'm hanging on by my fingertips," he said.

He rode about a dozen rodeos left-handed. All he made was $70 for a tie for eighth in St. George. Chances dwindling, he desperately went back to his right hand.

"I tried three rides," Jesse said. "Got 78 in Lewiston, Pasadena, and Pullayup—78 all three times right-handed. I had a cortisone shot to take the ache out of it. But I had no power in my arm to lift."

But, like Cody, he still had a chance to make the National Finals with a big performance in Omaha. He drew a stout horse, and it came out strong, with three big bucks before it reared and almost flipped. It stalled before the eight-second buzzer, then spun and dipped and "fucking lawn-darted me," as Jesse explained it. He was given a 67. He and others expected a re-ride option that never came.

"It's pretty sad when you're 67 at a rodeo that big and don't get a re-ride," Jesse said. "It sucks. I was pretty let down. I thought I could bear down and make the NFR. I was pretty down about myself."

CoBurn spent most of the season outside the top twenty, but

a streak of consistency and good health moved him into the upper teens by late August. Then he won in Blackfoot and Salt Lake City, made good money in Abilene and Tyler, and took home more than $2,000 from Pendleton. He tried to ignore the standings. Becca was a nervous wreck. He cracked the top fifteen, then bucked off in Amarillo.

"I thought, 'Gosh, I hope that didn't cost me the finals,'" he said when the season ended. "And then Jake called and said I made it. He had all the numbers figured out."

It was Jake who lent CoBurn money the spring before, when CoBurn was broke and thought he'd go home to find more reliable work. CoBurn couldn't afford to be away chasing bronc rides if he wasn't winning money to send home. But Jake put him up in a hotel one weekend and told him to keep riding, that he would finance him back into the black. That was when CoBurn started to win. He paid Jake back, and in a few more months, maybe CoBurn could pay off his credit cards, even afford the renovations to the house he had just bought in Milford, next door to Alex.

The strangest thing was not who would be there, but who wouldn't. Rusty had little memory of the National Finals without his father competing. Cody had made it every year since Rusty was eight, and part of life's routine was sitting in the stands in Las Vegas and cheering his father on. It was weird to him that this year the roles would be reversed. He had always hoped he would be there one day beside his dad, not instead of him.

■ ■ ■

The sound carried on the breeze, a thump and twang of country music coming from town. It caught Bill's attention, and he rose from the living room chair, put on his cowboy hat, and grabbed the keys to the truck. He steered out the dirt driveway, past the pen of bucking horses and the hulks of trailers, camper shells, and farm implements that baked in the Indian-summer sun. He made one turn down a gravel road and, within a minute, parked at the Milford Pavilion Park, near the rodeo ring with the sheet-metal sign honoring Cody Wright as a world champion saddle bronc rider.

It was Wright Night, a townwide party thrown by a Las Vegas casino that had signed on as a sponsor for most of the boys. A covered stage with colored lights had been erected behind the baseball field's backstop, and a five-man band filled the afternoon with country songs. There were bounce houses filled with air from whirring compressors and kids from all over town. The grass was dotted with tables covered by cloths. On the concrete slab, under a high aluminum cover that provided shade, were a few dozen shaded picnic tables.

People stood in lines for food, a choice of barbecued chicken or brisket, mashed potatoes, green beans, baked beans, and pecan pie. Large coolers were filled with bottles of water, soda, and beer.

"Help us cheer on Milford's own—Jake, Jesse, Rusty, Spencer, Cody, and Alex Wright—as they gear up for the National Finals Rodeo," The D Las Vegas Casino Hotel wrote on advertisements hanging around town and spread through social media. "Enjoy delicious food, live entertainment, and fun family attractions. The event is FREE and open to the community. Give a hand to these hometown heroes before they head to the NFR."

There was no announcement of who had qualified and who hadn't, and the faces of the boys did not reveal the verdict. Friends and neighbors and strangers approached each as a hero. They asked for autographs and took photographs. They shook their hands and told the boys what great role models they were for the children and what great representatives they were for the town.

No one dared express disappointment that Cody fell short, or said aloud how much of a shame it was that he and Rusty would not compete together. Even if people could tell Jake and Jesse apart, they might not decipher which one was headed to Las Vegas and which one was not—the one on crutches with a cast on his ankle or the one with a torn labrum that was hidden under his Western shirt.

The boys were all sorts of frustrated and injured, but they were not the type to show that to everyone else, not on a night when hundreds of people came to greet them and thank them for doing everyone proud. People lined up to congratulate Rusty for reaching his first National Finals, for winning $115,986 and being ranked second overall, and for the news that he and Morgan were expecting a baby come spring. There was no wedding date yet, because Rusty didn't want everyone thinking that the baby was the reason they were getting married. Cody and ShaRee, still in their thirties, were about to become grandparents.

"Mom said she wasn't surprised," Rusty told a woman who held his hand and smiled at him. "Dad didn't say much."

Under the brim of his black hat, Rusty wore an X-shaped scar on the bridge of his nose. It came from Ellensburg, when he was thrown off the front of his bronc and had the misfortune of landing face-first on a rock in the dirt. It always seemed that faces and ankles found the only rocks in dirt arenas. But the real problem was hidden under his shirt. His right arm was swollen to twice the size of the left. It was covered in bruises the color of painted sunsets, all purples and oranges and yellows, from his armpit to his wrist. He could not close his fingers to make a fist.

He got his upper arm stepped on by a horse in Pendleton, which forced him to miss Abilene, San Bernardino, and Omaha, probably costing him a chance at the number one spot on the money list. Doctors said there was a bone bruise and nerve damage, and Rusty said it wouldn't quit hurting. He sometimes wore a sling, mostly as a signal to tell others not to shake his hand, but he decided against it for the town celebration. Though he tried not to wince with every firm handshake and pat on the shoulder, every jostle sent a pierce of pain through him that he hid with a forced smile.

He walked with a limp, but no one notices a cowboy with a limp. Under his Wranglers, Rusty's left knee was swollen with fluid. Trying to get off a horse in Puyallup, he smacked the knee against the hard swell of the saddle. He hoped to ride in Waco in mid-October.

The better the boys did in the season standings, the worse off they looked. Jake had finished eighth, second among the Wrights, with $85,423, but he could not walk without crutches. He broke his ankle in Othello when he landed awkwardly on a dismount. His right foot was in a cast, his left in a cowboy boot, and he did not expect to ride again until he got to Las Vegas two months later.

Before the Fourth of July, Spencer was in second place in the rankings, but he hit the doldrums in midsummer and a pack of riders climbed past him. By mid-August, Spencer was in ninth place and falling. A win in Pendleton in mid-September broke a long winless streak and settled him into tenth place, with $74,338. Only about $20,000 of that came after Memorial Day. Whatever mojo he had discovered over the past year that carried him to the world championship had evaporated in the summer heat.

An owner of The D Casino Hotel, up from Las Vegas, all smiles and back pats, asked the band to stop the music. He had the Wright boys in a line and he bragged about their talent and gave them each a brown leather range jacket, lined on the inside. Each jacket had a name embroidered on the left chest, opposite the D's logo. They already wore shirts with the casino logo, too—all except Rusty, who had signed the deal on retainer but couldn't advertise the casino until he turned twenty-one, and Cody, who wasn't sure he was going to sign the deal at all. He wanted to make sure that it didn't conflict with any of his other sponsors. He was careful like that.

But after the jacket presentation and a series of photographs, in the awkward silence when no one knew what they should do next, Cody took the microphone.

"We just feel blessed that we've got so many great sponsors," he said. "We're just glad to be part of the D. Thanks again, and thanks everybody for coming out."

In the crowd, ShaRee shrugged.

"I guess he is signing with them," she said.

Within a few days, Cody was in Texas, and then Florida, to start accumulating money for the next season's standings. The rodeo year ran from October 1 to September 30, even though the National Finals weren't held until December. But Cody was riding well and wanted to keep momentum going, and money earned in October was the same as money earned in September, just like the first regular-season baseball game in spring is worth the same as the last one in the fall. The only difference was that the stakes start to show themselves at the end.

12

Run to the Fence

FALL WAS AS CLOSE to an off-season as rodeo had, and it arrived in Milford like a coal train crawling into town, predictable and steady. The sky was pewter and the leaves were yellow. Hay was baled throughout the valley and stacked like sugar cubes. Some was tucked into two-hundred-foot-long sheds or covered by vast tarps to keep the mildew away in the dampness of the season. Rain was coming, chased by a cold front. The Mineral Mountains were tipped in frost.

Their kids in school, Cody and ShaRee rumbled out of town in one of Cody's pickups. Cody had been raising and training cattle dogs, and two were leashed behind the cab. The pickup pulled a horse trailer made of brown metal, rusted in some spots and dented in others. It had a canvas roof and held nine horses, squeezed tight— probably one over its recommended capacity. Three belonged to Bill, two to Cody, two to Jesse, and two to Spencer. Cody wanted to deliver them to Smith Mesa. There were 270 cows coming for the winter next week from Beavers, and the Wrights needed horses to work them.

They got on the interstate at Cedar City and off at Toquerville, drove past where Evelyn had lived when she was a girl, past where she'd married Bill at the church, and turned up the hill toward Zion on two-lane Highway 9. The autumn sun was pale and without force, more a source of light than of heat. The road was emptier this time of year, without the summertime tourists in their campers and rental cars. It climbed diagonally up the side of the mesa, past the hillside H for Hurricane, past the striated lines of sedimentary rock in shades of red and pink and white and onto a high plain of red sand and sagebrush. The sheer walls of Zion's western boundary blocked the horizon in the distance. A van stopped on the side of the road and people spilled out to take pictures of themselves with the dramatic backdrop, like something from an old Western, not realizing that the views only got better.

For Cody, every spot held a memory. He grew up in Hurricane and had come this way to Smith Mesa ever since he could remember—thousands of times, probably. One memory that Cody might have been too young at the time to remember now was one of Bill's favorite stories, about the time that Bill wrecked a '68 GMC on that stretch when Cody and Calvin were young.

"I had put a new tire and tube on the truck the day before, and outside of Virgin, we had a blowout," Bill said. "We had three horses and I lost control, hit the hill, and flipped upside down. We come to a stop, and there was a huge cloud of dust. Calvin, he would just never shut up. He was all excited and goes, 'Boy, I never been in a wreck like that before!' But I couldn't see Cody, and I was lookin' all around the cab of the truck, yellin' for him—'Cody! Cody!' And there was so much dust, I still couldn't see him, but I heard his voice.

Somehow, he's outside the truck. And he says, 'I'm all right, Dad. I'm outside. I didn't like it in there.' "

Cody and ShaRee passed Fort Zion, a gift shop and petting zoo among a smattering of small-scale Old West buildings, and they passed the place with the sign saying it sold cactus jelly. They passed the Virgin post office, a tiny brick building with "Elevation 3552" painted on the side. They turned at the quiet corner where Cody's great-grandparents once lived, near the hardpan Pioneer Cemetery, where so many Wrights were buried.

Had they kept going for eighteen more miles, they would have passed the old Mormon settlements of Grafton, now a ghost town after a history of debilitating floods over the banks of the Virgin River, and shady Rockville, and then reached Springdale, the gateway to Zion National Park, filled with motels and restaurants and ice cream shops and traffic. Come summer, it was filled with European tourists and other sunburned adventurers who made up Zion's four million annual visitors, a number that rose almost every year. It was now one of the country's most popular national parks.

But the Wrights almost never went into the heart of Zion. Instead, Cody and ShaRee made the familiar turn on Pocketville Road, which wound past a few small and weathered homes and quickly broke free of what stood as the town of Virgin. Evelyn liked to joke about the beauty pageants and Miss Rodeo contests, and the poor young women who had to smile while wearing a sash that read "Virgin." They passed Bill's weathered corral of gnarled logs at the bottom edge of the range and crossed North Creek. Cody's truck downshifted as it hit the big hill where the road climbed atop the shoulder of a narrow ridge.

A man stood in the middle of the road where it broadened, in front of a barricade that read "Road Closed." There was construction on a few miles of road that led into the national park, and it included the turnoff to Smith Mesa. The road was closed from one to four, the man said. It was 1:15.

"I need to deliver these horses up here," Cody said through the open window of the truck. He smiled.

"You'll have to come back at four," the man said. There was no tone of compromise in his voice, and the two fell into an awkward silence. Minutes passed. Cody stewed behind his sunglasses. He kept the car running.

"He's just doing his job," ShaRee said to Cody.

Cody had thought that he'd drop the horses onto one section of the property, where they could roam for a few days with plenty of food, water, and mild temperatures. He and ShaRee had planned to go shopping in St. George, then drive two hours back to Milford in time for parent-teacher conferences and Statler's sixth-grade state-championship football game at the high school. They couldn't wait until four, and couldn't take the time to come back.

Cody leaned his head out the window.

"So if I just go past you, who gets in trouble: you or me?" he asked.

"You," the man said flatly.

"You'd probably do it if I wasn't here," ShaRee whispered.

"Dad probably had an arrangement with someone," Cody said to her. He tried to call Bill, but couldn't get a clear signal on his cell phone. He leaned out the window again.

"Any way you can call up there and see if it's clear to get through real quick?" Cody asked.

The man ambled to a walkie-talkie, with no sense of urgency, and said something into it that Cody couldn't hear. A voice squawked back. The man walked back toward Cody's truck slowly.

"Afraid not," he said when he got to the window.

Cody clenched his jaw. He turned the rig around in the road and headed back down the ridge. He stopped at the corral, backed the trailer to a gate, and checked the fencing to make sure it was intact to keep the horses penned. He let the horses out. But there wasn't much feed in the dusty corral, and little water. He'd have to come back the next day to move the horses up onto the mesa.

"Bill would have driven right past him," ShaRee said as Cody released the horses. "Calvin definitely would've."

■ ■ ■

A windy rain fell in the morning as the kids went to school. Cody was inside a horse trailer, wearing an apron and shoeing Champ, one of his dad's favorite horses. Sage, one of Cody's new border collies, lay in the trailer to stay out of the damp. The conversation turned to rodeo, and the cold realization that Cody would be at the National Finals to watch Rusty, but not to compete. There was melancholy in his voice and in his expressions, conflicting bits of pride and disappointment.

"I tried to make it," he said. "I should have rode better." He laughed. "It's disappointing, but it ain't nobody's fault but mine. And I've been there. Nobody wants to hear me whine that I didn't make it."

He felt worse for Jesse. He had just had surgery on his shoulder, and doctors found five tears in the labrum. The severity of the injury made Jesse feel better about missing the National Finals, even though it meant a longer recovery, maybe six months, before he was back on the circuit.

"He was so close," Cody said. "One win and he woulda been in. But everything happens for a reason. If he'd a made it, he'd never have had that surgery on his arm. And then you go to the Finals hurt, and who knows what happens."

Cody knew a thing or ten about injuries. He was thirty-eight now, old in rodeo years, and couldn't remember them all. The broken right fibula came from a bull in college, and left Cody with a steel plate and nine screws. He added a rod in that leg when he broke his tibia in Albuquerque, forcing him to miss what would have been his first National Finals. A horse fell on him and broke his left tibia and fibula a few years later. Both lower legs were propped up by plates, rods, and screws.

"I got a fair amount of metal in me," Cody said.

He had broken fingers when ropes caught them against the saddle horn, and broken hands when they got smashed between the bronc and the chute. He broke a vertebra once in Kansas City and thought he could tough it out until he woke the next morning and couldn't move. There were too many injuries to remember, but they popped back into his memory whenever he scanned his body for scars or felt the twinge of an old ache when the weather changed.

None of these injuries mattered to him, really, because they were just excuses, and rodeo was where excuses went to die. The only way to make a dime was to get on the horse. Anything less than eight seconds didn't really matter, and might as well never have happened at all.

The surgically repaired shoulder from the year before finally felt mended in July. But just as it felt good, Cody's left knee flared up. He hadn't told anyone about it, but when he was introduced at the Calgary Stampede, he could barely make the required jog into the arena. The trainers said it was out of joint, and they moved it around until it felt better, but Cody struggled with it for weeks.

"When I spur up in the neck, like in Dodge City, I got my spur up over my rein and it kinda tweaked it a little bit," he said. "Oh my hell, the next morning, I couldn't hardly walk on it."

His problems weren't just physical. During a swing through Wyoming the year before, he left his saddle with the saddlemaker to get fixed. After he picked it up and started using it again, Cody never felt comfortable. Bronc saddles were usually molded wood, sometimes fiberglass, covered in rawhide, and Cody couldn't figure out why the inside riggings felt off. No matter how he cinched it, it felt loose.

A saddle to a bronc rider was like a car to a race driver, something to be custom-fitted and fine-tuned until it felt like another body part. Unlike a race-car driver, who could test the car endlessly under perfect conditions, a saddle only got tested for eight seconds at a time, always on a different horse.

"I couldn't lead a stick horse to water in that thing," Cody said. "I didn't realize it until Lawton, when we watched the video. Rusty was the one who noticed it. He said, 'Look at that saddle. It's moving back and forth.' I switched saddles in Tremont. I placed there and started winning. I still don't know how the hell it got messed up."

He didn't like that the saddle issue sounded like an excuse. Cody had put eighty thousand miles on his truck and gone to eighty rodeos, but the bottom line was that he was not one of the top fifteen saddle bronc riders.

"I rode like shit," he said. "I started ridin' better at the end and started winning more money. I woulda had to win damn near everything to make it. But once I didn't win in Omaha, I knew. That's why I didn't go to San Bernardino. I went to Stephensville, but my first horse was lame. I got two re-rides, and I turned out the second. It was just me and Spencer, and he didn't want to go to San Bernardino, either. So I said, 'Hell, let's just go on home and call it a year.'"

■　■　■

On the two-lane road between Minersville and Cedar City, headed to Smith Mesa to move the horses that he and ShaRee had dropped into the old corral the day before, Cody got a call from his agent. It looked like a new rodeo tour was going to happen, something called Elite Rodeo Athletes, where only the best of the best would compete for big money. A few top veteran cowboys were behind it. The idea was to break free of the grind of the traditional rodeo circuit, where even the best cowboys had to drive tens of thousands of miles to compete in a hundred rodeos just for a chance to make a living.

They would compete in fifteen or twenty exclusive, big-purse rodeos in big arenas, all on television, a regular-season schedule followed by a five-night championship in Dallas. It was not unlike what top bull riders had done twenty years earlier. They had broken away to form the Professional Bull Riders tour, which was a smashing success. The PBR tour was based loosely on NASCAR, with a top tier of marketable drivers competing in a season-long series. Those who committed first would be shareholders. The Elite Rodeo Athletes organizers wanted the best bronc riders. They wanted the Wrights.

Cody was not persuaded. He had heard this kind of splintering talk for years, and he knew that the Pro Rodeo Cowboys Association would fight the idea with all its financial and political might. Earlier in the fall, the PRCA had changed its bylaws to say that anyone with a financial interest in a competing rodeo association could not buy an annual PRCA membership card. A card was required to compete in any of the association's six hundred rodeos in North America, including the National Finals Rodeo in Las Vegas, with its new $10 million purse. ERA countered by filing a class-action lawsuit against the PRCA.

Everything was in limbo, leaving some dramatic questions that could forever alter the rodeo landscape. Cowboys and cowgirls were trying to figure out if they'd be willing to give up a chance to compete at some of their favorite rodeo stops, including the big-money finals, for the promise of the untested. They wondered if the PRCA would really shut out dozens of the most accomplished and recognizable stars from all its events.

Cody's concerns were pragmatic ones. The ERA schedule was still under construction, and payouts were little more than promises. There were rumors that Wrangler, the biggest sponsor in rodeo and the title sponsor of the National Finals Rodeo, was pulling its contracts with cowboys leaving the PRCA. Wrangler sponsored all the Wrights, dressing them in denim, paying each of them thousands of dollars a year, and giving bonuses for their place in the standings. Winning the world championship, as Spencer had done the year before, was rewarded with a $25,000 bonus from Wrangler.

Cody also felt a sense of duty. Rodeo had been good to Cody, and he respected the tradition of it. He wanted to pass it on to his boys. This felt like a shortcut, an insult to the world he knew, a gamble not worth taking. Cody talked Rusty out of joining ERA, but Spencer and Jesse had committed to it.

"They think they're holding a lotto ticket," Cody said into the phone. "Each of those original guys who started PBR sold out for $4 million. But if you weren't one of them, you didn't get anything. "

The phone signal was weak because of where he was, and the call dropped. Cody called back a few minutes later.

"It's going to cause them trouble because the PRCA is fighting it," Cody said. "It's going to be interesting when they go to enter Denver, and you're Trevor Brazile or Spencer or Jesse, and they don't let you in."

He listened, but lost the signal again, and when he got close to Cedar City, Cody called Spencer, then Jesse, and told them the same thing. They listened to their older brother without argument. The conversations were quick.

"You guys need to figure out how you're going to make a living without your PRCA card," Cody told Jesse. "Maybe you can help Alex pour concrete."

Another call chimed in..

"Hold on," Cody said. "Dad's calling. I'll holler at you later."

He pushed a button and said hello to Bill.

"I shod the bay horse," Cody said, and he told his dad that he was on the way to Smith Mesa to move the horses from the corral to the pasture. Then ShaRee interrupted that call, and Lily got on the phone to talk. She just wanted to tell her dad about kindergarten that morning, and about Oatmeal, a kitten that she got the day before. She told Cody that she was pretty sure Oatmeal was a girl.

Cody stopped for gas and something to drink before the road to Smith Mesa closed for construction. He pulled into the gas station at the corner turnoff toward Virgin and Zion.

"Congratulations on your son," a man said to Cody as he stood behind him in line.

"Thanks," Cody said, with a sheepish smile. He searched the man's face for recognition.

"He's in second, right?" the man said. He knew all about the Wrights. He asked about Cody's shoulder. He said he looked forward to watching Rusty, Spencer, and Jake in Las Vegas. Cody nodded and thanked him on the way out.

■ ■ ■

Cody got to the lower corral and backed the horse trailer to the chute. He opened the gate, grabbed a switch to coerce the horses, and climbed over the fence into the corral. With a little encouragement, the horses fed themselves into the chutes and up the ramp into the rattling trailer. The last one tried to get in, but found no space. It fell back out, then leapt in and crowded the others, who shuffled forward to make room.

"Nine horses," Cody said. "That's one too many. That's a Bill Wright special right there."

He pulled the loaded trailer up the road, past the point where he was stopped a day before. There was no one there. The road had been widened slightly and repaved to a smooth ribbon leading up into the edge of the national park. The transition onto the red-dirt turnoff to Smith Mesa was perfectly flush, and the road itself, so often a narrow washboard with a cliff to one side, was graded smooth. Loose dirt was pushed to the side as a type of guardrail—a mental one, if nothing else, that probably wouldn't hold back an out-of-control truck with a trailer. The road was as passable as ever, at least until the winter storms and the spring runoff came and eroded it away again into something rutted and dangerous.

The pasture near camp was spiked with rye and sunflower, a riot of green and yellow, and as Cody approached, something moved and caught his eye. It was one of Calvin's pigs. Bill would not be happy to learn the pigs were eating his feed before his cows even arrived.

Cody steered the truck and the horse trailer past the branding corral at the L-turn and along the road that traced the edge of the wash to the left. He stopped at a cattle guard that bridged a small drainage ditch and was clogged with mud and branches from the runoff of thunderstorms. He pulled a shovel from the back of his truck and spent twenty minutes clearing the slats so that cattle and horses would not be tempted to cross.

At the big field on the right, he pulled the truck to a stop. In a minute, the gate to the trailer was open and the horses, one by one, hopped out and trotted into the freedom and warmth of the winter rangeland. Three horses were already there, and they came to greet the new arrivals. The dozen of them would wait until the truck of cattle came in a week, and they would be saddled and used to move the herd and check the water supplies and mend the fences. Cody lingered for a bit, the walls of Zion to one side, the sprawling landscape of Smith Mesa and the deep cut of the wash spread before him.

"I have a lot of memories here," he said. "But it's Dad's and my mom's. They can do whatever they want with it. If he decides to trade it off, it'll be for something better, hopefully."

He had been helping Bill look at other properties all fall, but nothing was quite right. Not yet. And maybe there was a chance they could find something close to Milford. But another question, part of the uncertainty that the Wrights faced, was how many of the Wright boys would be part of a family ranching operation. Even Cody wasn't sure what his brothers were thinking.

"Everybody enjoys doing it," Cody said. "That kind of lifestyle seems to be what everybody likes. Everybody seems pretty happy if they're outdoors on a horse. But we can't really grow the herd, the way it is now. We're pretty much maxed out. I like doing it, but I like doing it with the family. If I was doing it by myself, I don't know how much I'd like it."

■ ■ ■

Back in Milford, Kruz, Jesse and Aubrey's boy, was turning four, and there was a birthday party at their house that night. On the brown shag rug of the living room, he sat atop Rusty, who was playing the part of the bull, and held tight to the collar of Rusty's shirt. Rusty spun and bucked on all fours, and Kruz giggled and eventually tumbled off the side. Rusty spun to face him and dipped his head to gore the boy.

"You gotta run to the fence! Run to the fence! Get away from the bull!" someone shouted, and Kruz stood and ran to the side of the room, giggling uncontrollably. Ryder pulled cushions from the couch and made a chute. Kruz boarded Rusty again, and Ryder pulled open the cushion gate. Rusty bounded out. Kruz laughed until he fell, then stood up and ran to the side. Statler, on his knees, played the role of rodeo bullfighter, and stepped in front of the charging bull to protect young Kruz.

Jesse stood in the kitchen, his right arm in a sling, his left hand holding a beer. The labrum had torn in five places and he hoped to ride again by spring. Like all the boys, Jesse saw his latest injury as a mere interruption, a comma in his bronc-riding career, not a period. Still, more than most of them besides Cody, he had given consideration to his post-rodeo life. Maybe it was being the father of a growing family, with two kids and a third coming. But Jesse had always been the quiet and serious one, by Wright standards, the yin to Jake's yang. On the rodeo circuit, the twins were persistently confused for one another. To the Wrights, they were as distinctly different as any other two of the boys. Jake was out hunting elk with some friends for a couple of days. He couldn't walk because his ankle, fresh from surgery, was still in a cast, but he drove and would shoot at anything within range of the car.

Jesse knew that rodeo couldn't go forever, and he was investing in the family business. His Bone Hollow permit gave the Wrights an easy access point on the low spot of Beavers. Jesse liked spending time at Smith Mesa, and was quicker than most of the boys to help Bill with chores there, but he started to separate the family history from the future business.

"The key to making money on cows is finding a place to winter 'em where you don't have to feed 'em," Jesse said in his kitchen. Smith Mesa was just such a place, but there wasn't room for what the Wrights wanted to do. "There's a lot of awesome memories there.

But it's his to do with what he wants. I'd probably be bummed, but I wouldn't be upset."

Bill stood nearby, drinking water and eating a piece of birthday cake. It had been a tricky fall. Bill had found a way to raise cows the last couple of years without any of the physical work, by investing in cattle that he never saw. It was a bit like buying futures through a feedlot, and the company he'd found was in Kansas. He bought a pen young at one price, let the lot raise it, and then sold it again when the cattle were grown. The company took care of the expenses and labor and then split the profits with investors like Bill. Bill was just testing it out, and he had made pretty good money on the first couple of pens he bought. But he knew it was a gamble, putting faith in the cattle market and blind trust in other ranchers far away. The cattle could be mismanaged. A big storm could wipe out a pen. A drought could prevent them from fattening up. All the variables were still there, only Bill had no control over them.

"In Kansas, the cattle prices dropped in September," Bill said. "I made about $25,000, but if I hadn't hedged, I'd a made $50,000. I got greedy. I gambled it wouldn't go down, and it went down. I have a friend in this business who has been doing this for years. He lost a million and a half dollars in that one drop."

Bill's own herd was getting up toward three hundred head. He added to it every year, as space and permits allowed, almost like contributing to a 401(k).

"I once told an uncle, 'This is nothing but gambling. I might as well give this up and go to Las Vegas,'" Bill said. "And he said, 'You're right. But the Lord don't look down on this kind of gambling.'"

The feed in the mountains was still good, thanks to a wet summer, and the cows still grazed at the higher elevations. Bill wanted to get them down into the pasture above Bone Hollow before they were trapped by weather. The days were getting shorter. A cold front was coming. Snow was in the forecast. And the cattle pot to move the herd to Smith Mesa had been ordered for next week.

Bill had missed Statler's football game the night before. He had been at Beavers, riding his horse back to his truck at dusk, hoping to get home for dinner and over to the game, when he came across five cows in a dead-end corner of the mountain. He decided to move them in the dark rather than coming back the next day and looking for them again. By the time he got to Milford and parked at the high school, the game had ended. The next afternoon, the day of Kruz's birthday party, a chilled fog settled onto the Tushar Mountains and filled its high valleys. Bill had gathered twenty head, shuffling his horse in an arc behind them to keep them together and moving downhill. But the fog thickened in the afternoon, and in the course of just a few minutes, it swallowed the outline of the cows. One by one, they turned into hazy gray shadows until they drifted into the nearby trees and disappeared entirely, like ghosts. All of them were gone.

"I couldn't see where they went," Bill said. "Some of 'em had bells, and I could hear them getting farther and farther away in all directions, but I couldn't see 'em. I could hear them bells going this way, and could hear them bells going that ways."

A day's work was undone. Bill just rode away, figuring there'd always be a better day ahead. He laughed at that and took another bite of cake. There were worse ways to spend a day.

"Worst ride I ever had was better than my best walk," he said.

13

Flag Bearer

RUSTY CAME FLYING on horseback into the Las Vegas arena, the way he'd always seen his father do at the National Finals Rodeo. It was called the Grand Entry. One by one, in alphabetical order, the states were called—Alabama, Alaska, Arizona, Arkansas, and so on—and the cowboys and cowgirls from that state arrived at full speed on horseback into the sold-out arena, led by one carrying the state flag. It was manic and fast-paced. Within a minute, and certainly by the time they got to Kansas, a cloud of dust hovered toward the lights and hung there above the chaos.

The horses circled the arena once, then crowded into the center, bumping one another to cram together as tight as cows in a pen. Not every state had representatives, but most of them did, none bigger than Texas.

When it got to be Utah's turn, most years and most nights of the past decade it had been Cody Wright leading the way, a pole propped on his hip and Utah's blue flag flapping in the self-made breeze of a horse at full speed. But Cody was nowhere to be seen—not behind the chutes, not at the gate next to his father, not in the stands with ShaRee or Morgan, now five months pregnant. He was somewhere, just another face among eighteen thousand in the stands.

It was his oldest boy, Rusty, second in the world saddle bronc standings, who carried the Utah flag on opening night. He had just turned twenty. Close behind him was CoBurn. He was twenty-one. Rusty and CoBurn grew up about thirty miles apart, Rusty in Milford and CoBurn in Beaver, and they met through teenage rodeos. Now they lived on the same block in Milford. CoBurn and Becca had a baby girl, born the previous spring. Rusty and Morgan's baby boy was due the next one.

Rusty was less than $4,000 out of first place, which was about equal to nothing. Payouts had gone up, and each of the ten rounds were going to earn more than $26,000 for the winners, up from about $19,000 the year before. The other payouts and the big prizes for average, now over $67,000 for the average winner, were going up the same way.

The standings could flip with every ride, and the average tallied at the end could hopscotch contestants up and down the standings and turn all the happenings of the previous twelve months inside out. Anyone there could win the world title, even someone like CoBurn, ranked fourteenth out of fifteen riders to start—Spencer had proved that the year before. The key to the National Finals was getting there. Then you've got to get hot.

The opening-round draw had CoBurn coming out fifth on a bronc named Roulette. None of the first four riders managed a score, and CoBurn was nervous. Spencer leaned in to check his saddle and pat him on the shoulder. The horse bounded out, and CoBurn kept time, his feet up on the animal's neck and his right hand overhead, like a waiter holding an invisible pizza, every time Roulette came down on its front hooves.

THE LAST COWBOYS

"Now we've got a ride going," the television announcer said, but the bronc slowed the final couple of seconds. A pickup man rode alongside, and CoBurn leaned to him and slid off the side and dismounted perfectly on his feet. He clapped his hands and jogged to the gate, craning his neck to see the score come in—a respectable 81.5, good enough to be in the money, the kind of start any rookie would love.

Rusty climbed atop Nickels and Dimes, which leaned hard to its left and pinned Rusty's leg against the metal gate. Rusty winced. Jake and others tried to tug the stubborn animal straight, and when it finally put its weight evenly on all fours and unlocked Rusty's leg, Rusty raised his hand and nodded. The bronc corkscrewed and dipped its neck low on its first jump, and Rusty nearly tumbled over the front. He never recovered his balance and splattered into the dirt, face first and on all fours, after just three seconds. It was not the kind of start any rookie would love.

It went better for Rusty the next night, a solid 75 on a bronc called Major Huckleberry, good enough to tie for fifth and a split of the five-six payouts. But CoBurn won the round atop Curly Bill, which strode out of the gate like a racehorse, then stopped to buck and curl left. CoBurn was unfazed by it all and scored 83, and it held up through a procession of buckoffs and low-scoring rides. Just like that, in two nights, CoBurn had jumped from fourteenth in the standings to eighth, and now he was on the stage at the South Point, getting asked about marrying into the Wrights. Rusty was there, too, and he took the microphone, because he liked the microphone better than CoBurn, and he could explain it all better.

And so it went, for most of ten nights, Jake and Spencer unable to muster momentum, Cody and Jesse not competing, but Rusty and CoBurn making names for themselves under the heavy weight of being part of the Wrights. If it wasn't apparent before, it was then.

185

If world-class bronc riding hadn't just passed to the next generation, it certainly had blended with it.

Quick extrapolation told anyone paying attention that the Wright name was not just going to be part of rodeo's record books for a single era, from the start to the finish of some mix of seven brothers, from Cody to Stuart. Those brothers were having boys of their own, and those boys were just about starting to have boys, too. All of them would have the chance to become bronc riders, bequeathed the advantages of being born into such a family. Maybe some combination of evolution and shared experience would make the next wave even better than the last.

■ ■ ■

Rusty won Round 4 on a veteran bronc called Sundance. It was the same horse Cody won on in Round 4 nine years before, on his way to his first world title, and that Stetson watched over and over at home because it was his favorite of all the rides Cody had ever had. "My dad actually won a round on him a few years ago," Rusty told the television interviewer in the tunnel after all the rides were over. "I tried to drag as much information out of him as I could."

"Didn't you hook up your aunt with your new uncle-in-law?" Flint Rasmussen asked Rusty during the buckle ceremony onstage at the South Point.

"It kind of went that way," Rusty said. He was more attracted to the lights and cameras than his father. "I called CoBurn and asked him if he'd take my aunt to the prom and go with me."

"Man, if I had a nickel every time someone said, 'Hey, buddy, want to take my aunt to the prom?'" Rasmussen said. He asked Rusty to introduce the entourage lined up on the stage behind him.

"This is Morgan, my girlfriend," Rusty said. He pointed to her stomach. "This is my boy. This is my brother Ryder; his girlfriend, Cheyenne. And my little brother Stetson. Statler, my brother, and my little sister, Lily Jo. This is my dad, Cody. You guys know Cody."

"Two-time champion of the world," the emcee said.

"This is my mom, ShaRee, and her mom, my Grandma Betty. And my dad's mom, Evelyn, and Grandpa Bill. Spencer, Jake, Jake's wife, Loni."

They handed Rusty a framed buckle, just like the fourteen round-win buckles that his father had won. One of the buckles from Cody's first National Finals, thirteen years earlier, was on the belt that he wore almost every day. Rusty had a lifetime of memories of his father wearing that buckle.

They asked Rusty if he was old enough to accept the Pendleton Whisky. Before he could say anything, ShaRee stepped forward and took it. Back when Cody started to win rounds and brought his family onstage, the boys sometimes in their pajamas, Cody didn't even get offered the whisky. They just figured a guy from a big Mormon family in Utah wouldn't want it, until ShaRee stepped in and told them different. Now she did the same thing for her son as she had for her husband. She made sure they got the whisky.

CoBurn was not there. He had been sick, some sort of quick-moving flu that kept him in the bathroom at the Aria most of the day. Bill joked that CoBurn was hungover, taking advantage of his winnings and celebrating being twenty-one, but he swore he wasn't. His score of 72.5 that night wasn't worth any money, but it kept his average up among a dwindling number of riders with a score each night. CoBurn felt bad to miss Rusty's buckle ceremony, since Rusty had been at his two nights before.

But they were all back the next night, too, after CoBurn won for the second time in the first five rounds. He was assigned to Wound Up, a seven-year-old mare that bucked off both riders it drew the year before. Wound Up took CoBurn for a ride straight through the middle of the arena, with big, smooth jumps, arcing like a sine wave. CoBurn was in full command on top.

"Niiiiinnnnety points!" the arena announcer shouted when the score got posted, and the crowd roared its appreciation. It was the first 90-point ride at the National Finals since Jesse did it three years before, and just the fourteenth in history. When all the rest of the riders finished their turns, CoBurn was introduced to the crowd again, and he rode into the arena at a gallop, waving his white hat as he circled and disappeared into the tunnel again.

When the rodeo ended, CoBurn walked alone to the parking lot and sat in the chilly desert air at a table to sign autographs, an obligation of winning. He sat next to Kaycee Feild, a champion bareback rider from Utah. There was live music and a few booths advertising trucks and all-terrain vehicles and trailers. Coors had a big tent nearby, where people took turns riding a mechanical bull and women danced on the bar. Fans politely lined up to get their programs or T-shirts signed. Some of them came behind the table to take pictures with CoBurn. He thanked everyone who approached. His family watched from a distance, his mom and stepdad and father and three siblings and grandmother, a few cousins and friends, smiling and taking pictures themselves, all wearing yellow T-shirts that read "CoBurn Bradshaw." When the crowd thinned, and someone told him it was OK, CoBurn stood and walked back toward his car in the parking lot, where he found Becca and their daughter. The baby needed her diaper changed.

"She has what you had," Becca said.

CoBurn was fifth in the standings, right behind Rusty. They both had a chance to win the world title, and they knew it. CoBurn told Becca that The D Casino now wanted to sponsor him. Two months before, in Milford, he watched the casino throw a party for all the Wright boys, while CoBurn had been ignored.

"I don't know if they knew back then that I was part of the family," CoBurn said. He shrugged.

An hour later, a huge entourage of Wrights and Bradshaws crowded into the backstage hallway at the South Point. CoBurn's father, Travis, wore a cowboy hat and a fat mustache, and he told stories about CoBurn being a great baseball player and a kid who wanted to race horses at the local track but got too big. "But he was good at breakin' 'em," he said. The group was ushered onstage and smothered it, and for a moment, CoBurn was mixed in with all the rest. Jake, Spencer, and Rusty were there, and Jake joked with the emcees and did a break dance. CoBurn watched from the group until he was pulled to the front.

"We're giving you money and buckles," Rasmussen said. "Get out here on the damn stage."

CoBurn held his baby girl and wore the shiny buckle he'd won three nights earlier.

"Thanks for coming out," he said to the crowd. He couldn't see most of the faces, lost behind the glare of the spotlights.

"What a nice guy," announcer Randy Corley said. "He fits right in with that family of bronc riders."

■ ■ ■

Rusty drew Roulette in Round 6, the same horse that CoBurn rode the first night to an 81.5. In the crowd, Cody held Lily on his lap. Morgan was on one side of them, Statler on the other. They watched as Roulette leapt out of the chute and nearly left Rusty behind. If the horse could have been removed from the picture, Rusty would look like a man who had just slipped on a sheet of ice, flailing backward. He managed to keep his feet up and in the stirrups as his neck snapped back once, then again. On the third jump, Roulette dropped its head, pulling the rein taut and forward, and Rusty desperately tried to dig his heels into the animal to get a grip and restore his balance.

He never had a chance. Before the clock reached three seconds, Rusty was airborne, launched off the left side of the horse, and landed on the seat of his pants in the dirt. He sat for a moment, pulled the rubber guard from his mouth, and stood up. If Rusty knew the stakes, his face didn't show it. Two no-scores crushed his chances of making money in the average. Rusty knew that titles could depend as much on the horses you didn't ride as the ones you did.

But Rusty won the seventh round, and the eighth, too, and everything got interesting again in a hurry.

"This is the rank pen of horses, folks," the announcer told the crowd before the seventh round, as the chutes filled with bronc riders adjusting their saddles. "This is the one when you better have Velcro on the bottom of your britches."

Rusty's 83-point ride on Tip Off took him along the fence and dumped him, just after the buzzer, onto the dirt. It knocked the air out of Rusty, and he couldn't catch a breath. He slowly followed the fence back to the gate, lucid enough to hear the announcer through the din of the crowd.

"I heard the guy say, 'That 83 will sure make him feel better,'" Rusty said when he got out of the arena. "And I was thinking, 'No, it don't.'"

And after Rusty scored 87 on Lipstick N Whiskey to win Round 8, he was leading the money, first in the world with two nights to go. The projections had him finishing third, behind Jacobs Crawley and Wade Sundell, a pair of veterans who had each ridden all eight of their horses. Rusty needed them to buck off, but there's no rooting for bad luck in rodeo, so if he harbored such thoughts, he kept them to himself. Cody always said: Control what you can control, dust yourself off, and move to the next ride, whether it's the next night in the same big arena or a small ring a thousand miles away.

■ ■ ■

The night before the final performance that would determine who won the world title, Rusty went downtown with Cody and ShaRee, Ryder, CoBurn, and Becca. Like any other tourists, they rode a zip line through the neon glow of Fremont Street. Rusty didn't sleep much, through the night or into the daylight hours.

"I thought about it all day and all night," he said. "I didn't do no math. I just knew I had a chance if I had a good ride."

The final round featured the top broncs in the sport. Spencer rode Lunatic Fringe to 82.5 and sixth place, the only paycheck of a disappointing Finals for the defending champion. He finished the year in fourteenth. Jake took on Maple Leaf, which opened with a big drop that pulled Jake out of the saddle. He landed on the bronc's neck and was catapulted over its head. Jake flipped into the dirt in a somersault.

"I thought I was gonna puke right there," Jake said when it was all over and he had finished the season in ninth.

CoBurn mounted Kid Rock, which stalled in the chute for a few seconds, then leapt out as if it had stepped on a tack. His 79.5 didn't earn him money, but it meant that he had ridden all ten of his horses, a rare feat, and he finished second in the average. Over ten days, CoBurn won $153,576. With a year-long total of $229,722, CoBurn finished fourth in the world and won rookie-of-the-year honors, just as Rusty had the year before.

Rusty wasn't sure how the standings stood. He scooted nervously in the saddle atop Low Bucks. Spencer and Jesse hovered over him, cinching ropes and tugging at the bronc to get it to stand straight. A man with a television camera leaned in tight to catch Rusty's expression and broadcast it to screens around the country. Across the arena, ShaRee watched with her hands pressed together in front of her face, as if in prayer. Cody was next to her, and Lily was next to him, wearing a sweatshirt that read "Rusty Wright" in sparkly letters.

"This guy's barely out of high school, a two-time national high school champion," one of the announcers said. Rusty nodded. Spencer and Jesse backed away. Bill peered over the nearby gate. ShaRee pumped her hands. Lily screamed. Cody watched.

It was a good ride, enough for an 84, the kind of score that would have won a few rounds. But Rusty would have to settle for three go-round wins and third place in the world standings, with $244,448 in prize money for the year.

"I think his move was too late in the week to catch Crawley and Sundell, but I'll tell you what: tip your hat to that young man," one announcer said. "He is the real deal."

"Yeah, he's going to be really tough," the other said. "He's got a younger brother called Ryder, who's also a national champion. He's tough."

"My question is, how many Wright brothers, Wright family, are we going to see here at the Wrangler NFR?"

Back in the hallway, one by one, the bronc riders carried their saddles back to the locker room.

"You rode like a champ," Spencer told CoBurn. "What'd I tell you? You were so nervous on the drive down here. You were like, 'I don't want to go down there and freeze up.' I told you you wouldn't freeze up."

CoBurn smiled. Rusty asked Spencer about his ride, the only one of his that looked like the year before.

"What did you give him?" Rusty asked.

"A double," Spencer said. "I don't know if it was a bad measure-ment, but I was like, 'Whoa!'" He held his fist and an imaginary rein in front of his face and clenched his expression. "When she hit, she bring me up out of there and I missed the next jump. The flank strap come undone."

He turned to Jake, still feeling the jarring pain of landing on his bronc's neck, balls first, and flipping over its head.

"I shoulda warned you," Spencer said. "That's a stout bitch, huh?"

"Yeah, as hard as this," Jake said, and he rapped his knuckles on the concrete-block wall.

Cases of Coors Light were piled on the floor. Rusty had paid for the beer three times, but Jake and Spencer had had to buy it because Rusty wasn't yet twenty-one. Most of the men cracked beers, and whatever anxiety they had felt during the previous ten days disap-peared in relief and loud chatter. There were no enemies or rivals. There was no brooding over what-ifs and why-mes. It was on to next season.

"We get to wake up tomorrow and do it all again," Jake said, and he pulled a swig of beer from a silver can.

"How 'bout we take a vote and have ten more rounds?" Rusty called out with a smile.

"No," someone called back, flatly.

Rusty left the room with his bag over one shoulder and his saddle in his other hand. He took them out of the arena and put them in the back of his dad's truck. Had he finished first or second in the average, instead of sixth, he would have won the season title. The rides he would remember wouldn't just be the ones that won him thousands of dollars, but the two that didn't last eight seconds. That was the thing about rodeo. They didn't just get him nothing. They cost him.

He returned with a Sharpie and a metal NFR sign, the one

shaped like a highway route marker, with the number ten on it—his number, representing his ranking among all the contestants in all the disciplines before the rodeo began. Around his neck, Rusty wore a silver necklace that Morgan bought before National Finals started. A silver charm with the number-ten NFR logo dangled under his chin, in the opening above the top snap of his rodeo shirt. Morgan had a matching charm, hers made of copper.

Rusty was thirteen when Cody won his first world title, and he remembered a lot of years of heartbreak before it ever happened. If Rusty were to someday win a world championship like his father, he supposed, now his own son would be around to see it, too. It was hard to imagine it taking another thirteen years, but maybe that's how it was meant to be—him not winning a world title until his boy was in the stands, just like it had happened with Cody. Anyway, it would have to be that way.

"That's what I get for falling off," Rusty said. "I coulda done better." He braved a smile. "That's rodeo," he said. He looked around at the others, all older and harder men, but all smiling, drinking, and packing their gear, to see whose autograph he was missing.

14

Truck a Money

THE MOON WAS FULL over Smith Mesa, like a lantern hanging over the wash, casting just enough light from the heavens to give shape to the Earth. The landscape was as colorless as a pencil drawing. The cliffs were drawn with a straight edge, the junipers were charcoal ghosts, and the sand had lost its rich redness to the night.

The cows and their calves, some in the corral and most in the near meadow where Bill had herded them, cleaved the stillness with their moans and bleats. Cows called and calves answered. They could be heard for miles. But it was white noise to the cowboys, who slept hard until light over the cliffs touched their campers and color returned to the world.

Bill was the first one up, and he tugged on his jeans and buttoned the snaps of his shirt and slid his boots over his feet. He pulled a two-liter glass jar from the cabinet. It was filled with red liquid, the color of tomato juice, and hard-boiled eggs out of their shells.

He dipped his knife into the concoction of vinegar and hot sauce, stabbed an egg, and put it in his mouth. That was breakfast.

It'd been as interesting of a spring for him as it had for the boys. He felt a pop and tear in his belly when he tried to lift a wet bale of hay, a hundred pounds when they're dry, over the side of his truck. It was a hernia, and the doctor said he had two strangulations—"one just with fat in it, the other with four inches of intestines coming out that he had to poke back in," Bill said. The doctor also found bad arthritis in Bill's back and a swollen prostate. "A rodeoer's disease," Bill called it. "That's from all the ridin', I think."

The hernia surgery laid Bill up in bed for a couple of days, which was boring as all get-out for him. "They don't even want me pickin' up more than five pounds for three weeks," Bill said. "Hell, I can't even pour a glass of milk."

Bill trusted doctors about as much as he trusted federal rangers or rodeo judges.

"He always thinks he's fine," Cody said. "And he thinks he can diagnose himself better than the doctors can. He doesn't like doctors. I'm surprised he doesn't take himself to a vet instead."

Walking or standing wasn't bad, but it took a long time before Bill could sit comfortably in a chair or a saddle. He didn't believe much in pain pills, because they just covered up the problem and fooled you into thinking everything was OK. Let pain be your guide, he always told the boys. Eventually, he could lift seventy-five pounds, which wasn't much for the kind of work Bill did. The doctor said that he needed to drop thirty pounds. "Give me a half a pound a month, I'll be happy," the doctor told him.

So Bill got rid of the Smarties and the Cokes, and within a couple months he had lost ten pounds. He could bend over more easily, but his pants kept falling down, so he had to punch another hole in his belt so that he could cinch it with his old rodeo buckle.

"They tell me to have more sex, too," Bill said. "I said my wife wants to see that on paper."

Bill passed the time with a few trips to Smith Mesa. From his truck, he checked the herd and the water and fixed a few fences and put salt licks out. His neighbors knew that Bill was laid up, and they were patient with him when they found that some of his cows had wandered onto their land.

It was a hot and windy spring, and the forecast was for more heat and less rain. Bill was on his horse one afternoon, holding his phone to his ear and talking to Cody as he surveyed the landscape. His land had about thirty ponds scattered around it, most of which filled up only after a thunderstorm or a long stretch of soggy weather. Last fall, when he brought the herd down from Beavers, six or seven of the ponds held water. By spring, only one of them did.

"I'm worried about being out of water," Bill said. "It's going to be hot, and there's only one pond that has any water in it this year, and it'll be dry within a week. And I'm worried about my well drying up. It's just dry. We've had a good winter of moisture, but not the kind that'll fill the ponds. The feed looks good, but not the ponds. I'm just nervous. It hasn't gone dry on me before. But everything is dry in the wash and the springs aren't as good as they usually are. Seems like we're just getting a little drier and drier."

Bill wanted to get the herd up north earlier than usual, even earlier than the year before, and some of the boys had come to help. By seven, Bill had the horses loaded into the trailer and Calvin riding shotgun. Spencer rode the back of the trailer like a fireman on a ladder truck, and dust piled up behind them as they came out of the campsite, through a couple of gates, and to the main dirt road at Smith Mesa, rutted by winter rains and now hardened by spring's heat. At the hard bend in the road was the corral, filled with cattle.

"Let's get these separated," Bill shouted, and Jesse arrived on horseback, and four-year-old Kruz followed on Darla. The boy wore chaps and spurs and a belt buckle and a hat, like a miniature version of his dad. In the corral, Bill was on foot and Calvin was on horseback, a cigarette dangling from his mouth. He cut about a dozen of the cows away from the herd, flinging his horse side to side, letting them slide past him and Bill and leaving the calves in front of them. A cattle dog that belonged to Alex and Bill flitted about. Its name was Rooster, like the one-eyed John Wayne character.

"Stir 'em a little more," Bill said, and after a few rounds of cutting, there were forty calves wedged into one end of the corral. Bill closed the fence to keep them separated from the rest of the herd. They called for their mothers, and their mothers called back. The back-and-forth honking, at different notes and various octaves, sounded like midtown traffic. A dust cloud hung over the corral.

A cattle pot was backed to the loading chute. Its bumper sticker read, "Steaks Alive!" Calvin used nonstop patter and an occasional smack of his leather rein to persuade the calves to follow the throat of the chute in single file until they were swallowed by the silver trailer. The driver of the truck, a quiet man from Colorado City, used an electric prod to move the most stubborn ones. The calves moved up the ramp to the second level of the double-decker trailer, and walls inside divided them into compartments. The mothers came last, coaxed into the first level, their weight like ballast for the difficult ride off the mesa and up the interstate to Beavers.

It would take two days and five trips of the truck to get them to Beavers, and even then, Bill knew he'd leave some back, because some probably still wandered around the wash, looking for something green to eat.

"You got forty?" Bill shouted to Calvin through the din and dust.

"Was I supposed to be countin' 'em?" Calvin replied. He smiled. "I wasn't countin'. I was just lookin' at cows."

Bill pulled his cell phone from the leather holster on his belt.

"He's just leaving," he said to Cody, home in Milford. Cody loaded up a horse and headed to Beavers to be there when the cattle pot arrived at Bone Hollow.

■ ■ ■

All day, they repeated the process, bringing cattle from the pasture and dividing them up in the corral, dragging temporary fences through the dirt to create pens and keep them apart. Bill spent most of the time on his feet, directing traffic, sometimes with a long wand that had a plastic grocery bag strapped to the end like a flag of surrender. From under the brim of his stained hat, Bill studied the nervous animals, looking for pairs, making sure mothers were shipped with their calves. About ninety percent of his cows should have had calves. Bill studied their udders.

"That cow's being sucked," Bill said, pointing at the udder of one that scampered past.

"Looks like it," Spencer said.

"That little cow right there," Bill shouted toward another, "that might be her calf right beside her. Let's just set and watch her a minute."

He assumed it was a first-time mother because she was so small. The calf looked to be a couple months old. Bill worried about the mother's health, and reminded his boys about how a cow's body prioritizes how it expends energy—for milk first, then to grow, then to ovulate.

"Let's separate them," Bill said. "Take the calf to Beavers. He'll be bewildered for a bit, but he'll be OK. I think he's already

201

weaned, and then she'll spend more energy on ovulation and not
producing milk."

Bill's eyes fixed on a cow without a calf that had a huge growth
protruding from her jaw. Calvin called it the goiter cow, and Bill
figured the infection had started with cheatgrass and foxtail, good
feeds before they ripened and went to seed, when they turned
thorny and their sharp burrs stuck into clothes and hides. He had
been keeping his eye on the cow all spring. He hauled her into
town to the veterinarian and injected sodium iodine into her, but
now part of the growth on her cheek had hardened, and part of it
jiggled under her chin.

"The vet says I should just sell her, but I don't know if I'd get
anything for her," Bill said. "I thought about just operating on her
myself and trying to lance it, but I don't know. It's calcified now."

"You're not going to shoot her, are ya?" Calvin asked. He wore a
ball cap that read "Rodeo." Everyone else wore a cowboy hat.

"Yeah," Bill said. He did not turn to his son, but stared deeply at
the cow, the way someone might stare at a car after a wreck.

"Why don't you take her to the kill plant in Cedar? Won't they
take her?"

"I dunno," Bill said.

"Can't you eat her?" Calvin asked.

"She's got an infection."

Calvin leaned on his knee, looking down from atop his horse.

"I'd like to think that when I got a sore jaw, the rest of me is all
right," he said.

Bill changed the subject.

"Call Cody and tell him the truck just left," he said.

Calvin tapped into his cell phone and held it to his ear. His
brother picked it up a hundred miles away.

"Hey, Cody," Calvin said cheerfully. "Truck a money just left."

Calvin, four years younger than Cody, the fourth of Bill and Evelyn's thirteen children, might have been the best bronc rider of
them all. He shattered both cheeks, like eggshells, on a bull when
he was twelve and broke his ribs in college when he was one of the
best all-around cowboys in the country. His coach called him his
secret weapon. Calvin could do it all. Then he turned pro and the
injuries kept coming, and booze and pills tried to chase away the
pain, and the rodeo career for the Wright boys skipped from Cody
past Calvin and on to Alex, Jake and Jesse, and Spencer, and now to
another generation.

But none of them had Calvin's personality. He was as extroverted as the other boys were introverted. None of them lit up the
room the way Calvin did, as if his voltage meter ran higher. None of
them made Evelyn laugh like Calvin did. The seven Wright brothers
looked like brothers, but outside of the twins, none of them looked
just like any others. But Calvin looked a lot like Cody, if Cody had
just come wrinkled out of the dryer. They often got confused for
one another.

"I tell him a million times, 'Calvin, you're the most famous kid
I've got,'" Bill said later in his trailer, over dinner of burgers and cut
fried potatoes with bacon. "When I introduce myself, more people
ask me if I know Calvin than anything about bronc riding."

Calvin bounced around jobs, working ranches in Utah and
Nevada, but most never lasted long. He ran a few hogs on Smith
Mesa, which Bill used to do, too. He'd had about ten cows in the
herd, but in need of money, he'd sold them to Alex. He had four
kids with Stef, the oldest a teenager and the youngest not even two,
but the marriage had finally disintegrated through tears and broken
promises.

"He's having trouble with drugs, not for the first time, but it's gotten really bad in the last year," Evelyn said a few months earlier, when Calvin was in rehabilitation in Hurricane. "He called two nights ago. He said, 'I love you, Mom,' and then he started makin' jokes. I think he was just doin' it so he wouldn't cry."

Calvin had come out of rehab and was living on couches and in trailers around Hurricane. He had more time to help Bill, and Bill welcomed the help, because Calvin was a hard worker with a sense of humor, even if he sometimes wore Bill out with his constant talk and impatient ways.

A couple weeks before, at Smith Mesa, Calvin had been breaking a new horse. As he navigated it along the cliffs and down the steep trails into the wash, on his way to lure cattle out, the horse spooked and lost its footing. Calvin leapt off its back just before the horse plunged over the edge, a couple hundred feet, to its death. It rattled Calvin deeply, and at camp that night, Bill told him about how he'd lost a horse the same way once, one of his dad's racehorses, when he was sixteen. You didn't forget a thing like that.

"The rehab helped with the OxyContin," Bill said. "I can see in his eyes he's not takin' 'em. But his problem is that he likes the cowboy life too much—ridin' and horseshoein' and so on. And it's painful work. So, instead of taking OxyContin, he's goin' out and gettin' drunk. And I know about that. I used to do the same thing. It takes the edge off and makes the pain go away."

The thing that derailed Calvin from big-time rodeo years before, beyond the injuries and addictions, was his attitude toward the sport. Cody saw rodeo as a business. Calvin saw it as a party. The first few years on the circuit were full of temptations—the buckle bunnies, the honky-tonks, the drugs, and the drinks. Calvin, "too much of a people person" in Bill's mind, couldn't negotiate them cleanly. Cody did, and he was still going as he approached forty.

Most of his younger brothers followed his example and turned rodeo into their livelihood. But Calvin was still trying to piece together a life through the maze of odd jobs, divorce, and addiction. It was a wonder that he smiled so much.

In a way, Calvin was a big reason why Cody was still riding and still traveling the circuit with his boys.

"Cody wants to coach his kids through all that," Bill said. "He tried that with his brother, and it didn't work."

The boys were close. Calvin named one of his sons Cody Slade. When Cody held the baby the first time, he welled up.

"Don't you think you oughta name him after yourself?" Cody asked.

"No," Calvin said. "I think he should be named after you."

■ ■ ■

There was a pause in the work. Calvin asked his dad if he wanted him to fix him a Spark. It was a flavored powder, with vitamins and caffeine, mixed into a bottle of water. Cody drank several a day, and just about all the other boys did, too, instead of coffee and pop, during their long drives between rodeos. The men stood in the chute, to avoid the breeze and the dust, and fixed sandwiches made of white bread, ham, pepper jack cheese, mayonnaise, and mustard.

Two more truckloads would go up to Beavers the next day, so the men spent the afternoon sorting the cattle and making sure they were properly tagged before they were hauled north and let loose on the summer range in the mountains. They needed fly tags in their ears to keep bugs away, and they needed Forest Service tags so they could run on the Forest Service land up north.

Calvin ran them, one by one, into a narrow runway to the squeeze chute, and as soon as the head popped through the end, Jesse yanked the lever to shut the door around its neck, like a stockade, and Bill pulled the lever that squeezed the green metal bars around its midsection and closed the gate behind it. Spencer bent down to give a quick look behind the bellies, like a mechanic squatting to look at a chassis. He called out "steer" or "heifer."

The yearling steers didn't need anything, because Bill planned to take them to auction the next day. They usually got a few more cents on the pound because they gained weight faster and matured bigger. Jesse opened the gate for the steers, and Spencer directed them into their own pen.

For the heifers, Jesse leaned his body against their necks to hold them steady, and then punched their ear with a tag gun. They checked for brands, to make sure that none of them had been missed the year before, and when they found one without a Wright mark on its hip, they branded it with an electric brand, plugged into a generator. The smoke rose from the animal and smelled like burnt hide and hair.

Bill wanted bells on some cows, too. He pulled the square-shaped bells from a box, and a length of rope from another, and tied the bell around the neck of the occasional cow. He didn't do the yearlings, because their necks were growing, but he did the young cows, because they were the ones that tended to wander. He did just a few, because cows usually moved in small groups, a herd within a herd, and all you needed was one of them to have a bell to be able to find a whole lot of them. When Jesse opened the squeeze chute and let a belled cow out, the animal sometimes leapt and bucked, trying to shed the clanging weight around its neck. It quieted and stilled after a few seconds.

The goiter cow came into the squeeze chute, and Bill looked at her closely. The cheek bulged solidly, and it oozed blood and pus.

"Yeah, I'm going to have to kill her," he said. "Well, put her over here and maybe I can take her out and do it away from everything."

"You can't sell her?" Calvin asked. He wasn't ready to see a cow go to waste.

"Would you want to eat her?" Bill replied.

A Jeep marked with "Zion Tours" pulled up. The company took tourists on the rugged roads around Smith Mesa, extolling the views of Zion. A young man with a beard stepped out and came to the edge of the corral and looked in on Bill and Jesse at the squeeze chute. He had the look of someone whose other job might be at a craft brewery, or maybe a coffee shop as a barista.

"How ya doin'?" he asked.

Bill nodded, and his body language said that he didn't really have time for small talk.

"You guys got a pretty thick herd of coyotes around here," the man said. "I was out here the other night, about two in the morning, to take pictures of the stars. And there were about thirty coyotes out there in the pasture."

"Thirty coyotes!" Bill said, and his face lit up in a smile. "Well, I knew there was some."

The man said he could hear the howling, and if anyone had some ammunition and a searchlight, he'd be glad to help go after them one night.

"Well, I'd just as soon no one go shooting into the herd of cows," Bill said.

The man stood for a moment until the silence grew awkward. "Well, just thought I'd let you know," he said, and he returned to his truck and drove away.

"Thirty!" Bill said to his boys. He figured the man heard coyotes in the wash and saw the vague outlines of calves in the meadow. "I've seen three big ones, and I know there's a litter here, but there ain't thirty. And we don't have any cows without calves that have lost any that way."

Bill and other neighboring ranchers paid a dollar for each head of cattle they sold to fund a trapper hired by the BLM. The trapper had become a friend and lived off and on at Smith Mesa, parking his trailer next to Bill's.

"He caught fifteen coyotes on my property a few years ago," Bill said. "Then ten the next year. Then five. Last year, I'm not sure he caught any. Coyotes get blamed for a lot more than they do."

Last fall, Bill had lost a calf at Beavers and found it half-eaten by coyotes.

"I don't think the coyotes killed it," he said. "I think it died some other way and they just came to clean up."

Bill worried more about people than coyotes. More and more were coming, leaking out of Zion and finding their way to the sprawling landscapes on its edges. There were no fees, no crowds, and plenty of places to get lost in the wilderness. There were more empty cars parked at turnouts, for days at a time, and Bill sometimes stumbled upon people camping in the pines and on the shelves of the wash. It was a nuisance, finding trash on the ground or gates left open, but he was used to that. Things had gotten worse.

Just recently, the trapper found one of Calvin's pigs shot, and two others were missing. Then Bill found one of his calves shot in the shoulder, near the branding pen. Bill sometimes wondered if cattle that he never found, presumed dead in the desert somewhere, were actually stolen. A cow could feed a family for a year.

"I'm asking people in the area to write down license plate numbers," Bill said. "I called Fish and Game, and they're doing more patrols. They don't care so much about cattle. But I told them that I bet they'll find a bunch of deer shot and left there, too. People are just doing it for sport."

His voice rose and his words quickened. "That's a lot of money gone," he said.

A couple years earlier, in the middle of summer, Bill got a call from someone near Smith Mesa who said he had one of his cows and its calf. Right before that, another neighbor said he had three of Bill's cows, but no calves.

"That's fishy," Bill said. "I got a ninety-percent rate. But then I go to pick up that pair, and down at the bottom end by the creek, I see it looks like some cows had made a trail in there. I decide to go back and look around. I come across three calves, with my neighbor's brand on 'em, suckin' on my three cows. I went and talked to him, and his son was there, and I told him, 'I'm takin' those calves. They're mine.' His dad called before I got them to the brand inspector and said, 'Well, I sure don't want any problems.' I had the proof. When a calf is suckin' from a cow, that's proof."

Bill took a deep breath and turned back to the work at hand. The next heifer in the squeeze chute nearly slipped through before the gate and got caught by its back hips. Jesse tried to grab it around the neck like a steer wrestler and shove it back into the chute. The animal thrashed him against the fence, lifting Jesse's boots off the ground like a movie serpent.

"She fuckin' bit me!" he shouted.

"It's all right," Bill said, and he hinted at a smile. "You hurt your knee some more?"

"No, but I hit my back on these things," Jesse said, pointing at steel rods that stuck out of the chute. His shirt was wet with cow slobber. "Glad I brought two shirts."

Another cow trapped in the chute got eyeballed closely by Bill. He hadn't seen a calf with her.

"She pregnant?" Jesse asked.

Bill rolled a sleeve to his armpit. "Hold her tail up," he said.

He stood behind the cow and pushed his hand into the cow's ass and slid the full length of his arm inside. If she was pregnant, he would feel an umbilical cord through the inside wall. The thickness of the cord would tell him how far along she was. Sometimes you could feel the shape of the actual calf inside.

"Feel one?" Jesse asked.

"No," Bill said, and he slowly pulled out his arm, coated as if he had dipped it into a deep bucket of brown paint.

By seven o'clock, twelve hours after the work started, the corral held twenty head ready for auction the next day. About forty pairs of cows and calves were turned out in the pasture at camp to water and feed, and they would go on the first truck in the morning. Sixty yearlings were turned out in the lower pasture. The horses were watered back at camp as the late-day sun sizzled on the Zion cliffs. Smith Mesa was the rare place where the best view of sunset was facing east. Jesse pulled a Coors Light from the cooler of his truck. Spencer grabbed a rifle. He wanted to see if he could find coyotes over the cliff where Calvin's horse had fallen a couple weeks before.

"You serious?" Jesse said. Afternoon had turned to dusk. "It's like a mile to that ledge."

"Yeah, but I brought my tennis shoes," Spencer said, and he sat on a rock and swapped out his boots for white sneakers. "I'd like to try."

Bill warmed water over the propane stove of the trailer and used it to wash his hands. He began cutting potatoes into chunks with his knife. If he was close to selling Smith Mesa, if this was one of the last seasons he would run cattle on land his family had run for seven generations, he wasn't acting nostalgic. His father had homesteaded not far away, back in the days when the government offered 320 acres for a farm or 640 acres for a ranch, and they grew small grain— winter wheat, mostly, but later barley and millet. They put the cows on the wheat stubble and hogs behind them, and when the snow flew, they'd pull the hogs. For years, they ran fifty head of cattle year round and harvested tons of wheat. But things were drier now, and fifty head of cattle wouldn't be enough to support Bill and Evelyn, never mind the families of some of their children.

Calvin left to spend the night down in Hurricane, and Spencer came back through the dark without having spotted coyotes. He and Jesse built a campfire while Bill grilled burgers. Kruz went to bed in Spencer's truck, and Bill and two of his boys sat in the glow of the fire, telling old stories.

From over the edge of the wash, coyotes howled.

"Probably thirty of 'em," Bill said with a smile.

■ ■ ■

The next morning, everyone was back at the corral by the time the cattle pot rumbled up the road. The quiet man from Colorado City nimbly backed the two-deck trailer toward the ramp. He stopped it just as the steel bumper kissed the logs that framed the opening.

"How did you do that?" Calvin asked, amazed. The man shrugged. He and Calvin loaded up one deck and waited for Bill on the other side of the corral to decide which other cattle he wanted to include in the load. Calvin asked the man whether he thought the goiter-faced cow would be OK for eating. The man said he didn't really know.

Both decks were loaded within minutes, and the truck disappeared down the red road again, on its way to Cody. Bill backed his rusty trailer against the corral, and the boys helped him load twenty head of yearling steers to take to auction in Cedar City. Bill drove down the road, keeping all the wheels out of the sun-hardened ruts with one hand on the wheel. He drove into Virgin, turned right in La Verkin, away from Hurricane and through Toquerville, and pulled over before he got onto the interstate. He looked at the tires, and felt them with his hands to see if the bearings were hot. He squeezed into the shadow between the truck and the trailer and relieved himself. Soon after he got onto the highway, headed north, his phone rang. It was Calvin.

"They must be in the dry wash, is what I'm sayin'," Bill said. It had been a hard year of pulling the herd out of the wash, because there was feed and puddles in the shadows of the rock walls. Calvin wanted to know if his father wanted him to go dig deep in the canyon for more cattle, but Bill wasn't worried about leaving strays at Smith Mesa for a time.

"Well, a couple a guys can go in there and try to find 'em," he said, "but I don't think we'll have time today."

He holstered his phone and realized that cars were flying past him. He was driving fifty-five in an eighty-mile-per-hour zone. "I don't drive very fast when I bullshit. Evelyn says I don't multitask."

About an hour later, he pulled into the dirt lot of the Cedar Livestock Market on the west side of town. It was a building with a coffee shop in front of a maze of corrals. There was no one around—no branding inspector or anyone to give Bill a receipt. Bill unloaded his cattle into a chute and pushed them into a pen and closed the gate. He started to pull away, and then stopped. He climbed over a fence and wandered through the maze, opening gates, and then pushed his cattle farther, to a pen with water and feed. That bit of extra weight might bring another few bucks a head at the auction the next day.

The young steers weighed about six hundred pounds, Bill figured, less than half of what they'd grow to. He liked to keep his yearlings until fall, when they were about fifteen or sixteen months old and when they might weigh eight hundred pounds. You didn't get as much money as you would if you held on to them a few more months until they were fully grown, but you got more per pound. And when you included the extra cost of feed and permits and so on, the math showed that sixteen months and about eight hundred pounds was the optimal time to sell. That's how Bill figured it, at least.

But he didn't have enough summer feed at Beavers this year, because the big reseeded parcel was still off-limits. Bill expected the year-old steers would sell well, because they were healthy and had a lot of frame on them. He figured someone would buy them and put them on a range for a few months, just like Bill would have done, and then either sell them or send them to a feedlot for finishing rations for 120 days.

Whether they would eventually become choice beef or prime beef depended on how they'd be fed from there on out. Those labels weren't predetermined, and Bill didn't have much to do with it, either. But the steers were Black Angus, which had some marketing cachet that Bill himself thought was a little ridiculous, and they were grass-fed. *Angus* and *grass-fed* were trendy buzzwords.

"I've had steers like this sell for three dollars a pound," Bill said. That meant those twenty steers could fetch $36,000. "But I don't think it'll be that high. But they'll go for a premium. That's what these grass-fed people are looking for."

He closed off all the gates and left a voicemail for the man who ran the auction. Halfway back to Smith Mesa, Cody called. He told his father that a cow had come off the truck at Beavers with a calf sticking a quarter of the way out of it. She came off the ramp, lay in the grass, and gave birth. The calf had already started sucking for milk.

"Boy, I'm lucky she didn't have it in the truck," Bill said. The cow and the calf probably would have been trampled. "Anyway, all's well that ends well."

■ ■ ■

As he left behind the last of the small houses at the edge of Virgin, heading to Smith Mesa, Gooseberry Mesa came into view about five miles to the south, on the other side of the Virgin River. A road cut up its front face, a vertical stripe to the flat top, where a nephew had a permit that he let Bill use. The nephew had sold the permit a while back, but the guy who bought it let Bill use it. During the winter, Bill had driven a hundred head from the creek at his lower corral, across the Virgin River, and up that road. It was not prime grazing country, not as good as Smith Mesa, but it helped in a pinch as Bill's herd grew in a land of tightened options. Bill wasn't sure how much he'd be able to use it in the coming years. He heard that the BLM was trying to buy it back, figuring there was a better use for it than a bunch of cows.

More and more mountain bikers were coming to Gooseberry Mesa every year, including for an event called the Red Bull Rampage, one of the most daring and dangerous contests in the world. People saw this landscape now on YouTube, and outfitters were crowding into Hurricane, and there were hotels and fast-food joints and coffee shops sprouting up all over this side of Zion, and Bill saw firsthand how ranching and farming were not the future here. Not anymore.

The left side of the road, toward Smith Mesa, was a bigger worry. The county decided to improve a scraggly little road that went six miles into the dry wash, to a place where an old oil well was capped. Bill couldn't get an answer as to why. There were already strands of bike trails. There was a campground and a smattering of new houses along the road. People were coming.

He was already backed against the border of Zion, and the squeeze felt tighter than ever. Bill remembered the national park expanding its borders when he was a kid, swallowing up some of his father's land on Smith Creek that had once had a cabin belonging to John Doyle Lee, executed for his part in the Mountain Meadows Massacre of 1857. He couldn't help but worry that Zion might grow again. After all, the federal government seemed to be adding parkland all over the place, and especially in Utah. And if Zion didn't expand out, well, the outside world was closing in.

"That's the thing I worry about," Bill said, his elbow out the window. "They might think they've got a different and better use for this land than me. The thing is, those people are illiterate when it comes to cattle. They see these plants and this dirt and these cliffs and think this area is no good. But it's some of the best range in the country. You just have to know how to work it."

He got nervous every time one of his permits came up for renewal, because the government rarely added AUMs. It usually subtracted them. That meant that, even if he kept the rights to the same amount of land, the number of animals he could put on it trended downward. On one of his permits near the corral, at the edge of Zion, Bill was told he had to cut his AUMs by seventy-five percent, from twenty-four to six, because of the expanding deer and elk populations in the area. They ate some of the same plants as cattle. Bill threatened to fence his private property, which would impact their migration and access to water. The government responded by keeping the AUMs the same, for the time being.

"This private land gives me a lot of leverage," he said.

During the last National Finals Rodeo, a BLM ranger called to say that it looked like Bill had too many horses at Smith Mesa. She said he was only supposed to have six, but there were about twenty.

"I was so mad I decided I better not call her back, or I'd say something I'd regret," Bill said. "They don't get it. I called her after I got home and I said, 'Look, I have 72 AUMs for horses there. I put them horses down there on December 1. It hasn't even been a month, and that would be 20 AUM.'"

He smiled. "She's left since then," he said. He had outlasted them all, for now.

The cattle pot rumbled uphill for one last load to Beavers. Calvin steered the cattle onto the truck from his horse, and Bill, Jesse, and Spencer moved the cattle from pen to pen. Bill needed to figure out which ones went to Beavers now and which ones could wait a few more days, and which pastures to put them in so that he could gather them up quickly when he came back in a few days.

It was impossible to be precise. Bill had a series of permits for the winter months, and different ones, a hundred miles away, in the summer months. Each of them had their own restrictions on how many animals they would allow and when they would allow them. Bill needed to divide the right number of cows and calves and yearlings and bulls into all those fixed parameters. And not every head was equal—in the math of AUMs, three pairs of cows and calves were the same as four yearlings, for example.

Bill also wanted to sell off a few of the aging cows in the herd and replace them with promising heifers from the batch of yearlings. Bill had built his herd with Black Angus bulls and Hereford cows, because he was told long ago that it was the best cross for his type of operation in terms of size, quality, value, and temperament. He decided he wanted the newest cows to the herd to all be black, because those seemed to fetch better prices. Bill examined cows and looked for the healthiest all-black heifers. It was like a beauty contest to see who made the herd.

Calvin noticed the goiter cow in one of the temporary pens.

"You know he's gonna leave us to take care of her," he said to Spencer. "He's getting soft-hearted in his old age."

Bill coolly shuffled cattle from one pen to another inside the corral, and when he looked to have it figured out, Calvin began hustling the batch headed for Beavers into the chute to load into the cattle pot. In moments, that end of the pen was chaos. Dust swirled. Bill snapped.

"Slow down!" he shouted at Calvin.

"I thought we needed these eighteen on the truck!" Calvin

shouted back, and he thrust his horse into the center of a scrum and shouted for Jesse and Spencer to open one gate and shut another to keep two groups from mixing together. His brothers didn't move. They knew not to do anything until Bill told them to.

"God almighty, we're figuring it out!" Bill shouted at Calvin.

The men shuffled cattle back and forth, cutting them into subgroups inside the corral, sometimes swapping one animal for another. After the cattle pot was loaded and gone, the dust had settled, and Calvin was out of earshot, Bill turned to Spencer.

"Geez, Spencer, what'd you give him?"

"He said he had two and a half Sparks and a Crystal Light," Spencer said.

"He said he felt like he had fourteen cups of coffee," Jesse said.

"I'll say," Bill said. "He was going wild. Took a loud voice to slow him down."

Bill looked at one pen of cattle divided from the others.

"How many do I still have in here?" he asked himself as he counted with his chin. "Eleven? And one yearling? Shit. Do I not have a bull?"

Bill shook his head in exasperation. "All that back and forth, and I didn't leave a bull with these cows? I'm gonna have to bring one back."

"What're you going to do with this cow?" Spencer said, pointing to the one with the infected jaw. "Kill it?"

Bill thought for a moment. There was no time for that now. "Just let it out," he said. "I'll deal with her when I come back down."

15

Muffled Cracks

THERE WAS A CRACK when he hit the dirt, and when Cody went to grab where the pain came from, he could feel that the bone under the skin of his shoulder was in two unmatched pieces. That's when he knew for sure he was out, and in that moment he couldn't help but think that his time had ended just as Rusty's had started and Ryder's was about to. Maybe bronc riding wasn't something you did with your kids, but something you passed down.

Cody had been riding well, making money in Denver and just about every other place. He got to Fort Worth, one of the biggest rodeos on the circuit, and rode a tepid horse. The judges gave him a re-ride. Re-rides were tricky. You didn't have much time to learn anything about the bronc, and since the rodeo never slowed down, the re-ride just fit into any gap in the program. You felt like you had to get ready in a hurry.

Even Cody wasn't immune after all those years. The back cinch of his rig came undone in the middle of the re-ride. His saddle became an ejection seat, and it shot him off the front of the bronc and into the dirt.

He was lucky to have Rusty and Ryder there with him. Rusty was competing. Ryder was watching, having finished school midway through his senior year and waiting for his eighteenth birthday to come a few weeks later so that he could turn pro. But now their father was crumpled in the dirt, trying to make sense of the mismatched collarbone under his snap-button shirt. Suddenly, their three lives looked to be going in about a million different directions.

The boys drove Cody home to Utah through the night. The doctor in Cedar City put a plate and a few screws into the shoulder and told Cody he'd probably be out at least a couple of months.

The night after Cody got hurt, there was a baby shower for Rusty and Morgan, their baby due in a few weeks. While he waited for his baby to come and for his father to mend, Rusty went out and won rodeos in Rapid City, South Dakota, and San Angelo, Texas. He took big money in San Antonio. He went to the big rodeo in Houston and scored 81, 81, and 83 in the first three rounds to win his group. He flew back home just in time to see the baby born.

Rookie Scott Wright, they called him. The first name was Sha-Ree's idea. Then Rusty hustled back to Houston, where he won the finals and collected $29,000 and headed back home.

Ryder turned eighteen that week and got a permit to compete on the pro rodeo circuit. He needed $1,000 in winnings to be able to buy his card and start accumulating money in the official standings. He went to his first rodeo in Goliad, Texas, won the thing, and earned $902. Then he went to El Paso and won that one, too. That made him $541. Just like that, he could get his card. So he did, and he won in Cave Creek and Lubbock, and he began to climb the standings, chasing cowboys who had started the season months before.

It was a strange and eventful spring for all the Wrights, as if life was a deck of cards that needed shuffling once in a while. Jake won the Fort Worth rodeo, where Cody got hurt, and Alex earned a lot of money there, too. Jake, CoBurn, and Rusty were all ranked in the top ten, and Alex was in the twenties, thinking that maybe this was the year that he, too, made the National Finals.

But Jesse and Spencer were stuck in rodeo purgatory, nowhere in the rankings. Jesse couldn't ride until the first of March because of the surgery on his shoulder back in the fall. Even without that, he and Spencer were locked out of rodeos because, against Cody's advice, they had joined the Elite Rodeo Athletes tour. The ERA had dropped its lawsuit against the Pro Rodeo Cowboys Association, and as a result, the PRCA could keep out anyone with ownership shares in another circuit. So Jesse and Spencer gave up their ownership stakes to be able to compete in both, and devoted most of their energy to the PRCA.

"You can't make money just on ERA unless you've got an oil well in the backyard," Cody told them.

Cody, now a grandfather, was ready to ride broncs again by early April, and he drove down to Logandale, just on the near side of Las Vegas. He won the final round and the average and got $3,850. The same weekend, Rusty flew to Florida and was in Kissimmee for the circuit finals. He won the semis and the final round and got a check for $21,168. And in California, in a soaking rain in the Sierra foothills town of Oakdale, where the signs on the rodeo grounds proclaimed it to be the cowboy capital of the world, CoBurn, Jake, Jesse, Spencer, and Alex all finished out of the mud and in the money. Everyone was riding again. Everyone was healthy. And the chase was on.

■ ■ ■

It was a perfect, room-temperature day in Clovis. Behind the chutes, the conversation among the bronc riders turned to baby powder, as it sometimes did.

"I got baby powder, but it's not the silky soft," Jesse said. "It's frickin' terrible."

"You got that cheap Great Value stuff?" Rusty asked.

"No, it's Johnson & Johnson," Jesse said, reaching for it in his bag. "But it's not the silky soft."

"I didn't know there were two kinds," Rusty said.

"This one sucks," Jesse said. "It totally binds my latigo."

The smell of manure and baby powder filled the air as Jesse got on Lunatic Fringe, a top bucking horse. The best riders knew they'd draw any given bronc maybe once a year, and it hurt to squander the opportunity on one like that, especially for Jesse, buried at the bottom of the standings. Jesse withstood a huge skyward jump out of the chute that left him parallel to the ground, staring at the sky and holding on by just his spurs and his rein. A couple more big lunges and Jesse had an 82.

"God, it's such a sweet-ass horse," he said afterward, and adrenaline still bolted through him as he shed his chaps.

Rusty climbed atop Lunatic from Hell, the son of Lunatic Fringe, and didn't act nervous for the chance. The announcer, in the booth above the chutes, raised his voice in excitement as the action bounced away, and the crowd, a quiet one on a lazy afternoon, sensed something different from the other rides.

"How many? How many? How many?" the announcer shouted, and the score popped up. "Eighty-eight points! Way out front!"

Rusty smiled. No one would touch that score. He'd get $7,022 for it and move into the top five in the season standings. Halfway through the season, he almost had enough money already to qualify for the National Finals. He just had to stay healthy.

There was no time to waste. It was nearing four o'clock. By the time the calf roping ended, with the bleachers full of people and the parking lots filled with empty cars, two truckloads of Wrights were gone, on their way south to Springville. Cody, Rusty, and Spencer had a six o'clock rodeo to make. It was rodeo's version of a double-header, and most of the other bronc riders hustled out of Clovis, too. Jesse, Alex, and CoBurn weren't up until the next day, but they needed a place to sleep. Springville was as good as any, with its little rodeo arena wedged into a small hollow, its grandstands nothing but wood benches set on a natural hill.

Cody scored 78. Spencer got dumped at the seven-second mark and came back muttering to himself. Rusty had a ride that didn't stand out and wouldn't win any money.

"Man, rodeo is humbling," he said, tipping his hat back. "An 88 one ride, a 75 the next, in the same day."

The rest of the rodeo continued, now under the lights. In the shadow of the parking lot, the boys stood in circles at the back of trucks, talking with other bronc riders, most of them tugging on cheap beer.

"Spencer, should we go to Auburn?" Rusty whispered. Spencer paused. He usually let things sink in, which gave him the appearance of moving at a slightly slower speed than the world around him.

"We're only three hours away," he finally said. It was more than four, really, but it might as well have been next door, in rodeo geography.

Rusty hadn't been home in more than a week, and he had a new baby waiting for him. "Yeah, but that's three hours we could be closer to home," he said.

"Whaddya got in Auburn?" another rider asked, overhearing the conversation.

They talked about the bronc draw and compared notes. The

boys tried to decide if one more rodeo was worth it on this trip, or if they'd hit the point of diminishing returns. It wasn't just money they were calculating, but time.

In the end, before the rodeo ended in Springville and the cars snaked out of the lot, creating a rural traffic jam on the two-lane road leading out, Cody, Rusty, and Spencer were gone. When they got out of the little valley, they did not turn south toward Bakersfield and the route back home to Utah—they turned north toward Auburn. Rusty won the little rodeo there. He got the $820 first prize. Cody and Spencer got nothing.

■　■　■

Back behind them on a Saturday night in Springville, Jesse and CoBurn sat at a picnic table in an area cordoned off for contestants. Two women in a little booth served them spaghetti and bread on paper plates. Jesse and CoBurn talked about CoBurn's grandmother. Jesse knew her well because he had dated CoBurn's older sister for a time.

"Man, I loved her noodles," Jesse said as he smothered his spaghetti in ranch dressing.

"You remember, she also made those sourdough pancakes," CoBurn said.

"That's the first time I had anything sourdough," Jesse said.

Jesse was five years older than CoBurn. When CoBurn was about twelve, he tagged along with his sister and Jesse one night on a four-wheeler. They spotted a coyote. "Hold the wheel," Jesse said as he stood up and kept his foot on the gas. Moving at full speed, Jesse shot the coyote with a .22.

"Luckiest shot I ever seen," CoBurn said, retelling the story between bites of spaghetti. "Best shot I ever seen. But the coyote was still alive, so we go back and Jesse has his foot on it, holding it down, and he tries to cut its neck. The thing was squealing so loud. It took forever. I thought, 'Man, this guy is crazy.'"

Jesse and CoBurn's sister didn't stay together. Now, a few years later, Jesse was married, and he and Aubrey had just had their third baby, and CoBurn was married to Jesse's sister Becca, and they had a one-year-old girl and another baby on the way.

"A small world," Jesse said.

"A small county," CoBurn said.

Alex sat down with Ace, his toddler son, who had spent the evening wandering around the chutes in chaps and a tiny protective vest, like his dad. His little boots had tiny spurs. The bright lights of the of the arena were clicked off, and the reminiscing turned to rodeo and all the places where they'd slept on the road and all the campers they'd crammed into for a few hours of sleep. One well-worn story was about another bronc rider who woke up with Alex, dead asleep, spooning him from behind. What woke the guy up was that he had Alex's finger in his mouth. Everyone at the table laughed.

CoBurn told about how he broke his tailbone on a fall when he was fourteen. For years, when he rode broncs, he would reach back and push the loose fragment that floated around out of the way. Finally, a doctor took it out.

"I kept it," CoBurn said, and having such a conversation over a meal didn't strike anyone as unusual. "I keep it in a jar. Since it wasn't connected to the blood supply, it was all dead. But it had this shriveled-up meat on it. So I boiled it off. I grabbed a pot that I'd never seen my stepmom use. Then I cleaned it real good. I bleached the bone with peroxide."

By ten, Alex and Ace were sitting in the front seat of CoBurn's truck, lit by the glow of a DVD player mounted on the dashboard, playing *Lonesome Dove*. Ace fidgeted in the driver's seat while Alex propped his feet on the open window frame, a cigarette dangling out the truck door. The Coors Light was gone, so CoBurn went to the back and found a twelve-pack of Keystone Light and sat in the back seat of the cab.

They knew the six-hour tale by heart—the old Texas Rangers Gus and Call leaving Lonesome Dove, the epic cattle drive through the plains north to Montana, the death of Gus, and Call's pledge to return him to Texas to be buried. After a while, they decided to watch something different. CoBurn dug out a huge case of discs from the back seat and flipped through them. About half of them were old Westerns, the others forgettable comedies of more recent vintage. They decided on *Paint Your Wagon*, but after a few slow minutes Alex popped it out of the player and they decided to watch *They Call Me Trinity*, a spoof about a couple of outlaws defending a band of Mormons.

"This movie's hilarious," Alex said. More than his brothers, Alex had the look and mannerisms of Bill. He walked with his arms out and his chest up, like someone entering a rough and unfamiliar saloon. His mouth didn't open far when he spoke, and his voice had a bit of gravel to it. His natural expression was a faint and crooked scowl. But he intimidated only those who hadn't met him. The smile clicked on like a lightbulb, and he had a hearty laugh.

By midnight, Ace was asleep in the driver's seat, and the boys decided to go to bed in the camper. They left their boots at the door and hung their hats on hooks, next to a rod that held their pressed rodeo shirts. Alex, Ace, and CoBurn slept in bedrolls on a huge mattress that extended over the cab of the truck. Jesse had gone to town with some bull riders, and when he came back, he slept in the back seat of the cab.

They stepped into the daylight of Sunday morning to the sounds of a sanitation truck emptying the portable toilets and generators humming electricity into nearby campers. Horses roamed loose. The lot was emptier now than it had been at midnight, and more cars and trucks were leaving. The lot was sprinkled with piles of beer cans from where cowboys had partied and slept before heading out.

After a bit, an announcement advised that church services would start soon on the other side of the arena, followed by the faint sound of country gospel. A hot breakfast was served at the booth, and the boys sat at a picnic table. Ace ate instant oatmeal sprinkled with Doritos. A cowboy sat down without a smile.

"You go out in Clovis last night?" CoBurn asked him.

"Nah," he said. "You?"

"We came down here to watch Cody and them," CoBurn said. "We just watched *Trinity* and *Lonesome Dove* and went to bed."

The cowboy nodded knowingly.

The rodeo started at two. CoBurn popped out from behind a gate atop a bronc called Silk Tassel. It was a good, clean ride with a bit of a stall in the middle. The judges gave it 83.5 points. The announcer told everyone it put CoBurn in first place, and then moved on to the next contestant.

"He is part of the Wright family, a brother-in-law of the man you're about to watch," the announcer said. Alex settled into his saddle, and CoBurn was already by his side, helping him get adjusted. Jesse leaned in and tugged. The horse was anxious and banged against the metal chute. Alex grimaced, and when the bronc settled for just a moment, he raised his hand, leaned back, and nodded. The score came back as a 72.5, not good enough for any money.

Alex was in a cycle where he was riding well, but not getting much attention from the judges. He had won in Glen Rose, Texas, but otherwise was usually hoping just to get in the money. He had Megan and two young boys, and the dream of the rodeo and the stability of the concrete business made for a difficult dance. Another season was drifting toward concrete.

"Nice ride, Alex," CoBurn said afterward. He had won the $921 first prize.

"That thing came out of the chute queer," Alex said.

"It bucked queer," CoBurn said. "Did this little sideways thing. A little hop-skip. I thought you rode it good. They coulda given you more."

Alex shrugged. They walked back toward the truck, carrying their saddles. Ace followed along. They dropped their gear in the dirt and went about cleaning it. They used lighter fluid to remove the sticky rosin, and stretched their reins and cinches and folded them neatly. Alex shook his head and started talking about his stirrups.

"I can't decide to let 'em out or tighten 'em," Alex said.

"I thought you got 'em right," CoBurn said. "You wouldn't be able to spur 'em like you did."

"I don't know," Alex said. "That was a stocky horse."

CoBurn looked over at Alex, trying to read his face.

"Don't be getting headsy on me," he said.

The truck pulled out of the lot before the rodeo ended, and when it got to Porterville, it turned toward home, not another rodeo. They all had young families to get back to, if only for a day or two. It would be a long summer.

■ ■ ■

Rusty heard it, a muffled crack, but he wasn't sure what was broken. He'd bucked off and landed in the dirt, and when he tried to move, he could feel the bones in his left leg grind together. He didn't know that a bone was sticking out of the skin above his ankle, under his shin guard and his sock and his boot. He didn't know that both his tibia and fibula were fractured. But he felt something wet inside his sock. He just about got sick to his stomach.

His mind raced, even before the medics got to him. Rusty was in second place in the saddle bronc standings. In those helpless moments in the dirt, he realized that his chances of riding in the National Finals Rodeo were probably over. His hopes for a world title were broken in pieces at a little arena in Bremerton, Washington, in late August.

He had been on Urgent Delivery, a big bay bronc that had bucked off Spencer at the Calgary Stampede. Rusty had never been on it. He got a little forward midway through the ride, up and out of his saddle, and when he spurred his legs back, his left foot caught underneath him. He sat back down, heard a snap, and tumbled to the ground.

"My butt broke my leg," he said.

He waved for medics. Cody and Spencer were there, behind the chutes, and Cody knew Rusty was hurt because he could see it in his son's eyes. Rusty was lifted away and helped into an ambulance, and on the way to the hospital, Cody told Rusty about the time he had broken his tibia and fibula. Doctors put a rod and screw in it, and Cody missed a few months and came back, about as good as new. Rusty worked the calendar in his head: September, October, November, December. He had a little more than three months.

Then Rusty casually told the medics in the ambulance that his foot felt wet, and they cut off his pants and cut through his boot. That's when they saw the bone sticking out. Cody almost got sick. Rusty couldn't look. Surgery couldn't wait. About midnight that night, Rusty posted a photo to Instagram and his twenty-five thousand followers, showing him in a hospital bed, Cody sitting by his feet, the left one wrapped thick in bandages.

"Had some bad luck here in Bremerton, Washington, tonight! Going in for surgery! Get patched up and be ready for the finals come December!"

Among the comments were those from ShaRee ("Love ya bud!") and Morgan ("I love you Rust!") and other bronc riders like Jacobs Crawley ("Get well soon my friend") and Heith DeMoss ("Dead gum it! Get well soon").

ShaRee posted the news on Facebook. "I know this is part of the game and things like this happen but it's never an easy pill to swallow," she wrote. "I am just so thankful that it's only a break and he will recover and with God's good grace he will hopefully be back riding at the NFR! You can't keep a good man down!!!"

Rusty tried to be optimistic. "I must have needed some time off," he told *ProRodeo Sports News*, "and now I have it." Miss Rodeo America came to visit him in the hospital, and she and six other rodeo queens surrounded his bed for a photo. Rusty smiled with his foot wrapped and his thumb up. "Rusty is in great spirits and already talking about his plans for Vegas," ShaRee wrote on Facebook. "Please keep him in your thoughts and prayers as he heals."

■ ■ ■

By then, Cody was long gone. He and Rusty had talked about it in the hospital. Rusty was in the National Finals, easily. He would make Las Vegas as long as he was healthy enough to ride. Cody would make it only if he got on the road immediately. He needed a big push to get into the top fifteen by the end of September.

Ryder did, too. He had made his move in June, when he won in Delta, Utah, and placed high in Reno. At the start of July, in West Jordan, Utah, Cody, Rusty, and Ryder went one-two-three, and by the time the onslaught of rodeos during Cowboy Christmas ended, with Ryder winning in Elko, Nevada, Cody and Ryder were ranked in the teens. For the first time, it seemed possible that Cody would not just return to the National Finals, but compete alongside at least one of his sons, and maybe two.

What Cody didn't tell anyone was that his ankle had been broken in August, and he wasn't sure it would hold up. He had gone weeks without a win, or even so much as a decent paycheck, and didn't have time to get it fixed or let it heal. When he got to Bremerton, he was out of the top fifteen. He got fourth place and $732 the night Rusty was hurt. He needed a lot more than that.

ShaRee's brother offered to drive to Washington and bring Rusty back home to Utah. So Cody left and headed to more rodeos, in Utah, Colorado, and Idaho. And when Cody won almost $12,000 in San Juan Capistrano a few days after leaving Rusty behind, he practically secured his place in December. Cody and Rusty, father and son, had qualified for the National Finals.

Ryder faced more of a scramble. He won in Heber City and Douglas. He nosed into the top fifteen at the start of September, but fell back out by the middle of the month. He had $60,000 in official winnings, but that wouldn't be enough. Ryder had established a pattern of either winning or getting bucked. There weren't a lot of conservative rides, the kind that got him a few hundred bucks and slowly added up over the course of a long season. Ryder made money in bunches, between droughts. With just a few weeks left, there was no time for no-scores, and not a lot of time for middling ones.

Cody saw Ryder suffering, quietly and stoically, with the pressure. There was a unique anxiety to searching for a perfect eight seconds and then spending the next twenty-three hours and fifty-nine minutes thinking about the next chance. It wasn't easy, as Cody knew better than anyone, to push through the pains and sleepless nights of aches and worry, all for the real possibility that it wouldn't be enough, anyway.

When Cody was twenty-five and had three young boys at home and had yet to reach the National Finals, he finished sixteenth in the season standings. That season hurt as much as the world titles felt good. And now he knew it hurt more to watch your sons go through it than to experience it yourself.

"What you're going through now is why I wasn't sure I wanted you to rodeo," Cody said to Ryder. "Because I've been through this and I know what it feels like."

But you couldn't stop when you'd come that far. In the middle of September, they hired a six-seat charter plane so that Ryder, Jesse, and Jake could fly from the short round in Pendleton to the rodeo in St. George. Jesse won in Pendleton, and that clinched his spot in the top fifteen, a big comeback after a slow start of his own. Cody drove the distance in the truck and met them back in Utah. The pressure was on Ryder. He needed a few thousand dollars in the last two weeks of the season.

He did it by taking second place in four consecutive rodeos in four different states. He got second in St. George, Albuquerque, Othello, and San Bernardino, all in the space of a week. They weren't big rodeos, but they added about $7,000 to his season total. It was enough to leapfrog Ryder from seventeenth in the rankings to thirteenth, right when it mattered. Ryder became the youngest of the 120 rodeo contestants, across all events, to qualify for the National Finals.

"And then there were six," *ProRodeo Sports News* reported. CoBurn had passed Rusty for second place. Rusty was in third, Jake in fifth, Jesse in tenth, Cody eleventh. Ryder ended up fourteenth. Alex, in thirty-eighth, and Spencer, in forty-fourth, each won more than $20,000, but fell short of qualifying for the National Finals.

No family had ever come close to dominating a rodeo event they way the Wrights had smothered saddle bronc. Ryder was the rookie of the year, just as CoBurn had been the year before and Rusty the year before that, and Spencer two years before Rusty and Jesse three years before Spencer.

But the season had shown something else. Rodeo could be passed down, like a family tradition, like land and manners, but it could spit you out, too, without warning. Rodeo was rooted in the past, but it had no sentimentality. All the years and all the successes, all the rides and sweat and blood and miles on the tires bought you no guarantee beyond the next stop. Cody was a rare survivor. Everybody else had better start thinking about what happened if the next ride was the last.

16

Missions

A FEW DAYS AFTER finishing third in Utah's high school rodeo championship behind Ryder and Stetson, Stuart received a large, white envelope in the mail. It came from the Church of Jesus Christ of Latter-day Saints in Salt Lake City. Bill and Evelyn had raised their children with the Book of Mormon and a forty-four-page booklet called *For the Strength of Youth,* which established standards of behavior and expectations. It had sections on dating, dress and appearance, education, entertainment and media, family, friends, gratitude, honesty and integrity, language, music and dancing, physical and emotional health, repentance, Sabbath Day observance, service, sexual purity, tithes and offerings, work, and self-reliance. It encouraged clean living. It warned against the use of tobacco, alcohol, and drugs, and the evils of pornography and homosexuality.

"My children have grown and have used their agency to choose their own way," Evelyn wrote in a letter about her faith, with the elegant cursive handwriting of someone who teaches it to grade-school children. "At their core, they are still Latter-Day Saint people, with strong pioneer blood running through their veins. On both sides of their family, our forefathers were pioneers, full of faith and sacrifice. When I read their story, I am amazed at their fortitude. They were forever firm in their faith and sacrificed all for their beliefs."

She took a picture of Stuart holding the envelope and told family and friends that he had received his mission call from the church. None of the Wright boys had served a mission. Cody had planned to when he was young, and he used to sneak into his father's pants pockets after Bill got undressed at the end of the day and take the coins out. He told his mother he was saving them for his mission. Bill said that Cody just always knew how to work his mother.

Cody went on to rodeo instead, finding no time for a mission, and his brothers followed. If Evelyn was disappointed that they didn't take religion as seriously as she did, she never showed it. She figured she had infused them with faith and knowledge, and it would build inside of them as they grew older and they had children of their own.

But there was something about Stuart, the last of the thirteen, the last of the boys, growing up under the expectations set silently by his older brothers, but doing something so different than all of them.

The house filled with people at three the next afternoon, and they sat in a circle in the living room and crowded into the doorways and down the hall and into the kitchen. Bill thought that Stuart would get assigned to somewhere in Canada, because when he first got a passport the year before, it was just for Canada. They got it so he could go to the Calgary Stampede to watch his older brothers ride.

Evelyn started to record on her camera. "All right," she said. "OK, Stu."

Stuart, in a blue T-shirt, Wranglers, and a silver rodeo buckle, stood and read from the letter. "You are hereby called to serve as missionary of the Church of Jesus Christ of Latter-day Saints," he began.

When he got to the part that said "Ghana," Evelyn whispered, "Ghana?" and laughed a bit under her breath.

"Where's that?" several others said. Stuart kept reading. He was to report in October. "Watch out, Ghana," Evelyn said. "Here comes Stu."

While his brothers and two of his nephews—all the young men in his immediate family—spent their time trying to earn their way to ten days in Las Vegas, Stuart spent it preparing for two years in Ghana. On a day in October, Bill and Evelyn drove Stuart up to Provo and pulled up to the curb at the Missionary Training Center.

"They don't even let you say goodbye," Bill said.

"We pulled up and popped the trunk, and he took out three roll-on bags," Evelyn said. "I hugged him quick, kissed him on the cheek, and he was gone."

And six weeks later, Evelyn was in a fancy hotel room in Las Vegas, just her and Bill, preparing to watch three of her sons, one of her sons-in-law, and two of her grandchildren compete in the $10 million National Finals Rodeo, and she was reading emails from her baby boy in a tiny village in Africa. The emails from Stuart came only on Mondays. For the first few weeks, they were long and full of details about the living conditions, the work he was doing, how hot the weather was, and how kind the people were that he met. Every week, though, the notes got shorter. Bill and Evelyn weren't sure if that was because he was busier or was just running out of things to say.

Evelyn cried as she opened up the latest email. "How're you gonna replace a kid who sings at the top of his lungs in the shower, who sings the national anthem at the football games, who dances around the kitchen because he knows how to swing dance like no other?" she asked.

Bill put his arm around Evelyn. A housekeeper knocked on the hotel room door, opened it, and said that she would return later. Evelyn read the email to Bill. Stuart had written that he would be thinking of everyone at the rodeo in Las Vegas. He had been there, too, most years of his life, watching his brothers compete, thinking that someday he might be there in the chutes, not in the crowd. Bill and Evelyn figured Stuart would come home in two years and go to college. He had a standing scholarship offer for rodeo from a small school in Arizona. But two years was a long time, especially away from the influences of family and culture. They could only guess what Stuart would become.

In the email, Stuart didn't say much about his brothers competing in rodeo.

"Tell Calvin I'm rooting for him half a world away," Stuart wrote.

Evelyn sighed. Bill clenched his jaw and shook his head. Calvin was in jail in St. George.

"I'm the one who put him there," Bill said, and he pulled Evelyn close.

■ ■ ■

Most of the fall, Rusty wasn't so sure he'd be riding in Las Vegas with everyone else. When he got home to Milford, his shin was bowed back, kind of concave, and his foot was cranked out to the side, with his toes pointing out. It was as if someone had screwed his lower leg onto his knee, but stopped before it was tight and pointed forward. And it hurt like hell. X-rays showed that the breaks weren't lined up. The doctor in Cedar City said that if he didn't try to fix them, Rusty might never be right.

The doctor took out the eight-centimeter metal rod, fitted the bones back together tight in the three places where they broke, and secured them with a ten-centimeter rod and new screws. He wanted to see Rusty back in six weeks, which would take him into November. The National Finals started on the first of December.

So Rusty sat in his little house on Milford's Main Street as fall came, the leaves turning and the winds getting colder, while his dad and Ryder scrambled to the season's last rodeos, and Stetson and Statler went back to school and played on the football team, and Grandpa Bill began pushing the herd down from the pine forests at Beavers ahead of the winter storms. He was stuck doing nothing, which didn't feel right at all, and he was stuck at home for weeks in a row, which was strange, too.

Rodeo took the boys away for more than two hundred nights a year, a lot of them between about March and September. Rusty got to spend more time with Morgan and Rookie than he had in the six months since the boy was born. But there was an unnaturalness to the new rhythm of life, and it put a strain on Rusty's long relationship with Morgan. After six months of taking care of Rookie on her own, she had Rusty to take care of, too. She didn't feel fully appreciated. Come to think of it, she never really had. She was a safe anchor back in Milford, stuck in place while Rusty chased his rodeo dreams. She felt like little more than an option in Rusty's life, not the center of it, not even a partner. He'd never married her, after all. He had plenty of chances.

By the time Rusty turned twenty-one in November, Morgan was gone. She and Rookie moved back to Minersville to live with her family there. She changed her hair from platinum blonde to jet black, as if to highlight the mood. They stayed friendly, though, and the door felt open to a reconciliation. Morgan brought Rookie to Milford often, and Rusty was at his happiest when he was with his round-faced son, waiting for the bones in his ankle to grow back together and a chance to see if he could ride again.

It struck Rusty that his father had gone to twelve National Finals Rodeos in a row, didn't get to his first until he was twenty-six, and won his first world title when he was thirty-one. Rusty was still a decade away from that age, and already he wondered how much luck and grit it would take to last. With some of his winnings the year before, he bought eighteen head of cows and a bull for the herd. Now he, too, was not just interested, but invested. He didn't know for sure that ranching was what he wanted to do down the road, after rodeo ended. He and Ryder thought they wanted to be stock contractors, to raise the kinds of broncs and bulls that they grew up riding. That seemed to go pretty well with raising cattle.

"Maybe we can do both," Rusty said. "I don't mind what my grandpa and dad do with the cattle. I still want to be in rodeo when I'm done rodeoing."

The day before Thanksgiving, Rusty, Stetson, and Jake drove up to Ogden, about four hours away. A stock contractor friend met them at the indoor arena there, and Rusty got onto a bronc for the first time in three months.

"Pull! Pull!" Jake shouted at Rusty, and Rusty pulled hard on the rein and kicked his feet forward and back, again and again. "Yeah!" Jake screamed as Rusty rode away and made it through without a hiccup. Rusty pronounced himself ready for Las Vegas. It hurt when he pointed his left toes out on the bronc's neck, and his entire leg hurt the next day, but Rusty didn't see those as adequate reasons not to join his brother and dad in Las Vegas and see if he couldn't win a world title.

■ ■ ■

Calvin had spent time in drug rehabilitation, but when he came out, he fell in with his old crowd in Hurricane and Milford and into his old habits with booze and drugs. The episodes grew scarier, more violent, and more tortured, with Calvin tearing apart rooms and screaming at invisible demons.

Bill confronted him one night in Milford, and the two stood toe to toe, screaming at one another until the cops came. Bill told them to take his son away. He figured jail had a better chance of keeping him safe and steering him straight than anything else.

But a girlfriend bailed him out, which disappointed the Wrights, and Calvin went back to Hurricane, where nothing got better and the demons got worse. Cops came again during one fit, and they found drug paraphernalia and a torn-apart house. Calvin was in jail again, and Bill and Evelyn weren't sure how long he'd be there. But they hoped and figured it was for the best.

Bill hadn't talked to Calvin. "He's madder'n hell at me," he said. Evelyn heard from him time to time, when he could make a call, and she told Calvin how much she loved him, and he said the same back to her and tried to make her laugh.

And in the hotel room in Las Vegas, waiting for the next round of the National Finals Rodeo to start, Evelyn sat at the table, writing an email to Stuart in Ghana and a postcard to Calvin in jail. The only postcards she found to send him had pictures of towering sandstone formations, like the ones near Smith Mesa. They were postcards of Zion National Park.

17

The Kid

CODY'S FIRST RIDE took the early lead. He rushed back to the chutes, past Bill at the gate, and found Ryder was in Chute 2, on top of a horse called Times Up. Cody squeezed past a cameraman, who didn't want to miss what was to happen next, either, and leaned in over his son. He told him to hold his feet and then get them moving. It was just another ride, he said.

For Ryder, everything up until then felt like it always had, every year since he was five. There was a drive to Las Vegas, a long overnight stay, daily afternoon trips to the arena for a night of rodeo. But instead of sitting in the stands, watching with his mom, brothers, and little sister, Ryder was on a horse, and everyone was watching him.

Ryder wasn't that nervous, but he knew he should be. A year before, Rusty bucked off in Round 1, and it ended up costing him the world title nine days later. The misses cost you more than the makes get you. But Ryder was in fourteenth place, somewhere in the happy-to-be-there pack. Only Ryder didn't think that way.

The announcer said something to the crowd about Ryder being the youngest cowboy there, about competing in high school rodeos all summer, about his famous father and his famous uncles and his older brother and Utah and whatever else. Ryder didn't hear any of it. He had his one hand on the rein, the other on the gate, and he looked across the arena to see that it was all clear. He wiggled hard into the saddle and clenched his thighs against it. He leaned back and raised a hand in the air. He nodded. He had no expression at all. He looked like he was in the backyard ring in Milford.

The horse swung out to its left with a leap, and Ryder's spurs were dug into its neck when its front feet hit the dirt. The first three jumps were tight knots, but then Times Up stretched its legs and bucked and kicked hard across the dirt, angling to its left as if it was out of alignment. It was all big jumps and high spurs, the only glitch about midway through, when Ryder's boot stuck on the saddle the way Rusty's had in August, but it only cost Ryder a stroke. It didn't matter. The crowd knew it. It cheered before the eight seconds were spent, and the volume level doubled as Ryder slipped onto the back of the pickup man and landed on his feet.

Cody spent the ride shouting, his insides and his face contracting with every buck, and when it ended, he ran behind the chutes to the gate next to Bill with a huge smile. Ryder acted like nothing special had happened, but the faces of his father and grandfather gave away the secret. Cody smiled bigger than he ever did for one of his own winning rides.

"How about 87 and a half points for the high school kid!" the announcer shouted, and Ryder had knocked Cody out of the top spot. Cody gave Ryder a fist bump, because even if Ryder didn't quite grasp what had happened, his father sure did.

"Just shows you that he's got ice water in his veins," Rusty said after he swallowed Ryder in a bear hug. "I was watching him up on the big board and he just leans back and nods. I was like, 'Bear down!'" Rusty laughed. "He's so mellow."

The first-night scoreboard was lit up in Wrights—Ryder, Cody, and Jake going one-two-three—when Rusty's turn came. "His younger brother is winning the round, his dad is second, and his uncle is third," the announcer said, and it sounded as ridiculous as it looked in the lights.

Rusty had been on just one horse since he broke his leg in August and the bone came through his skin. He was yanked out of Chute 7, next to Bill, who couldn't hold his stoic look and cheered the kid on. Rusty's ride took him diagonally across the arena in powerful arcs, and he didn't feel the pain in his leg through all the adrenaline. It wasn't until he landed and walked off with a limp that he felt it again. The score was 82.5, good for fifth place, a much better start than the year before.

"This man shattered his leg in about twenty-seven places," the announcer said as a send-off, and every night when it was Rusty's turn, that number grew.

Ryder got the victory lap, and he circled the arena on a horse just as he had seen his dad and his uncles do so many times, and Rusty and CoBurn the year before. He waved his hat and pumped it toward Section 110, where his family sat—where *he* would have been sitting, had he not squeaked in back in September. He dropped his saddle in the locker room and was taken immediately for interviews, the first one on the live broadcast.

"It's awesome," he said. "You know, it's something I've been dreaming about since I was a little kid." A man escorted him down a back hallway, where Ryder stopped for another interview, and another, and another before he landed in a big gym that had been converted into a press room. He was surrounded by reporters, and they wanted him one at a time. At one point, Ryder stopped himself in mid-sentence, because he realized he had used "awesome" about a hundred times and probably needed a different word. Most reporters asked what an eighteen-year-old would do with a $26,230.77 first-place check. Ryder said he hadn't really thought about it.

"When it comes to talkin'," one reporter told him, "you say a little more than Spencer, but maybe not as much as Jake and Jesse."

And when it came time to take the stage at the South Point, Ryder was no longer just another face among the Wrights, lined up perfectly in order of their ages like the children in *The Sound of Music*, as Flint Rasmussen said. He was the man of the moment, handed the microphone. He coolly introduced everyone there, flubbing only when he called ShaRee by his girlfriend's name, Cheyenne. Everyone laughed.

"Gimme a break, it's my first time," Ryder said, and he kept on going.

Afterward, ShaRee held the whisky. Lily asked Ryder why he called their mom Cheyenne. Ryder wondered aloud if the buckle was going on his belt or on his wall. And Bill remembered that, the year before, he was at the South Point six times. "This year, we're going for ten," he said, and it sounded like a joke, but it wasn't.

The Wrights smothered the world standings behind the leader, Jacobs Crawley. CoBurn was still second, Rusty third, Jake fourth. In one night, Ryder had gone from fourteenth in the world standings to sixth. Cody was seventh. But if any of the overnight hoopla rattled Ryder, he didn't show it. He went out in the second round and rode Get Smart, the three-time Canadian bucking horse of the year. The two popped out of Chute 7, and Get Smart was as consistent and jerking as a cardiogram. The bronc threw Ryder's hat off and did a looping clockwise circle until it deposited him in front of Chute 3 a hair after the buzzer, barely heard over the roar of the crowd. The score of 86 took over first place and held on to it. Ryder won again.

"I seen him once with my dad," Ryder said afterward. "I don't remember what year it was, but he circles and circles. Not very many horses get my hat off, but he did. I just kept throwin' my feet to the front."

Two rides had almost doubled his season earnings, and Ryder leapfrogged up the standings again, right behind Rusty, who bucked off. CoBurn bucked off, too.

"All year, I been fightin' to get into the top fifteen," Ryder said. "Then I came here, and in two rounds I go up to number four. It's awesome. I guess everybody's gonna get pretty good Christmas presents."

Two nights in, Ryder was the story of the rodeo, the buzz of Las Vegas, and the kinds of people who wore cowboy hats into casinos talked about the Wright kid, about the show he was putting on, about how he might be better than them all. And one day bled to the next and the next, as it did in Las Vegas.

■ ■ ■

On the third night, a Saturday, as Ryder rode straight away from the chute on Lipstick N Whiskey. Cody was left behind to gyrate and pantomime his son's moves. The horse did a few midair twists, then jumped ninety degrees to its right, but couldn't shed Ryder. Cody and the stock contactor hugged as Ryder came off the pickup man and landed on his knees in the dirt. He pulled his mouth guard out, slipped it inside his vest, and stood. Fans were already on their feet.

"Give it up for the kid!" the announcer shouted above the commotion. "Oh . . . my . . . goodness!"

If there was lingering doubt that a transition to a new generation of Wrights had taken place the year before, all while the old generation was still in its prime, there was no doubt now. Ryder was the first rookie to win the first three rounds of a rough-stock event at the National Finals. Only three saddle bronc riders had ever won the first three rounds, and the other two were in the Pro Rodeo Hall of Fame.

On the fourth night, Ryder in second place in the world standings, the building buzzed as he climbed aboard Sundance. It was the same horse Rusty drew the year before in Round 4, and Rusty won with an 85.5. It was the same horse Cody had ridden to victory in Round 4 ten years before. As Ryder had done each of the three nights before, he calmly nodded, held his feet on the bronc's neck, and pumped his way to the winning score, an 85.5, just like Rusty.

Cody was so excited that he left his chaps behind the chutes and didn't realize it until he got to the locker room. He came back out and ducked behind Ryder as he was being interviewed on television.

"I took 'em off to help and forgot 'em," Cody said. He beamed. "Rookie move."

"But you get a cut of his winnings, don't you?" a man asked.

"I wish," Cody said, and ducked past Ryder again to stay out of the television shot.

The whole week had thrown Cody off. He had never competed with his sons at the National Finals, and now he was there with two of them, and his mind was scattered. He worried more for them than he did for himself. Before that night's rodeo, he arrived without his number badge, the one he had to pin to his back in order to compete. He hadn't done that since he was a rookie. ShaRee had to drive back to the hotel to get it, and she missed the start of the rodeo.

A television crew attached a microphone to Ryder's shirt, and a cameraman followed him through the back hallways and listened in on his interviews. Ryder got handshakes and fist bumps from most everyone he passed—old contractors, young bull riders, people he had never seen before. A rodeo clown in full makeup stopped to congratulate him outside the medical room, where Cody was prone on the table, getting his neck worked on.

Only Robert Etbauer, twenty-five years before, had ever won four saddle bronc rounds in a row outright, the way Ryder had. No one had won five in a row. And while Ryder finished first-first-first-first the first four nights, none of the other saddle bronc contestants had even been in the money four times.

Ryder was still second in the standings, behind Crawley, but his average put him first in the projections. Reporters wanted to know what his family thought about it all, what he would do with the more than $100,000 he had made in the first four nights, and, mostly, how he explained his extraordinary success.

"I must be livin' right," he said to the first.

"Well, whatever you're doing, don't change it," an interviewer said.

Ryder got more talkative every night, and he told reporters that he might buy a nice truck with his winnings, and that he didn't feel too bad about not giving anyone else in his family a chance to win. He invited them to finish second any time they wanted. One reporter wanted Ryder to detail his workout routine and the prep work he did each day. He tried to avoid the topic, a bit embarrassed that his pre- and post-ride meals had been McDonald's or Jack in the Box every day, and that he never worked out.

"I shoulda given her a bullshit story," he said as he walked away.

And for the fourth night in a row, Ryder took the limo to the South Point, introduced everyone on stage, was rewarded a buckle and a bottle, took the limo back to The D, ate something, and went to bed. He didn't change anything, mostly because the same thing kept happening and there wasn't a whole lot else you could do after midnight in Las Vegas when you were eighteen.

His draw the fifth round, Spring Planting, was an all-or-nothing ride, a familiar bronc to the Wrights. Cody rode it hurt in Round 10 two years before, and Jesse won a round on it the year he won the title. The horse wouldn't align itself straight in the chute, and Cody leaned in to try to tug it upright. It got settled eventually, and Ryder leaned back and nodded. But the first big jump pulled Ryder forward, and it looked like he might go over the top, like a biker over the handlebars. He managed a couple more bucks before he dumped off the side, his winning streak done in the dirt. Fans gave him a standing ovation, knowing that something historic had come to an end.

In his hotel room the next morning, Bill complained about the judging. Cody and Rusty missed their marks the night before, according to the judges, a huge blow to their championship hopes. "I'm going to make a copy of the rule book and highlight the part about the mark out and give it to them judges," Bill said.

"To qualify," the Pro Rodeo Cowboys Association rule book read, "rider must have spurs over the break of the shoulders and touching the horse when horse's front feet hit the ground on its initial move out of the chute." If the horse stalled, it added, the rule could be waived. That happened to CoBurn the night before. He had a flag, finished his ride, and found out that his score counted. But cowboys usually saw the yellow flag out of the corner of their eye, and it took some discipline to keep the ride going as if they hadn't.

Bill had seen questionable mark-out calls cost Cody a couple of world titles, and Jake one, too. He didn't understand why mark-out calls shouldn't be subjected to video review. Even some small rodeos had started doing that. Bill went to a rodeo over at the Orleans Hotel and Casino that day to watch Spencer ride, and it allowed cowboys to request a review. A lot of sports, from football to baseball, had replay reviews. With the technology available, and with the stakes growing higher, it made no sense to Bill that the premier event in rodeo couldn't keep up.

"It's bullshit that you can't challenge it," Bill said. "It not only costs you day money, up to $27,000 here, but it costs you in the average. A world championship shouldn't be riding on one guy's judgment. That's horseshit."

A lot of rodeos, like the Calgary Stampede and the big indoor one in Houston, didn't even have a mark-out rule. Cody always wondered if it made sense to abolish it. If you didn't mark the horse out, he figured, then you missed a stroke and you were going to be out of balance and rhythm for a bit, anyway. The score would show it. The Elite Rodeo Athletes made a rule that a missed mark didn't disqualify a rider, but cost him ten points. That kept him in the average, at least.

Cody kept those opinions to himself. Rodeo was run by old-timers, and tradition trumped change. The National Finals had been run almost exactly the same way every year he'd been there, from the prayers to the pre-show entertainment to the grand entry to the structure of events, the announcers, the music, the post-rodeo interviews, the locker rooms, the people who trolled the back halls. Only the contestants changed, but not even them so much.

They still timed steer wrestlers and calf ropers to the tenth of a second, by hand, and there were ties practically every night. Bull riders and bronc riders had no recourse if the calls were wrong, even if everyone at home knew it. But there was no serious talk of changing anything. Rodeo didn't care much for controversy. It cared less for complaining.

Cody never said much, but the rules were impacting his boys. Cody started to see what got his dad fired up all those times. It was different when it was your kids.

Ryder missed his mark out the next night. So did Jake, who had been leading the average. "That could be a $70,000 bobble right there," the television commentator said. Rusty had a great ride going until his foot slipped out of the stirrup, which threw him off the horse just before the buzzer. Jesse scored out of the money. Only CoBurn and Cody made something, but not much.

When Cody got to the parking lot afterward, ShaRee was in the truck, keeping warm from the unseasonable chill in Las Vegas. Cody stood at her window, and someone asked about his missed mark out the night before.

"I was mad about it all night last night," Cody said, "and I was mad about it all day. Then Rusty showed me a replay and I said, 'Oh. Well, I guess I did.'"

He smiled. He knew he needed to stay positive to keep his boys focused.

"I don't mind getting called when I miss it," he said. "I just wish they'd be consistent with it."

ShaRee wondered if people weren't just tired of the Wrights. She couldn't help reading comments on social media, and there were some who said that the Wrights got all the breaks, and that Cody's boys were there only because their last name was Wright. No matter how many times Rusty or Ryder won, people wondered if they weren't somehow given an advantage by judges.

"I can handle it when they talk about Cody," ShaRee said, "but when they start talking about my boys, my mama bear comes out. It's hard not to respond. But they're just couch jockeys. They don't know."

"Look at this," Rusty said, interrupting. He had been staring at his phone, looking at video replays, and now he thrust it in front of his mother. "Ryder didn't miss him out!"

The bronc had hesitated, which might have earned Ryder a wave-off of the rule, but it didn't. The bronc took a couple of strides out of the gate, and Ryder's spurs were up on the neck. When it bucked the first time, hardly its initial move, Ryder clenched. Sha-Ree fumed. Cody shrugged.

"Nothin' you can do about that," he said. "Nothin'."

■ ■ ■

For the second night in a row, none of the Wrights earned a trip to the South Point. They all returned to The D. The casino had put ads for the Wrights all over, on billboards and marquees, and the boys couldn't go far without seeing themselves smiling back at them. As part of the deal for the rooms and the money and the promotions, some sampling of Wrights signed autographs at The D every afternoon.

A tall, round table was set up at the edge of a bar and within reach of slot machines. It didn't seem to matter that Ryder was eighteen. People wanted to come see him, sitting next to his dad and brother, to shake his hand and get his autograph on a National Finals program and take his picture and tell him how much they enjoyed his first four nights.

On other days, Jake and Jesse sat there, or it was Alex, Spencer, and CoBurn. Over the course of any hour, the line waned and the boys sat awkwardly as people milled around them, carrying buckets of coins. If the gamblers noticed the cowboys in their cowboy hats at all, sitting in front of a banner with their pictures on it, they looked at them confused and blended back into the machines. Sometimes, a minute later, there was a line, or some old man in a cowboy hat telling old stories.

Sponsorship obligations never stopped. One afternoon, all the Wrights and CoBurn were at Cowboy Christmas to sign at the Wrangler store. The line to meet them was deep, and others crowded around, which drew others to wonder what everyone was looking at and just added to the crowd. Some stood back, afraid to approach, so they took pictures and whispered to friends about which one was which. Morgan was among them, holding Rookie. Bill and Evelyn stood to one side, talking to friends.

Evelyn didn't show it, but her ankle throbbed from standing on the hard convention center floor so long. She had broken it just before school started, on a four-day ride up at Beavers with Bill. They were doing an eighteen-mile loop, putting out salt, when Bill's horse kicked up some ground wasps. Evelyn's horse began jumping and bucking before she understood why.

"Get off!" Bill yelled, and Evelyn stepped off fine, but that was when she realized she was in a swarm of wasps.

"The wasps bit me all over, even on my lip," Evelyn explained as her boys signed autographs. "It looked like a bad Botox job."

When she backed away and turned to run for the wasps, her foot got caught in a fallen log. She felt two pops. She and Bill rode five miles down to their camp at Duncan Creek, and Evelyn slid off the horse into Bill's arms. He carried her to the truck and drove her down to the emergency room in Cedar City. That was why she was on crutches on the first day of school, and she still didn't think it was healed right.

A woman interrupted. "Can I just come over and shake your hand?" she said. "I just think you are the most wonderful mother in the world."

Cody, Rusty, and Ryder were guests on Flint Rasmussen's daily talk show from the convention center, in front of a few hundred people and broadcast on television. Before the segment with the Wrights started, Rasmussen welcomed everyone back from the commercial break.

"And thanks to the guy in the front row with his arms crossed, looking so excited," Rasmussen said. "Oh, that's Cody Wright's dad."

They talked about Rusty's broken leg, and how Cody gagged when he saw it. Rasmussen asked Cody if he was distracted from his own riding because of his boys, and he said he probably was, but he didn't admit to forgetting his number badge in the hotel or losing his chaps behind the chutes. Rasmussen razzed Ryder about finishing second in the high school nationals. Rusty, still sore about the night before, said that some people thought he and Ryder were successful only because of Cody.

"Ryder, you won what—$114,000 this week?" Rasmussen said. "We know it's because of your dad."

"They're just insulting the judges," Ryder said.

Rasmussen ended by asking about other Wrights. Cody said he expected Spencer back at the National Finals, and Alex could be there, too. And Stetson was maybe two years away, if he got serious, he said.

"Great," Rasmussen said. "We'll have, like, ten Wright brothers. Everybody else will just quit."

■ ■ ■

The best ride of the National Finals that didn't count for anything came that night. Ryder came out on Killer Bee, a rank bronc with a history of big wins and, mostly, big falls. Its back feet kicked high above Ryder's head, and its jumps had such hang time that the animal might have spent more time in the air than touching the ground. Killer Bee carried Ryder to the middle of the ring. People stood, recognizing that something special was happening.

About six seconds in, Killer Bee stopped moving forward and bucked and kicked straight up in the air, throwing Ryder around like a rag doll on a trampoline. He lost all control of his upper body. His feet kept moving, but his head snapped back and his free arm flew around like a pinwheel. The buzzer sounded and fans erupted as they had for no other ride. There was talk that the ride would score in the nineties, maybe threaten the all-time rodeo record.

But there was a flag down. Late in the ride, a judge ruled, Ryder's wild off hand brushed Killer Bee's side. The ride was awarded no score at all. Most of the fans didn't see the flag, and their standing ovation nearly drowned out the news from the announcer.

"Fans, he slapped him with his free arm," the announcer said, and he repeated himself so that everyone heard. "But if you think you know the heart of a champion, let's tell Ryder Wright he's a special young man."

Ryder walked gingerly to the gate to the type of ovation few ever receive.

"That horse was scared of you," Bill told Ryder. "It got sick of the iron you were puttin' to him."

After the last saddle bronc ride, the officials huddled on the outside of the fence near the chutes. They assured themselves that it was the right call. There was no restitution if it wasn't. Ryder wasn't really sure. In the parking lot, someone asked him if he touched the horse during the ride.

"That's what the judges said," he said.

"He's learning," Cody said, and he seemed as proud of the boy for staying on as he did for winning any of the four rounds before.

"It just seems to be chicken or feathers," he said. "I hope he keeps lettin' it all hang out. You can't be playing it safe, just takin' mediocre rides."

CoBurn won that night, the seventh, getting the Wrights back on a winning streak after two nights off. Crawley had a big lead in the standings, and Ryder was second, his hopes for a title likely detonated by three straight no-scores. CoBurn was in third, in line to make money in the average, but he needed broncs to dispatch Crawley a time or two, and maybe Zeke Thurston, the young rider from Alberta, who was in fourth but leading the average. Jake still had an outside shot. Rusty was in sixth, and his riding was as unsteady as his limp.

It was coincidence of the draw the next night that landed Cody on top of Lipstick N Whiskey, the same horse Ryder won with five nights earlier and the one that Rusty won with in Round 8 a year before.

"I'm excited to get on her and see if I can still ride," Cody said.

Cody and his boys sat together in one corner of the locker room, the familiar corner to the right where the Wrights usually parked themselves, year after year. Cody asked Ryder his rein, and realized that Ryder had never asked *him*, even though Cody had been on Lipstick N Whiskey plenty over the years and had notes on the bronc in his book. Ryder told him X plus 2. That was a bit longer than Cody had, but he joked that Ryder was younger and more flexible and could lift and move in the saddle a bit more than Cody could anymore. Still, of all the brothers and sons, Ryder rode the most like Cody. They were cool in the chute, keeping their upper body still and their arm in the air as if they were holding a platter of drinks that they didn't want to spill.

Cody rode the horse even better than his boys. Judges gave him an 88, and Cody had his first National Finals go-round victory in three years.

"That's a thirty-nine-year-old bronc rider on the high-mark horse of the rodeo!" the announcer said, and Cody received the kind of warm ovation reserved for familiar and respected champions.

He got the victory lap and took his time in the interviews, as buoyant and talkative as he'd ever been, especially when he was asked about the boys, which he always was. As long as they tried as hard as they could, Cody said, he didn't care what happened. He praised Rusty for toughing it out and still doing well, even though his title hopes were gone, still broken in that dusty arena in Bremerton. He said Ryder was going big or going home, having won four times and then getting no-scores four times, and that made him proud, too.

"I don't think there's anything better than watching your kids do good," Cody said.

He credited the boys with helping him, too. They motivated him to stay in rodeo, to keep riding and competing. And now that they were every bit as good as he was, just a lot less experienced, they helped him out.

"Just because I've been doin' it twenty years don't mean I know everything," Cody said. "Don't tell them I said that. But I learn from them. I ask them how I look, and they tell me what I'm doin'."

Ryder drew a bronc named Alpha Dog on the second-to-last night. He had never been on it, but Cody had a few times. He told Ryder that it bucked flat, and that if you didn't stay back, you wouldn't be able to spur very high. He said to keep his head down and throw his feet as hard as he could.

Ryder did as Cody said, and he won the go-round. And even though he probably wouldn't win the world title, he was the breakout star of the rodeo. Before Ryder, only Billy Etbauer and Dan Mortensen ever won five rounds in saddle bronc at the National Finals, and they were in the Hall of Fame.

"To be born into this family, to have all this help all the time, whether it's in the practice arena or driving down the road or behind the chutes, you can't ask for better," Ryder said.

An interviewer tried to put it in perspective. He told Ryder to imagine that he rode for twenty more years, and kept riding well enough to win at the National Finals, and had some boys along the way who got so good that they got there and won, too, at the same time. Ryder didn't know what to say. He admitted that it was all a little hard to believe.

The final-night math was hard to figure. Crawley held a big lead and was second in the average, a combination that made it almost impossible for him to lose. Ryder, CoBurn, Jake, Rusty, and Cody were all in the top seven, but only CoBurn had a real chance. He'd probably need to win the round and have Crawley buck off.

But CoBurn had bad luck in the draw and an ordinary ride in the arena. Jake bucked off. Rusty and Ryder both got called for missing their mark outs. Thurston put himself in the picture with a big ride. Crawley just needed a score to win and hold off the coming onslaught of Wrights for the second year in a row.

He was on Spring Planting, the same horse that had ended Ryder's four-night winning streak a few days before. The bronc hesitated, and when it sparked to action, it nearly got hung up on the open gate. Crawley clenched his boots to hold on. A flag dropped. The mark-out rule wasn't waved off, and Crawley finished the ride and slumped out of the arena. He had led the standings all season long, all the way through nine nights of the National Finals, but lost on a missed mark out. Thurston slipped past Crawley in the standings by $2,831.39. He was world champion.

Among the Wrights, though, the night belonged to Cody. He won the tenth round with the best score of the rodeo, a 90.5 on Wound Up. He ended up in sixth place in the world standings. All of the Wrights finished in the top 10—CoBurn third, Ryder fourth, Jake eighth, Rusty ninth, and Jesse tenth. A keg and some bottles of whisky made their way into the locker room.

Cody slipped out to meet ShaRee in the parking lot. Rusty and Ryder had come out, too, not much for the beer chugging and wrestling going on back in the locker room. There was no buckle ceremony at the South Point on the final night, and Cody realized that he hadn't picked up his go-round buckle, the fifteenth of his career. He didn't want to go back in. Everybody would want to stop and talk.

"Hey, Stetson, do me a favor," Cody said. "Go back in there and ask someone where it is and get it for me, would ya?"

Jake came out to sneak some friends into the locker room to the party. He said that they'd talk their way past the security guards, and the group headed down the dirt ramp, past where trucks waited for the livestock to be loaded, and disappeared into the bowels of the arena. Cody shook his head. He was mad at Jake because Jake didn't show up to the autograph signing that day at the Wrangler booth.

"That reflects on all of us," he said. "And now we have Stetson coming up, and I don't want anyone to think any less of us. We should leave things better'n we found 'em. That's what Dad always says. If you're doing something, whatever it is, even if you're just spending the night at someone's house, leave it better'n you found it."

A truck pulled up next to Rusty and a window opened.

"Hey, are you Ryder?" someone asked from inside.

"No, I'm Rusty," Rusty said with a smile.

"Oh," the voice said, and the window went up and the truck drove away. Cody thought it was hilarious.

"Champ to chump in a jump," he said.

As Cody stood there with Rusty, waiting for Stetson to come back with his buckle, he couldn't help but wonder how many more times he would be there, in that arena parking lot, having just won at the year's biggest event alongside his brothers and sons. It was the kind of moment he never expected, and he had no real reason to expect it again. Cody was riding better than he had in years, but he knew that the next ride could be the last. That was true for any of them, really. Rodeo had a funny way about it. It made no promises. Momentum came in eight-second bursts, nothing more. Maybe this was it for him. Maybe there would never be more Wrights than this competing at the National Finals. Maybe this was as good as it got.

ShaRee put on Cody's leather contestant jacket to fend off the night's chill. She and Cody talked about all the things they had to do now that the National Finals were over. The kids had to get back to school and make up all the work they'd missed. They needed to check on all the animals, the horses and goats and dogs, including a new litter of puppies. There was unpacking to do and Christmas gifts to buy.

And there were rodeos between then and Christmas—a big one in Montana the next weekend—because the season never really ended. Rodeo never stopped until you decided it did. And Bill still had some cows at Beavers that he needed gathered and brought down to Smith Mesa. Cody planned to help, maybe when the kids were at school.

It felt like a straddle of time, and Cody recognized it. He'd just competed with his kids, not against them, at the biggest event in the sport, and they had done him proud. Just as he thought about the National Finals, and wondering how many more he had in him, he considered Smith Mesa, and how many more times the family would gather there. Someone was going to come along and offer a price that his dad couldn't refuse. Someone else was going to offer a place that Bill couldn't resist. He just knew it.

"I try not to stick my nose in it," Cody said. "But I like that we have that place—a place where we can all go and be together."

Stetson returned with the buckle. The parking lot was mostly empty and the cool air was still and quiet. The lights of the Strip glowed to the west. Cody and ShaRee realized that they were alone among the Wrights. All the other brothers would come out of the arena and want to go hit the blackjack tables and drink and be out till dawn. The kids were in the truck, which was running with the heater on.

"It's our chance to get away," ShaRee said. "We can go sleep."

Cody smiled. He never gave the impression that he was in a hurry to leave, and he seemed especially content there in the night. It was just another rodeo parking lot, but it felt like a moment to cherish and hold, or at least slow down a little. The moments, they piled up fast, and the world changed with every passing one. You couldn't control them all. You could try to guess where the few moments of a ride would go, but you didn't really know. You could try to steer your kids through the countless moments of childhood, but you couldn't always say where their lives would end up. You could try to pass something down from generation to generation, a million moments tied by blood and tradition, but you couldn't know where it all would lead.

Cody carried his buckle and followed ShaRee to the truck. He drove his family away, and the moment went with them, rolling toward the next.

EPILOGUE

THERE WAS A LOW SPOT on the property, just before the southern edge of Smith Mesa crumbled toward North Creek. All those Wrights all those years ago ran cattle from Virgin, up the creek, across the mesa to Kolob Terrace, before any of that land belonged to any of them. For years now, almost forty of them, a big swath of it was owned by Bill and Evelyn Wright.

Rain and snowmelt drained into the low spot and made a pond that sometimes went dry, more these days than it did a few years ago. There used to be a one-room cabin next to the pond. Bill's parents had built it with friends in a single day, as a homestead to claim that part of the mesa. The cabin stood there for years, until Bill and his father lifted it up on logs and dragged it uphill, a mile deeper onto the property, into a shaded hollow.

It still stood there, tucked against a hill, facing the red cliffs of Zion. No one had lived in it for decades. Its windows were broken, and its floor was covered in droppings and pieces of the ceiling and walls that crumbled from the unrepentant force of time.

But it was where the family gathered for the yearly branding—or used to, when they still held it on Smith Mesa. They parked their trucks and campers in the meadow, set up camp around a fire ring, and ate meals together there. There were kids and grandkids and horses. In the mornings, everyone walked up the hill to the flat spot where the big basin of water was and where the horses were kept and where Bill parked his trailer to stay in the winter. In the evening, they gathered again for dinner, and Bill usually led the prayer.

Bill wanted to stop by Smith Mesa with Evelyn on the way home from Las Vegas. Most of his herd was there, brought down from Beavers before Thanksgiving, but he hadn't checked on it for almost two weeks. He worried about the usual things—water, mostly, but also the feed and the fences and the gates. Someone had called and said they had a cow of his, and Bill wanted to fetch her. He'd probably be spending more time at Smith Mesa than usual this winter, because he had an idea, and the plan was already percolating. There was something he wanted to try.

Evelyn knew about it, and Cody, too, but he hadn't shared it with many others. He had been chewing on it for some time, giving it a lot of thought as he wandered around Smith Mesa on horseback, wondering how it was all going to go when push reached shove and Bill was faced with offers he couldn't resist or shouldn't refuse.

It always felt wrong that the Wrights were being forced to make a decision between the past and the future when, in their minds, they were the same thing. This land, their land, had only outlived its usefulness in the minds of outsiders. All they wanted to do was something much like what their ancestors had done: raise cattle and build something together. It wasn't that the Wrights had changed.

The outside world had changed, and it closed in on them and threatened to chase them away.

Maybe it didn't have to be that way. Maybe, Bill figured, the future didn't have to be one or the other, but everything.

That little cabin in the hollow gave him an idea. Las Vegas was just a couple of hours away, and more and more people were coming, including tourists from around the world in search of the last vestiges of the shrinking American West. More were coming to St. George, and more still were coming to Zion in record numbers. But there weren't a lot of choices for places to stay. Springdale was clogged with motels, and Hurricane and St. George, too, but there was nothing unique about another Super 8 or a Hampton Inn. There were campgrounds scattered about, but besides those in the national park, they were either in hard-to-reach places, designed for backpackers and adventurers, or roadside ones, for motor homes.

A woman had approached Bill a few months back, looking all around the region for a place to set up some tents for tourists. She talked about big tents, the kind with a pole in the middle and with wooden floors and cots, maybe each decorated with a different theme. She was thinking about ten or twelve of them, available for nightly rental in the spring. Bill would get a cut. Bill pondered it for a time. He didn't see what he had to lose. He thought the end of the property by the hollow might be a good place for them, in the shade and with the views of Zion out the front flap. He told her she could do it come spring.

And he started thinking that he and the boys had plenty of horses, and it wouldn't take much to offer horseback rides to any tourists who came along. He could do them in the spring, the same time as the camping, before the heat and the gnats got bad. If enough people signed up in the busy season of summer, and it was worth his while, he could come down from Beavers to lead them around. Bill knew the land better than anyone, and he knew a few trails he could loop together and just how long it would take to ride them.

A few other places did horseback rides, but Bill figured he could offer something different. The tourists could help him round up cattle. A real cattle drive, with real cowboys, against the backdrop of Zion. Bill figured people might pay a hundred bucks for a couple of hours, and if he got groups of six to go, and did it three times a day, well, then he might have something.

None of it would take much investment or extra work, he thought. He could probably do most of it himself, but some of the boys were usually around, too, especially in the spring before the rodeo season got too busy. And Cody's boys could help sometimes, and Calvin's oldest was about to be sixteen, and he was a good kid and lived pretty close. And if Calvin could get himself right, the tourists would love him and his funny stories and his good nature.

Bill wasn't sure how much he wanted to advertise the family name and its saddle bronc success when it came to all that. It went against his nature, such self-promotion, but maybe folks would like to know that they could ride alongside real rodeo cowboys, and not just any rodeo cowboys, but world champions, the best bronc riders around. Bill asked around to some friends for advice. Yeah, people told Bill. To stand out, let people know that these are the Wrights— *those* Wrights. There was no harm in that. Bill still wasn't sure. It felt like bragging.

He hadn't told most of his boys about all of that. What he decided about Smith Mesa wasn't theirs to haggle with, not yet, and he might not need to get them too involved at the beginning, anyway. It might just be a temporary thing. Maybe nobody would sign up. Maybe an offer to sell would come that Bill couldn't refuse. Bill didn't want to get bogged down. But he didn't want to sit around and do nothing, either. All the hard work in the world wasn't going to stop time. You couldn't just let the future happen to you.

■ ■ ■

Bill and Evelyn got to Smith Mesa. Bill always liked it that time of year, at the start of winter, when the sun was pale and the cool wind whispered through the junipers. The cows were scattered across the mesa, not yet chased into the shadows of the wash by the heat of spring and the promise of greener grass.

It could be hard to be at Smith Mesa and not think of time backwards. The place felt like something stuck in the past. After all, it hadn't really changed in 150 years, or probably a million years before that. It was the same as it was when Bill was a boy. That's what he liked about it. It felt timeless. Only the people changed. Only the world on the outside changed.

Bill had come to realize that maybe he didn't have to sell Smith Mesa to grow the herd. It no longer had to be one or the other. He could probably sell off the permits—or some of them—and have enough money to buy cheaper land and permits somewhere else. He could sell just part of the private land at Smith Mesa and keep the rest for the family to use, with or without cows. The boys might keep pitching in, too. He'd never ask them to, but six of them had just made more than half a million dollars over ten nights in Las Vegas. They might be able to make a move without giving up Smith Mesa. If that were the case, it changed everything.

Bill, standing there with Evelyn at the center of their property, looked forward. Not back. Bill had been in that shady hollow a million times, ever since he was a boy, and never thought much about it. Now he did. Next to the crumbling cabin, he saw a future. Bill let his mind wander deep, like cattle into a foggy forest.

He'd been to the rodeo in Springville, out in the California foothills, and seen its little arena tucked against a hill. There wasn't much to it, really, just an arena like the one Bill had in his backyard, and rows of wooden bleachers built into the hill on one side.

And he'd been over to Bryce Canyon National Park, a couple of hours to the east, on the other side of Zion. One of the resorts there, called Ruby's Inn, did a lot of trail rides for tourists. But it also ran a rodeo four nights a week in the summer. Some of the Wright boys rode in it and worked it from time to time. The rodeo charged tourists about $12 each performance, and a few hundred of them sat in the grandstand and got their up-close cowboy experience to remember for a lifetime.

There wasn't much like that around Zion, Bill thought. It wouldn't be hard to do, to build a rodeo arena in the shady hollow, with rows of wooden bleachers built into the hill on one side. And as good as the Bryce rodeo was, it was off a busy road next to a bunch of motels on a high, open plain. It didn't have million-dollar views, nothing like the way the hollow stared out at the majestic walls of Zion, so close you felt like you could touch them. And as the boys retired, they could run a rodeo school, teaching younger generations how to ride and rope. People were always asking them about doing that. They just never had the time. People might pay to be taught by them during the day, and pay to watch them ride at night.

He went so far as to think about a dude ranch on Smith Mesa. There could be horseback rides and cattle drives, campfires and cookouts. He had mentioned it to Cody, but Cody wasn't sure he wanted to be the public face of a dude ranch. It wasn't really his thing. But he liked to ride the range and run cattle, and he was getting more and more involved with training cattle dogs, which seemed like a good fit for what Bill was thinking. And Rusty and Ryder were interested in stock, and there were plenty of the kids and grandkids to help, including some of the girls. And there were always more of them on the way, the family growing exponentially, faster than the cattle operation could ever multiply.

Maybe they could build a lodge someday, and a few buildings and make it a real ranch, at least a small version of what they did at Beavers or wherever else Bill decided to take the bulk of his operation as the herd grew.

Smith Mesa could remain a place for the family to gather, which was really what he wanted more than anything. That's what Cody always said, too. Bill had been thinking about all that. Maybe it was just a ridiculous dream. Maybe he wouldn't be around to see it. Maybe someone would drive up tomorrow and offer $20,000 an acre, or someone else would put their ranch up for sale and it would be just what Bill wanted.

Bill felt good about moving forward. He was tired of waiting. If the world was closing in on Smith Mesa, maybe it was time to take advantage of it instead of running from it. Maybe the past really was the answer to the future.

■ ■ ■

If he could see as well in front of him as he could behind, Bill might have known how things would go in the coming spring and summer. He'd see the five big tents set up on the property, each with a queen-sized box spring and mattress, a fire pit, and a solar shower. And he'd see them filled most nights, once by a Hollywood couple that said they'd be back again. And he'd see the sites where people could bring their own tents, and those were filled up a lot of nights, too. Not everybody'd love it, of course. There'd be folks from New York who packed up and left in the middle of the night after they saw a coyote. But most everyone did, and they'd put stellar reviews online about a hidden gem on a real ranch at the doorstep of Zion that they'd discovered, as if it was something brand new.

He'd look out and see himself and Evelyn, leading a trail ride through the red dirt and sagebrush, telling stories about their family and the history of the area. And Bill would see himself leading groups, some from as far away as England, through that movie-scape of a setting. He'd hear himself telling stories of the old West, and see their faces light up at this authentic cowboy with the easy manner, and read their five-star reviews of his trail rides on the website. He'd be getting hundred-dollar tips left and right, and he'd tell Evelyn that he never got a hundred bucks total in all the years he'd spent leading people on mules down the Grand Canyon.

He'd see a couple of signs posted on the road, advertising the trail rides and the camping, and wish he had the time to do some better promotion, if only he didn't have to spend so much time at Beavers, mending fences and pulling his cattle out of the high country, where they weren't supposed to be until August. If he could just get more business cards to people in Hurricane, or get people to turn off the road in Virgin, or hell, if he could get himself to Springdale and hire someone there, they could load people up in a van and bring them to Smith Mesa.

He'd see there were a couple more four-wheel-drive companies starting up, driving by his place, loaded with tourists, sometimes stopping at the hard turn at the corral and saying that this was where a bunch of world champion bronc riders had their cattle operation. He'd see that he needed to put a sign there.

And he'd see on the road up to the mesa, down by his lower corral along North Creek, that someone had bought two hundred acres there, and they drilled a well, and they were building a whole bunch of platforms for big tents, and they had plans to build showers and a clubhouse, maybe even a pool. He might wonder if that'd take business away from him, or if it might mean more demand for trail rides, but he'd guess that it didn't hurt the value of his property either way.

And Bill would know that Cody was still riding strong through the summer, though Rusty had broken his arm in the chutes so badly that he needed a rod put in it and was out for the year. But Rusty and Morgan were back living together again, raising Rookie, and engaged to be married. Ryder and Cheyenne had bought a house in Milford and just had a baby daughter, and Ryder, still only nineteen years old, would win four rounds at the National Finals and become the fourth Wright to win a world title. Stetson was about to turn eighteen, but still wasn't sure if he'd go pro to ride the bulls or the broncs—or both. Bill would know that Alex, Jake, Jesse, Spencer, and CoBurn were on the circuit with them, more Wrights than ever, all of them going long distances on lonely highways for nothing more than another chance.

And he'd know that Stuart was doing so well in Ghana that they'd made him a trainer of other missionaries, and he'd hear Stuart tell Evelyn not to worry, because when he got back in another year he'd be the same old Stu, and Bill would see Evelyn cry and hear her tell their youngest son that no, no he wouldn't ever be the same, which was exactly the point.

And Bill would see himself riding along with Calvin, out of jail and working his way out of the woods, or so everyone hoped. Bill would watch him banter with the customers on the trail ride, and listen to the customers laugh, and think to himself just how good Calvin was at that sort of thing.

But it was still December, and Bill couldn't see all that yet. He wasn't sure where any of it was headed. He only knew that he'd spurred life forward a bit. He couldn't know where the ride would take him. Life could turn in a moment. You just held on and tried to find the rhythm in it.

■ ■ ■

Bill and Evelyn pulled back into Milford, over the train tracks and past the newly rebuilt sign that welcomed them to the home of world champion bronc riders Cody, Jesse, and Spencer Wright. The signs on all three roads into town had been redone, designed to accommodate plenty of additions.

They got back to their empty house, but there was work to be done. Bill needed to get things ready for the winter back at Smith Mesa and find some cows still left up at Beavers. Evelyn had to get back to school for the last days before the holiday break. And as she did every year, she invited everyone over to celebrate Christmas early.

There were too many people and too many in-laws and cousins and things to have everyone over on Christmas Day, and they all liked to do their own thing at home, anyway. So Evelyn had her thirteen kids and their families over every year on the Sunday before that. It was no small thing. With the children and their spouses, the grandchildren and the great-grandchildren, about sixty people came to the house. Along with branding day, it was a Wright holiday that everyone was expected to come to if they could.

The timing didn't work out too well with the rodeo schedule. Six of the boys were in Billings, Montana, the night before. Cody wasn't supposed to go, but Rusty decided to take time off to heal his leg for the bigger rodeos to come later in the winter. So Cody took his place and went, along with Alex, Jesse, Jake, Spencer, and Ryder, and he won the thing. And then they all drove in two trucks, twelve hours through the frigid night and over the snow-blown roads, to make it back home in time to celebrate Christmas.

Evelyn cooked a honey-baked ham and a turkey and made dozens of rolls. The day before, she made six banana cream pies, one apple pie, and one berry pie. Bill helped her peel and cut the potatoes. Their girls brought salads and sides, and soon the counters were smothered in casserole dishes and Tupperware. Everyone piled the food on paper plates.

Bill asked Evelyn to give the prayer before everyone ate. But she missed Stuart so much that she was afraid she'd cry, so she asked Bill to do it instead. He closed his eyes tight and everyone bowed their heads and held hands, and he thanked the Lord for all the blessings they'd received and for each other's company.

They took up a collection, and gathered some presents, and put them in a box and delivered them to a family in town that had come across some hard times. They made gingerbread houses out of graham crackers, glued together with frosting and decorated with candy and gumdrops. They had a talent show, and the children performed skits and some sang and danced and played the upright piano.

And they crowded into the living room and read from the scriptures—Luke, chapter 2, from the Book of Mormon. The children acted it out, and one of the babies was given the role of Jesus.

"And she brought forth her firstborn son, and wrapped him in swaddling clothes, and laid him in a manger; because there was no room for them in the inn.

"And there were in the same country shepherds abiding in the field, keeping watch over their flock by night."

Bill leaned over to Evelyn, the way he did at times like this, when everyone was together and he could take stock of the family they'd created. "And to think," he whispered, "I almost missed all this."

He still had a couple dozen cattle up at Beavers, and he worried over them. There was three feet of snow at the top of the Tushar Mountains, and the ski area at the upper edge of his range was already open. Down closer to Beaver, down in Bone Hollow, there was a little bit of snow, but temperatures fell hard into the teens at night. A snowstorm was predicted for Christmas Eve.

The herd had grown to well over three hundred cows, and Bill didn't want any of them to get ledged out and hung up by the snow behind them. It might take a few days to track the ones he hadn't moved yet, but he'd go up that week and gather them, a few at a time, and put them in his rusty trailer for the ride south. He hoped that Cody could come with him.

And they'd unload them on Smith Mesa for the winter, where the cattle would graze on the green grass next to the red cliffs, and Bill could camp nearby and look after them while waiting for the world to close in.

Acknowledgments

IWAS LATE THE FIRST TIME I went to Smith Mesa, but I didn't know it. Bill Wright was expecting me, and he said he would send Calvin down to the Virgin post office at 9 a.m. to lead me back to the family property. I got there right on time—or so I thought. Turns out I hadn't accounted for the change from Pacific time to Mountain time during the drive from Las Vegas. I was an hour late.

Calvin never said anything, and neither did Bill or anyone else. It was only at the end of the day that I realized I had left everyone waiting. I was appalled.

The episode spoke loudly about the Wrights. Over more than three years, and too many visits and conversations to count, every member of the family greeted me with warmth and treated me with patience. I kept showing up at family gatherings, branding weekends, and rodeos all across the West. The only consistency was the manner in which I was treated.

The boys squeezed me into the cabs of their trucks for long

drives and into the campers for short nights. Bill let me ride shot-gun in the truck wherever he went, and even saddled up an extra horse when necessary. Evelyn treated me like another son, smoth-ering me in kindness and good cheer. ShaRee, the other critical counterweight who keeps the Wrights centered, helped keep tabs on Cody and the boys and always provided an honest assessment of family dynamics. Spouses and significant others of the Wright brothers and Cody's sons—strong and supportive women such as Megan, Loni, Aubrey, Kallie, Morgan, and Cheyenne—did not blanch when I showed up on their doorsteps or at a family func-tion. When I called or cornered any one of them into a conversa-tion about the lives they led or the things they had been through, they acted as if they had all the time in the world. The same can be said of Stef, Calvin's former wife, and Bill and Evelyn's six daughters: Selinda, Laurelee, Michaela, Monica, Kathryn, and, most especially, Becca.

The only family member who questioned me was Monica. She approached me at a graduation party at Cody's house one warm night before we had been introduced.

"Who are you, and what are you doing here?" she asked. I laughed at her bluntness, and we got along great from that moment on.

Others were either too polite or too busy to really ask what I was doing all that time. For a year, they knew that it was for some sort of story for the *New York Times*. For more than two years after that story was published, they knew it had something to do with a book about them.

This is a work of nonfiction. Everything in it was witnessed by me, researched by me, or passed along as a story by someone who was there and verified by me to the best of my ability. It was a jour-nalistic enterprise, and as such, there were no arrangements with anyone in the book about its direction, contents, or tone. There were no promises about what it would or would not contain or reveal. No one in the book was paid for his or her time or cooperation, or has a financial stake in this story's telling. Journalistic ethics wouldn't allow any such arrangement.

That means, of course, that the book does not happen without the family's trust. The only thing I could offer in return was a promise to be fair and accurate. I hope they and others find that to be the case. All the Wrights—across all generations, and including the sprawling tangle of in-laws and friends—have my everlasting gratitude and respect for opening their homes, minds, and worlds to me. Their trust in this stranger will remain an inspiration.

Beyond the Wrights are too many people behind the scenes to possibly name. Any list begins with my family. My wife, Cathy, and our kids, Joe and Ally, bore the brunt of my sporadic but frequent inattention to their worlds as I focused on this project. They spent vacations, weekends, and late nights either watching me read and write or being dragged around the West to rodeos in far-flung towns. They got to know many of the Wrights, too, and I know that they will treasure the memories of meeting people they otherwise would not know, of riding horses across vast landscapes, of going behind the chutes with some of the best cowboys on Earth. They already do.

Other friends and family saw and felt glimpses of my distracted life, too, in scuttled plans and shortened conversations. Writing a book is hard, but it's also hard on those around you. I hope they know I recognize that.

A special thanks to Matt Weiland, my editor at W. W. Norton, for his quick and decisive interest in this book. His steady hand, honest assessments, keen advice, and quick quips were invaluable to both the transcript and my attitude. My literary agent, Luke Janklow, has my ongoing gratitude for believing in this idea, and in me.

ACKNOWLEDGMENTS

Few things make me prouder than being able to say I work for the *New York Times*. This project only became envisioned as a full-fledged book after it was published as a newspaper story. Sports editor Jason Stallman saw the potential in it years ago and allowed me to pursue it. *New York Times* photographer Josh Haner worked alongside me for a year. He brought his usual journalistic zeal and good humor, and I'm proud to call him a friend and frequent collaborator.

A large part of reporting this story depended on gaining access to and understanding of the worlds of ranching and rodeo. The staff of the Professional Rodeo Cowboys Association was persistently helpful throughout the years, especially at the National Finals Rodeo. Rodeos of all sizes welcomed me, often without notice, and granted me access to people and places, almost always behind the chutes. Too many other bronc riders to name allowed me into their trucks and conversations so that I could understand the culture of rodeo. I leaned on experts to teach me the intricacies of cattle and horses, such as Lori Lee O'Harver of Bronc Riding Nation and longtime rodeo reporter Brett Hoffman. Jason Davidson, the agent for Cody and others, was nothing but supportive. I trusted in serendipity and the good graces of strangers, which wasn't a big leap in a culture where helping others is second nature. Everywhere I turned was someone willing to explain federal grazing permits, to show me how judging works, or to lend me a cowboy hat to give the illusion that I might fit in behind the chutes.

Finally, a few words about Charlie Waters, to whom this book is dedicated. Charlie was one of the great newspaper editors of the West, mostly unsung, a bit of a cowboy himself. He was raised in Kingman, Arizona, and worked his way through papers of all sizes. He was executive editor of the *Fresno Bee* when he hired me from Colorado as a sports columnist. We'd stand outside the newspaper's dock doors in the brutal heat of summer or misty cool of winter and swap stories as he smoked cigarettes. When I left for the *New York Times*, Charlie remained a mentor and friend. We made a habit of meeting for breakfast whenever I was in Las Vegas, where he later worked and then retired.

He knew that I thought rodeo was a writer's paradise, with its color and characters, and he followed the sport a little bit, tracking the standings and personalities. He once sent me a long note about the Wright family of Utah, with a band of brothers beginning to dominate saddle-bronc riding. He thought it could be a good story for me and for the *New York Times*.

I agreed, but it took a couple of years before I carved out the time to work on it over a year between other assignments. About midway through, Charlie called to ask how things were going. He had been sick with cancer for some time, and his voice was weaker than I had heard it before, but he didn't want to talk about himself. He wanted to talk about the Wrights. He lent me ideas and support. He knew just where the Wright boys were in the standings. He wanted to talk about my latest trip to Milford and to Smith Mesa. Then he told me goodbye. I didn't know it would be the last one.

Charlie died a few days later. My great regret with this story is that he did not live to see it published. I wish for one more breakfast with Charlie, and a chance to pull this book out of my bag and hand it to him. I can picture his crooked smile.